TEEN-
PROOFING

A Revolutionary Approach to Fostering Responsible Decision Making in Your Teenager

JOHN ROSEMOND

Andrews McMeel
Publishing

Kansas City

To my darlin' Willie

 For information, write Andrews McMeel Publishing, an Andrews McMeel Universal company, 4520 Main Street, Kansas City, Missouri 64111.

www.andrewsmcmeel.com

99 00 01 02 RDH 10 9 8 7 6 5 4 3 2

LIBRARY OF CONGRESS CATALOGING-IN-PUBLICATION DATA
Rosemond, John K., 1947– Teen-proofing:
a revolutionary approach to fostering responsible decision making in
your teenager / John Rosemond.
p. cm.
ISBN 0-8362-2765-4 (pbk.)
1. Parent and teenager—United States. 2. Adolescent psychology—
United States. 3. Child rearing—United States. I. Title.
HQ799.15.R57 1998   98-27069
649'.125—dc21   CIP

Designed by Kathryn Parise

CONTENTS

◆

v

THANKS TO:

Everyone at Andrews McMeel, especially Donna Martin, Tom Thornton, and Katie Mace.

Everyone at The Center for Affirmative Parenting and Affirmative Parenting, Inc., especially Mary Cox, Marietta Dolman, Pam Fettig, Micki Fortner, Janet Moss, Mary Ellen Dillon, and Shannon (or is it Shayna?) Baxter.

Everyone at *Hemispheres* magazine, especially Randy Johnson and Lisa Fann, from Mr. Cantankerous, with a K.

Everyone at the *Charlotte Observer,* the Knight-Ridder wire, and the newspapers who continue to support my heresy by carrying my weekly column.

Dr. Bill Varley, for keeping me on the right track.

My supportive, loving, and most lovable wife of thirty years and getting better all the time, Willie.

My children, Eric and Amy, without whom I could not have written this book and because of whom I almost didn't.

INTRODUCTION

◆

Since 1955, two statistics concerning America's teenagers have increased more than threefold:

1. *violent crimes*—assaults on peers, teachers, parents, and society in general.
2. *depression*—as indicated by a tripling-plus of the teen suicide rate. (Statistics on teen depression from as far back as 1955 are highly unreliable, which leads some to assert that the threefold increase in teen depression is a function of more accurate reporting techniques. However, the teen suicide rate, concerning which fairly reliable records exist from 1955, *and which is a marker of teen depression,* has more than tripled since that time.)

Further, these increases have taken place *across the demographic spectrum.* In the 1950s, the kid who was likely to act out aggressively or develop serious emotional problems could be spotted a proverbial mile away. Almost always, he/she came from an obviously troubled family that lived on the "wrong side of the tracks." As in: The mother had run off with a traveling salesman, leaving the children in the "care" of a father who was a frequently unemployed alcoholic. The kids were generally unsupervised, undisciplined, and did poorly in school. No one was surprised when the oldest child was sent to reform school at age fifteen for robbing a store, and everyone felt it was just a matter of time before the younger siblings developed serious antisocial behaviors as well.

In a little over one generation, teen problems that were once isolated to specific pockets of obvious socio-familial pathology have spilled out into every nook and cranny of our society. Today, the child who, as a teenager, develops serious problems might have grown up in an upscale neighborhood within an evidently healthy family that never misses church on Sunday.

Items: A fifteen-year-old Kentucky boy, shy, but with no obvious family or emotional problems, comes to school one day, pulls out a pistol, and shoots five of his classmates, killing two of them. Several months later, a similar incident happens in Arkansas, this time involving two fifth graders who methodically shoot four classmates and one teacher. Several months later in Mississippi, an eighth-grade boy approaches a teacher at a school function, puts a gun to the teacher's head, and pulls the trigger.

Item: A fourteen-year-old boy—good student, good athlete, lots of friends—from an upper-middle-class family that everyone in the community agrees is "loving," hangs himself in the basement one day, leaving behind no note of explanation. This is not fiction, either. It concerns the child of a friend, who continues to be heartbroken and mystified.

That the above sorts of tragedies are becoming less and less the exception is nothing short of frightening. When I was a teenager, growing up in a middle-class Chicago suburb in the early- to mid-sixties, my peers and I were mischievous.

We got away with what we could when adults weren't looking. But today's teens aren't just mischievous; rather, they have become downright dangerous, to themselves and others, and there's no way of knowing which teen is going to go "off the deep end" next.

What's going on here? How does one explain why, in the world's most successful country, children are so at risk for serious problems? Actually, I have an explanation, one that involves a fairly simple psychological axiom known as the "flight or fight principle" (FFP). It's one of the few psychological principles that has been documented to the point of no longer being considered theory, but fact. Like most *valid* psychological ideas (and they are few and far between, in my estimation), it states what is already common sense: *When threatened by some thing or set of circumstances, an individual will either try to avoid the source of threat (flight) or aggress toward it (fight).* In other words, threat causes some people, in some situations, to flee—to try and put distance between themselves and the source of threat—while others try to suppress the source of threat through use of force. The actual response depends upon personality, situational, and historical variables, but in either case, the idea is to *reduce or eliminate the impact of the threat*—to, in effect, make it go away. FFP explains a broad range of human behaviors, but one illustration will do: Two businessmen decide to take a shortcut through an urban park at night. Suddenly, a man with a knife confronts them and demands their wallets. One of the businessmen immediately turns tail and runs. The other, enraged, lunges toward the mugger and tries to disarm him. Both men, each in his own knee-jerk way—one flees, one stands and fights—try to mitigate the threat posed by the mugger.

Before I tie all this into increases in teen violence and depression, a bit of historical background is in order:

Once upon a time not so long ago, there was no such thing as adolescence as we conceive of it today. Children were expected to be responsible, self-disciplined, and in many cases, to even help support their families (as did both my father and father-in-law) by their early teen years. This state of affairs explains why, in almost all cultures, rites signifying the transition from childhood to adulthood took place at age twelve or thirteen. Child labor laws and compulsory schooling changed all of this. Suddenly, the period of a child's dependency was extended well into the teen years. Since World War II, a steadily rising standard of living has further contributed to the creation of contemporary adolescence—a six- to eight-year period of relative leisure that only children of the fabulously rich (and not all of them either, mind you) enjoyed seventy-five or more years ago. To make matters worse, adults have generally responded lazily to teen leisure. Instead of confronting teens with hard realities and helping them develop mature decision-making skills, today's adults indulge and enable. As a consequence, compared with his grandparents when they were teens, today's teen is an emotional toddler—irresponsible, narcissistic, and oblivious to risk. Worst of all, today's teen is irrelevant—*worthless*, in the sense of *lacking worth*. Let's face it, there is no *point* to being a teenager today, unless the point is to be as irresponsible as possible. As the teen years have become increasingly devoid of meaning and purpose, adolescence has transformed into a period of profound emotional vulnerability. Forty years ago, when I was perched on the threshold of my teen years, these vulnerabilities were kept in check by an adult community that still stood together where child rearing was concerned. Today's kids, on the other hand, enter adolescence with at least three strikes against them:

1. *Weakened disciplinary policies and procedures*. Adult discipline of children has significantly weakened in just forty

years. This is the result of (a) disingenuous psychobabble to the effect that traditional child-rearing practices were psychologically harmful (a canard cut from whole cloth, let me assure you) and (b) an adult community that is no longer unanimous concerning how children should be dealt with under any circumstances. People of my parents' generation often tell me they are appalled at the behavior of their grandchildren and wonder how such well-behaved children (theirs) could be rearing such undisciplined kids. Not only do today's kids exhibit far more behavior problems than did children in prior generations, but they are also lacking in responsibilities (e.g., household chores). Then there's the ubiquitous parent who, when his/her children misbehave, protects them from accountability instead of assigning it dispassionately. Grandma called the undisciplined child a brat; today we say he has attention deficit disorder.

2. *A climate of moral relativism,* promoted by the media, lawmakers, jurists, public schools, and even some churches. *Example*: Sexual practices that almost everyone regarded as deviant fifty years ago are today regarded by many, if not most, as morally neutral—in some cases, even *chic*. The result of this sort of moral sleight-of-hand is that today's children are entering the teen years without a clear concept of right versus wrong. *Example*: In my day, when one of us cheated on a test, we *knew* we'd done wrong. A recent poll of high school students reveals the majority of them think cheating is actually okay under certain circumstances.

3. *A host of extra-family influences and temptations* that were simply not acting upon or available to teens in previous generations. I speak here of such insidious things as the contemporary family sitcom, where when kids sass their parents, the laugh track rolls, and drugs, which are more dangerous today both in terms of potency and kind than the sixties' hippie ever dreamed of.

Less disciplined, lacking a firm sense of right versus wrong, and more exposed to and tempted by unsavory influences; that's how today's all-too-typical child enters the teen years. Not just "still wet behind the ears," but more like "still wet all over."

In short, we're thrusting children today into the most vulnerable period of their lives having deprived them of the defenses they will need to make sound decisions, while at the same time bombarding them with a host of temptations. Inadequate moral, emotional, intellectual, and behavioral defenses render anyone, much less a child, highly susceptible to intense feelings of insecurity. Insecurity equates to a pervasive feeling of threat, and threat, remember, activates the *flight or fight principle.* In this case, the symptoms are a tremendous upsurge in both depression and violent behavior among teens.

So, what's a parent to do? After thirty years of marriage to the wonderful Willie, with whom I reared two children, Eric (now twenty-nine) and Amy (now twenty-six), and twenty-six years of experience as a family psychologist and parent educator, I am bold enough to say I have some answers to that very question. I am fully aware that any solution is easier said than done, but I am completely confident that the advice contained herein will work for those parents who are willing to work at it.

What, Pray Tell, Is "Teen-Proofing"?

Good question! The title came to me one December evening on a remote island in the Bahamas as I lay shivering under the covers with a 102-degree temperature. In my life, high fevers have always lent themselves to very creative—at times, downright *bizarre*—word association exercises, and so, having absolutely nothing better to do, I began one such exercise with the word *teenager.* Immediately, *werewolf* and *boarding school* came to mind. Shaking those off, I remembered that my intention was to write a book on how to manage teenagers such that they take responsible control of their lives.

I worked out the rather libertarian (but by no means "permissive") ideas contained herein while my two children were teenagers. Once formulated and field-tested on the Rosemond children—Eric and Amy—the concepts were further refined through my counseling work with parents of teens and the teens in question themselves. Once I reached the point where I was certain that any further attempts at refinement would be obsessive, I began writing this book, *sans* title.

Anyway, there I was, on a beautiful tropical island, quasi-delirious with fever, and I'm thinking about helping teens take responsible control of their lives so they (for one thing) are more likely to say "No!" to various forbidden fruits. I suddenly begin hallucinating about Adam and Eve, graced with the Only Perfect Parent, eating of forbidden fruit after being told in no uncertain terms not to eat of it. (They were there, in the bedroom with me, I swear it!) It occurred to me that the parenting style I'm putting forth by no means *guarantees* teens won't ever taste forbidden fruit, because that's pie-in-the-sky. After all, even the "best" of teens is likely to say "Yes" to temptation on an occasional basis. Rather, it's a parenting model that imparts to teens the ability to make decisions that are to their own long-term advantage, thus *minimizing* the likelihood of *big* problems.

The word "minimize" caused me to think of "immunize," which led straight to "inoculate." (A fever can be a wonderful thing!) My own experience with two teenage children had taught me it was indeed possible to *inoculate* teens against the sorts of hazards they're going to encounter in these interesting times. Inoculate—hmmm (I'm thinking!)—as in *to protect.* At this point, my two young (at this writing) grandchildren popped to mind, and I thought about how one *protects* a toddler by—what's this?!!—*child-proofing!* Of course! You can't teach toddlers to make good decisions about what to touch and what not to touch, where to go and where not to go, etc.; therefore, you protect them by "proofing" their surroundings—removing from their reach things which could cause them harm. Protecting teens from harm is not so simple, because in the final analysis, teens must protect themselves. Eureka! Managing teens so they make self-protective rather than self-destructive decisions is Teen-*Proofing!* And that was that. So I have the Bahamian Headless Chicken Flu, or some such thing, to thank for the title.

The analogy isn't perfect, I admit. My dictionary says that to *proof* means to make "invulnerable" or "impervious." Well, I won't pretend to go that far. You can guarantee a two-year-old can't get into a certain cabinet, but there's absolutely nothing a parent can do—short of putting a child in solitary confinement from ages twelve through eighteen—to *guarantee* a teen won't use drugs, or shoplift, or get drunk and crash a car, or whatever. A teenager, after all, has a mind of his own. In the final analysis, you can "proof" your teen only so far. Beyond that, you can only pray that your child, with God's help, will do the rest of the job himself.

I hope you enjoy reading this book as much as I enjoyed writing it. My wife, Willie, says I'm the only person she knows who can make himself fall on the floor with laughter. To tell the truth, there were times during the writing of this book when, true to form, I laughed hard enough to put a less physically adept person on the floor. You should know, however, that I turned fifty during the writing of this book. It may well be that as I get older, I laugh at sillier things. The fact is, however, the subject of teenagers doesn't cause too many people—parents or otherwise—to laugh; this despite the heroic efforts of Bill Cosby. I hope this book makes you laugh half as much as I laughed while writing it. After all, the teenage years are a serious matter, but teens themselves are taken much too seriously these days. In that regard, I'm fairly convinced of the following things:

1. Teens don't know adults take them *too* seriously, but they know adults take them *real* seriously, nonetheless.

2. The more seriously we adults take teenagers and the things they do, the more seriously they take themselves and the things they do.

3. The more seriously teens take themselves, the more convinced they become that the parent-teen relationship is a war which they have to win, no matter the cost.

4. The more seriously we adults take teenagers and everything they do, the more convinced we become that the parent-teen relationship is a war we have to win, no matter the cost.

5. Occasional parent-teen skirmishes are inevitable. All-out war is not.

6. The cost of parents going to war with a teen is paid mostly by the teen. Why? Because whereas parents try to win such wars by doing *self-defeating* things, teens invariably try to win such wars by doing *self-destructive* things.

7. We can't expect teens to understand the cost of going to war with us, but we should understand the cost of going to war with them. It follows that whether or not the parent-teen relationship becomes war is completely up to the parent. The big guy.

I've written this book with the above in mind. I am confident in saying that if you take it to heart and bring it to life it will help you stay out of war with your teenager.

Enjoy! Please!

SECTION ONE:

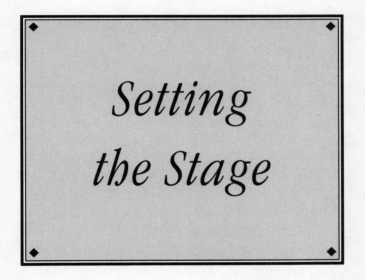

Setting the Stage

CHAPTER ONE

◆

Putting It in Perspective

Let's face it, you're not reading this book out of curiosity. Rather, you're hoping that by doing so, you'll learn how to parent your teenage child—or your child *when* he or she becomes a teen—so as to prevent him or her from (in escalating order):

1. becoming secretive and uncommunicative
2. becoming insufferably argumentative and defiant
3. falling in with the wrong crowd
4. using drugs and/or alcohol, becoming sexually active, and/or running away
5. making suicidal gestures or actually following through

On the other hand, you may be reading this book because your teenager is *already* secretive and uncommunicative, insufferable, etc., and you are hoping to find *The Answer!* within. In short, you are reading this book because you are presently suffering somewhere on a continuum between *anx-*

ious as all get-out and *scared to death*. When parents find themselves trapped on this emotional continuum, sliding erratically back and forth along its reach, they have already lost the ability to put matters into proper perspective. Nothing, let me assure you, is more important to effective management of a teenage child than putting and keeping things in proper perspective. So, we will begin by doing exactly that. Well, no, that's not exactly true. Because I have *been there, done that* with two children who are now young adults, I can *put* things in proper perspective for you. That's not a problem. I can't, however, *keep* them in proper perspective. That's completely up to you. But as regards the *keeping,* I have what I think is a helpful suggestion which I'll share with you at the end of the chapter. Bear with me, please, while I deal first with the *putting*.

Put It in Perspective Principle Number One: *Be assured, you are a responsible parent!*

Occasionally, someone will ask why I never talk or write about parents who don't care—parents of the lazy, irresponsible, good-for-nothing sort.

I answer, "Because by definition that sort of parent is not part of my audience. Any parent who is (a) willing to give up the time and money to attend one of my public presentations, (b) a faithful reader of my newspaper column, or (c) who has taken the time to read one of my books is obviously caring and wants to do a good job. There's no point in my talking about lazy, good-for-nothing parents because they aren't listening. What, pray tell, would they gain if I talked about them behind their backs? Furthermore, if I *did* talk about lazy, good-for-nothing parents, I'd wind up conducting an exercise in self-congratulation for those parents who *are* in my audience, which is definitely not what they need from me."

In short, I assume that you—the parent reading this book—can be accurately described as responsible, committed, well intentioned, caring, and hardworking. You are not a perfect parent, but you are a good, decent parent. You want to do your best. Your family is not perfect and, if you are married, neither is your marriage. But neither, I will assume, are your family and/or marriage more than just normally messed up. This book is for you and parents like you—normally messed-up parents who create normally messed-up families and rear normally messed-up kids who, when they become teens, occasionally do normally messed-up things. This is not—I repeat, *not*—a book about . . .

- teens who get into serious trouble all the time (i.e., juvenile delinquents), abuse drugs and/or alcohol, are promiscuous, or make frequent suicidal gestures—rather, it's about how to form a relationship with your teen that will prevent such things;
- teens who live in super-dysfunctional families where such things as alcoholism, spouse abuse, or other forms of destructiveness toward self and others are standard fare;
- cross-dressing fathers who date their teenage daughters' boyfriends;
- any other "far out" issue.

This *is* a book about how caring, well-intentioned parents often become their own worst enemies when it comes to teenage children, and what they (you!) can do to avoid getting hoisted on their own (your!) petards during their (your!) children's teen years.

I will not, I promise, bore you to tears with theory or psychobabble. I'm going to share real-life stories with you from the annals of my own family and other normally messed-up families with whom I've worked over the years.

It is my intention to give you a road map of sorts through your child's teen years. I can't guarantee a completely smooth journey because there isn't such a thing. I'm confident, however, that reading this book will help make the years you spend living with a teen or teens a lot smoother than they currently are or otherwise might be. In effect, this is the book I wish I'd read before my kids became teens. Then maybe I wouldn't have had to learn this stuff the hard way.

Put It in Perspective Principle Number Two: *Teens can do bad things (even things you never find out about) and still turn out okay!*

To prepare for writing this book, I developed a presentation entitled "Understanding and Managing Your Teenager." Not surprisingly, it was and still is a popular topic. The typical attendee is a relatively well-educated, thirty- or fortysomething parent whose standard of living could be described as "comfortable," but who is definitely *not* comfortable with this particular stage of his or her parenthood. "Nervous, angry, scared, and confused" are more like it: *nervous* over what the teen in question is capable of doing, *angry* about what he or she has already done, *scared* of what's to come, and *confused* over what to do about it.

I begin the presentation by asking for a show of hands from those people who, as teens, "did something pretty bad that your parents never found out about." As nearly everyone begins to laugh, a few hands go up, then a few more, until more than half the audience members have admitted to one youthful indiscretion or another.

"Keep your hand up," I then ask, "if yours was a reasonably healthy family where you learned good values." If some two hundred fifty hands are raised (assuming an audience of four to five hundred people), perhaps five will go down.

"Once again, keep your hand up if you never again did the 'bad' thing in question." Generally, three of every four hands remain in the air.

The results of this informal poll are indicative of several important considerations:

1. There's a fairly good likelihood that even a teen from a good family background, one in which proper values are effectively taught, will occasionally do something outrageous. Therefore, the mere fact that a teenager does something really *bad* doesn't mean his parents have been deficient or negligent in some way.

2. As exemplified by the parents who come to my presentations, most of these same teens grow up to be responsible members of their communities. Therefore, the mere fact that a teenager does something really *bad* doesn't mean he or she is going to grow up to be a bad person.

3. Most teenagers who do something really *bad* eventually, if not immediately, regret having done it, *even if their parents don't find out*. Therefore, when a teenage child who possesses basically good values does something really *bad*, the likelihood is he will feel bad about it (feel penitent) and learn the appropriate lesson even if he is never "caught." Another way of saying this: *A teen with a well-developed conscience never gets away with anything.*

Parental nervousness, fear, anger, and confusion don't prevent teens from doing bad things, but this mix of emotions

7

most certainly prevents parents from acting effectively when they need to do so.

As the once-upon-a-time parent of two teenagers, I found that in order to act effectively in the face of the almost inevitable *really bad thing,* one needs to keep one's cool. I also discovered that it's nigh unto impossible to keep your cool if you think everything your teenager does is a reflection of you. For parents of teens, emotional survival hinges on remembering the words of Proverbs 22:15—"Foolishness is bound in the heart of the child"—and remembering also that in these "modern" times, this foolishness generally peaks during the early teen years. If you've done your job reasonably well to this point (and the typical reader of this book probably has), your teen's foolishness will probably run its course in due time. Just as yours did.

Put It in Perspective Principle Number Three: *You are not the only force in your child's life!*

That may seem blatantly obvious, but I know from personal experience that parents of teens—parents of children of all ages, really—lose sight of it very quickly, if they ever have it in sight at all. Today's parents, whether they realize it or not, have been heavily influenced by Sigmund Freud's (1856–1939) pseudo-scientific gibberish. Through the first half of the twentieth century, Freud's ideas concerning the significance of childhood experience on the development of the human psyche were of interest primarily to academicians. In the mid-1950s, a number of writers began popularizing his ideas in the media. One such author was Selma Fraiberg. In 1956, Fraiberg wrote a best-selling book for parents entitled *The Magic Years,* in which her explanations of child development and corresponding advice to parents were rooted primarily in Freudian mystification. Almost overnight (but not entirely due to Fraiberg), the terms *ego, id, superego, Oedipus complex,* and *subconscious* entered the vernacular. More "psychoanalytical" parenting books followed, all of which convinced middle-class American parents that for every parental action there was a corresponding subconscious re-action in a child's psyche. Parents began to think that one error could mar a child's emotional makeup forever, resulting in some permanent sexual neurosis or deviation (anal retentiveness, penis envy, homosexuality).

The actual result of "parenting according to Freud" was not so much neurotic children but highly neurotic parents. For the first time in the history of any culture, parents became anxious en masse. They, and the culture in general, began intellectualizing something—child rearing—that is not intellectual. Rather, child rearing is, was, and forever will be commonsensical. But no matter. Thanks to Freud and parenting "experts" like Fraiberg, parents began thinking "psychologically" about the rearing of children—and anxiously so. They began obsessing about doing everything "right" so as not to ruin their children. It is impossible, of course, for inherently faulted beings to do anything perfect. Parents make mistakes. The "new" parent, however, instead of forgiving himself/herself, became consumed with guilt. This, too, was the first time anything of the sort had happened in any culture. Instead of focusing on the here and now, American parents began ruminating on their past child-rearing "sins," and worrying endlessly about the scars those sins had supposedly created. An epidemic of *God Almighty Syndrome* (GAS) swept through America's parents. This peculiar psychological affliction is characterized by the belief that everything your child does is a consequence of something *you* have done. In effect, the parent afflicted with GAS believes he or she has God-like power in his or her child's life.

A parent who suffers from GAS has a bogeyman hiding in a dark closet in her head. Every time her children misbehave or come down with any sort of problem (developmental, social, academic), the bogeyman bursts out of the closet and screams, "It's all your fault!!!" (Note: I emphasize the female pronoun because Freud made it seem as though any psychological aberration stemmed back not so much to *parental* errors, but *maternal* errors. As a consequence, mothers are far more likely than fathers to suffer from GAS—to be anxious, obsessive, and racked with guilt.) The moment the bogeyman pops out of his closet and begins his rampage, the parent in question becomes beset with mental paralysis. She doesn't know what to do about the child's misbehavior (or problem) because she doesn't know whose misbehavior (or problem) it is. Is it the child's, or is the child's misbehavior simply a response to her own parenting sin, whatever that sin might be? Without exception, this confusion/paralysis prevents effective action. Whether literally or figuratively, the parent just "stands there," trying in vain to hear herself think over the bogeyman's clamoring.

Parents who suffer from recurrent GAS also have a habit of passing the buck whenever their children misbehave. To protect themselves from the guilt that comes from feeling that their children's misbehavior is all their fault, they become desperate in their attempts to pin blame on someone or something else—a teacher, a playmate, a grandparent, a television show the child watched, aberrant genes, allergies, and so on. One frequently hears such parents saying things of the following sorts:

- "He's never had this problem with any other teacher."
- "She only acts this way after a visit from the grandparents."

- "He sees [some other child] getting away with it, so he thinks he can get away with it too!"
- "He can't help it! He has attention deficit disorder [or an allergy, or a biochemical imbalance]."

Whether these parents are paralyzed into inaction or pass the proverbial buck, they fail to assign responsibility for their children's misbehavior to their children. So, their children continue misbehaving in the same tiresome and increasingly annoying ways. Thanks a lot, Sigmund, you old Fraud! May you be made to do penance in a purgatory filled with the souls of parents endlessly screaming, *"It's all your fault!!!"*

The fact is, by the time a child is a teenager, his behavior is, for the most part, a function of three competing influences:

1. *Inborn temperament,* otherwise known as *personality.* Anyone who's ever had more than one child knows that each and every child has a distinct personality from day one, and that no two children are the same. You can make every effort to treat two siblings "the same" and they will still turn out as different as apples and summer squash. And anyone who has even one child knows a child's temperament never really changes. At this writing, my children are twenty-nine and twenty-six. As I've often told them, there are times when they do things that remind me of when they were toddlers. Obviously, parents can't change a child's temperamental makeup. It comes with the "deal," and is—in part—what Grandma meant when she said *a child has a mind of his own.* Over time, parents can *temper* a child's temperament. They can, in other words, act so as to smooth the rough edges. Nonetheless, they are powerless to make a shy child into a gregarious one, a moody one into one who is perpetually sunny, or one who's easily frustrated into one who takes life as it comes. Don't get me wrong. A shy child may eventually *become* a

gregarious adult, but not because of parental effort, let me assure you. In fact, in such cases, the less parental effort, the better. Furthermore, as every gregarious adult who was once a shy child (me included) will tell you, "Deep down inside, I'm still very shy, really." In other words, behavior can overcome personality, but the personality is still there.

2. *Parenting.* This is the only variable parents can control—*themselves.* But again, whereas parents are very influential during infancy, toddlerhood, and early childhood, their influence has waned considerably by the teen years, by which time the third variable (below) has become dominant.

3. *Other Influences,* including extra-family experiences, other adults and peers—especially *peers!* Children, like adults, want approval. When they are young, they want their parents' approval. As they get older, they become increasingly needy for approval from peers. Nothing new here.

Figure 1:1 shows the relative strength of these influences over time. During infancy and toddlerhood, it's all temperament and parenting. Through early and middle childhood, the influence of the peer group strengthens. By the time the child is a teen, the peer group rules! It's not that parents have no influence over a teenager, it's that their influence is less than that of the child's peer group, which is why it's so important that parents use their influence wisely *before* a child becomes a teen.

Put It in Perspective Principle Number Four: *You can do the right thing, and things may still go wrong!*

Despite the fact that his parents divorced when he was three, leaving his mother to parent alone for the next four

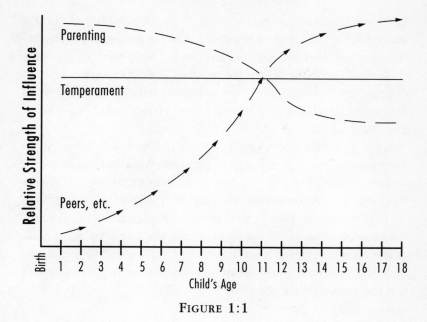

FIGURE 1:1

years, "J" had a happy early childhood. His mother and step-father formed a family that, while not a model of family health, was not a prime example of dysfunctionality, either. Whatever their faults, his mother and stepfather modeled good values—honesty, compassion, charity, responsibility, respect for others, and so on. While they did not believe in spending lavishly on children, they supported "J" in just about anything he wanted to do. When he wanted to play the trombone, they bought him a trombone. When he started thinking of becoming an inventor, they bought him a chemistry set and an Erector set. They bought him whatever books he showed an interest in reading. They encouraged him to be curious and creative. They were strict, but they gave him a lot of freedom. "J" was almost always a "straight-A" student. Despite all these advantages, by the time "J" was eighteen he (a) had been a guest in the town jail on two separate occasions (the first time

13

for participating in a "public affray," the second for stealing a road sign), (b) was smoking marijuana on a regular basis, and (c) was seemingly unable to drink beer without getting "falling down" drunk. By the end of his sophomore year in college, this former A student was decimal points away from flunking out of school. He was having too much "fun." Actually, he was lucky to still be alive.

The "J" in the above story is yours truly. My story is by no means unique. During my four years of "kick out the jams rebellion" (comprised of my last two years of high school and my first two years of college), I ran with lots of equally rebellious pleasure-addicts who'd been brought up in reasonably healthy families. This was the infamous late-sixties, as you might have already guessed.

What happened? Obviously, our turns for the worse were not the result of parental mistakes. One can list, as possible contributing factors:

- A cynical rejection of the values of our elders in response to (a) the assassinations of President Kennedy, Robert Kennedy, and Martin Luther King, and (b) the feeling that the Vietnam War was "un-American" and therefore unsupportable.
- The media's glorification of the "counterculture."
- College professors who encouraged our rebelliousness because they wanted to be seen as "cool."
- College administrators and politicians who caved in every time we threw a collective tantrum.

One thing's for certain: Our pot-addled excesses had nothing to do, in most cases, with how our parents had reared us. I'm clear that where my indiscriminate rejection of conventional values was concerned, my parents were completely innocent. I was not acting out some family dysfunction, or trying to resolve some nagging childhood "issue," or crying out for more parental attention/unconditional love. I was fully responsible, as was each and every one of my peers, for the decisions I made. Our parents (in most cases) had shown us the right path. They'd even walked a considerable distance down it with us. Given the first possible opportunity, we took the wrong path. Thank God most of us had the good sense to walk it for only a relatively short time.

So you see? You, like my parents, can do the right thing, and things may still go wrong—for a time, at least. Or maybe forever. Who knows? Everyone knows of a child who was brought up properly who, when he became an adult, went off the proverbial deep end and never returned. Likewise, everyone knows of a child who was brought up in family circumstances that—by any standard—were "horrible," who, when he reached adulthood, became a shining example of good citizenship. Again, it's not all up to you! Your child has a mind of his/her own! You can be a great and wonderful parent and your child may go "wrong" anyway. Then again, as was the case with me, your child can do really bad things and still turn out okay (however presumptuous that may sound).

This idea—that with proper parenting, everything during the teen years will go smoothly—is "between the lines" of many a book and article on teens. It is—hear me clearly—so patently absurd as to make one wonder how otherwise intelligent people (the authors of those books and articles) could even suggest it. It implies not only that parents are omnipotent but also that a child bears no responsibility for the direction and tone of the parent/child relationship. This is tantamount to saying that an employee bears no responsibility for how things go within the employer/employee relationship. Both ideas are equally preposterous. A child is not putty in his parents' hands any more than an employee is putty in an employer's hands. A human child is an independent agent (another way of saying he has a mind of his own). Being human, he is imperfect—in the-ological terms, *sinful*. He is not imperfect/sinful *because* of his parents (although they can certainly make matters worse); rather, he is imperfect *because he is human*. For all these rea-sons, a child is completely capable, at an early age, of doing things that bear little relationship to how well (or how poorly), by some standard, he has been "parented." Parenting is not sculpting; it is management. The trick, if you will, is to manage the child toward making functional decisions, while always re-maining cognizant of the child's inalienable freedom (not *right*, mind you, but *freedom*) to go off on a tangent, whether through ignorance or by design. Authors who commit the error of im-plying that parents are all-powerful are, I'm sure, trying their best to (a) motivate parents to do their best, to hang tough in the face of the aforementioned "tangents," and (b) convince parents that there is no problem so difficult it can't be solved. Unfortu-nately, their good intentions aside, these authors ultimately cause parents to feel tremendous guilt for the simple reason that *good parenting does not guarantee a good outcome*. Further-more, no matter how well you parent, *certain things will go wrong*. Parents who think a child's behavior is a mere reflection of how well they have carried out their responsibilities are (a) indulging themselves in God Almighty Syndrome (albeit unwit-tingly) and (b) setting themselves up for a big fall, indeed. God Himself could not create children who would not disobey! If you think you can parent well enough to prevent a child from ever doing something outrageous, then I am moved to ask you, "Who *do* you think you are?"

Coda

As this book unfolds, I intend to return fairly often to these four Put It in Perspective Principles (PIPPs). Sometimes one or more of them will be implicit to the text, sometimes I'll reference them more explicitly. I'm going to gently hammer them home because I'm keenly aware of the fact that parents can't be reminded of them often enough. As promised at the beginning of this chapter—I have a suggestion which lots of parents have told me is more than just a bit helpful when it comes to *keeping* these important principles in mind: Write or print the four PIPPs on a standard-size sheet of paper. When you're done, it should look like the example in Figure 1:2. Affix your personal PIPPs poster to the refrigerator or kitchen bulletin board where it can slowly but surely be absorbed into your Freudian subconscious, thus facilitating your constant remembrance of where your responsibilities end and your child's begin. (By the way, any similarity between the aforementioned acronym and Gladys Knight's backup singers is purely a matter of a shared affinity for great rhythm and blues.)

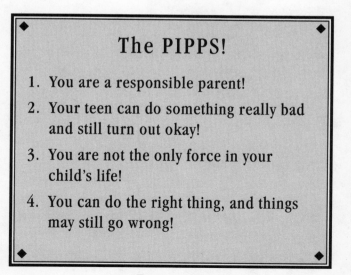

The PIPPS!

1. You are a responsible parent!
2. Your teen can do something really bad and still turn out okay!
3. You are not the only force in your child's life!
4. You can do the right thing, and things may still go wrong!

FIGURE 1:2

CHAPTER TWO

◆

The Big Picture

In doing the research for this book, I noticed that most authors who write on the teen years commit a common error: taking the tween/teen years out of context, as if they can be considered independent of the stages of development that have gone before. That's akin to thinking you can understand someone who's married by looking only at his/her behavior since the day of that person's wedding. The fact is, teenagers are *children,* which is something too many people in this day and age seem to forget (which perhaps explains why so many of today's teens seem to think they should be treated as if they were adults). Adolescence is a stage of *childhood* and cannot be understood by taking it out of that larger context.

You Are Not One Parent, but Three!

Over the course of a child's minority, the parent-child relationship goes through three distinct *stages,* separated by two major *transitions*:

STAGE ONE: Infancy and Early Toddlerhood—Begins at birth and lasts approximately two years.

Transition: **Late Toddlerhood**—Often called the "terrible" twos, one of the two most potentially tumultuous, precedent-setting times in the parent-child relationship.

STAGE TWO: Early and Middle Childhood—Ages three through eleven, approximately.

Transition: **Early Adolescence (The "Tweenage Years")**—Begins around the child's twelfth birthday and lasts from one to three years, depending on too many variables to enumerate. (Note: In *Parent Power!* [1981], I replaced the dry, academic sound of "early adolescence" by coining the term "tweenage years." I did so to make clear that during this time, however long or short, the youngster is betwixt and between childhood and true adolescence. The term "tweenager" has since made it into the vernacular, which has provided a tremendous boost to my self-esteem.)

STAGE THREE: True Adolescence—Begins at the resolution of the early adolescent transition above and lasts until the child is emancipated. (That's right! A child is not a bona fide adult, regardless of age, until the child is self-supporting.)

During both of the above transitions, the parent-child relationship is being redefined. (Actually, emancipation—the passage from dependence to independence—is a third "redefining" transition, but I choose to let it remain implicit. After all, the purpose of your reading this book is to properly prepare yourself and your child for exactly that.) Therefore, because the people involved must shed old roles and adopt new ones, some degree of upheaval is latent in both the "terrible twos" and "terrible tweens." Within some parent-child relationships, the upheaval is chaotic and painful. Within others, it's barely noticeable—a more deceptive state of affairs perhaps. Regardless, implicit to both transitions are critical issues which demand resolution. These issues are "stumbling blocks" which throw the parent/child relationship off balance. Sometimes the "stumbling"—the turmoil that attends major adjustments—is short-lived, sometimes it is long-lived, and sometimes it's permanent. Whether or not the parent-child relationship regains its balance by the close of any one of these transitions has great influence over how smooth the "sailing" will be from that point on. If, for example, an issue that begs for resolution during the late toddlerhood transition is not successfully resolved during that year, matters will almost certainly worsen from there.

The Big Picture, Part One:
Infancy and Early Toddlerhood

During the first two years or so of a child's life, responsible parents (Remember, that means you!) treat the child as if he/she was the Second Coming (or the First, depending on one's point-of-view about such matters). Their job title is *caretaker,* and their job description can be summed up in one word: *serve*. The child makes a loud noise and they appear at his side, basically asking, "How may we serve you, m'lord or m'lady?" On demand, they provide food and/or liquid refreshment, change diapers, entertain, fetch, soothe, comfort, or simply provide respite from boredom. In short, they are at the child's beck-and-call. Furthermore, they allow him to interrupt conversations, indulge him in all sorts of behavior that in an older child would not be tolerated, and wheel him through shopping centers and other public places in a portable throne. (And total strangers kneel before this throne and beg the child's blessings in the form of a smile!) Add that the infant/early toddler has no sense of history, no idea the world was in existence long before his or her arrival, and you've got a two-year-old who believes the world, created when he opened his eyes, is his exclusive preserve, and everyone exists to do his bidding. It takes just short of two years to create this fantastic impression; it takes at least sixteen more years to correct it! And that, paradoxically, is a parent's job: cause his/her child to believe in this fantasy, then burst—albeit gently—the child's bubble.

Bringing the fantasy into being "roots" the child in the world. In so doing, parents make the infant/toddler feel not just special (as in, "We've all been waiting just for *you!*"), but *powerful,* and with absolutely no limits or strings attached to either! All-special and all-powerful are an intoxicating mix, one the child is not likely to give up without a fight. But give it up he must, because socializing the child—adjusting him to the realities of life in civilized society—requires that this infantile fantasy be annulled. Quite simply, it is impossible to properly socialize a child who is allowed to wallow indefinitely in the belief that the world revolves around him. Self-centeredness is incompatible with respect for others, which is the linchpin of social responsibility. Furthermore, because one must first give respect away in order to manifest it within, self-centeredness is also incompatible with respect for self. Egotism is not self-respect, it is self-delusion, and it leads to self-indulgence. The properly reared child, however, is permitted this delusion for nigh unto two years. Then, for his own good (as well as the common good), the delusion must be exorcised, lest it become a demon-in-residence. To extend the above metaphor, the responsible parent "roots" the child in the world during the first two years of his/her life, then, once the child's root system is strong, begins the all-important "pruning" process.

The Big Picture, Part Two:
The "Terrible" Twos

As the child's second birthday approaches, his parents initiate—or *should* initiate—a revolution. (Note: For the purpose of the following discussion, I am going to describe what happens within the parent/child relationship when parents do what they are *supposed* to do, notwithstanding that many parents either never begin the transition/revolution in question, or never finish what they start.) This revolution is commenced as they begin shifting out of *caretaker* and into *authority figure*. Oh, they will continue to do caretaking—albeit less and less as time goes on—but their primary function now becomes that of *teaching social values*. During the first two years, the only teaching done was of the "don't touch that, don't climb on that" sort. It wasn't *social* teaching. Now, however, the child's parents must commence teaching him the much larger concept of *right versus wrong*. This requires that they take upon themselves the mantle of authority. This, in turn, requires shifting the center of attention in the parent-child relationship from child to parent. Slowly but surely, the parents begin taking the child out of the center of *their* attention and putting *themselves* at the center of *the child's* attention. For the first two years, the child was treated such that self-centeredness—the belief the world revolves around him—was inevitable. Unbeknownst to the infant/toddler, however, for whom everything during these first months is hunky-dory, his life is actually upside down. At this point, it is his parents' job—their obligation to him *as well as to the rest of us*—to begin turning his life right side up. As a consequence, everything changes—Everything! For the first two years, the parents paid inordinate amounts of attention to the child; now, they begin expecting *the child* to pay the greater share of attention to *them*. For the first two years, they were at their child's beck-and-call, creating the illusion that he was in control of the relationship. Now, they make clear that they are taking control. They begin to discipline the child in earnest (previous attempts being sporadic) in order to turn him into a disciple—*someone who will follow their lead.*

Understandably, the typical toddler does not take to this turnabout easily. He screams bloody murder, hurls himself to the ground, thrashes from side to side, bites himself, bites his parents, beats his head against hard objects, and otherwise proves, beyond a shadow of doubt, that his primal ancestors were savage beasts. His parents have pulled the proverbial rug out from underneath him, and he does not take it lightly. He tries every desperate means to maintain himself at the center of his parents' attention and, as such, to maintain his control of the relationship; in short, to keep things the way they were during his first two years of life. If, however, his parents stay the course—if they realize that his reaction to what they are doing is inconsequential, irrelevant, and will pass in time—then by the time the child is three (or thereabouts), his parents will have succeeded in communicating three essential understandings. More accurately, they will have succeeded in communicating *one* understanding in three parts:

1. *From this point on in the relationship, you, child, will pay more attention to us than we, generally speaking, will pay to you.* His parents will continue to supervise him well, and they will give him all the attention he requires (which is diminishing rapidly) along with a relatively small amount of the attention he simply wants, but it is now time for him to assume the role of *student/disciple*. It is time, therefore, for *him* to pay the greater share—the *much* greater share—of attention. Why? Because . . .

- his parents are now *teachers*, and
- you cannot teach someone who is not paying sufficient attention, and
- a child will *not* pay sufficient attention to someone who is acting as if it's his/her job to pay as much attention and do as much for the child as possible.

It's as simple as that.

2. *You will do what we tell you to do.* He is free to disagree, to dislike what his parents tell him to do, but he is not free to disobey. Not that he *won't* disobey, of course (Remember, not even God could keep His first children from disobeying!), but he's not *free* to disobey. When he disobeys, and he will, his parents will make sure he learns that disobedience is not free. How? By making him pay a price.

3. *You will do what we say not because of threat, bribe, promise, or "good" reason, but simply because we say so.* He can question his parents' decisions, but he cannot question their authority. Why? Because their authority is legitimate, and therefore not open to question.

At this point, I must briefly digress. If you are shocked concerning the above assertions, you must be unfamiliar with my writings. Indeed, as I have admitted in previous books, I am a heretic, one of the few psychologists in the U.S.A. who thinks psychologists have done much more harm than good to the rearing of children. I believe—the unsubstantiated claims of most modern psychologists aside—our foremothers and forefathers, who reared children unsentimentally and nonintellectually, reared them about as well—generally speaking, of course—as children have ever or will ever be reared. We of the apostate generation would do well to repent and begin again to honor our mothers and fathers when it comes to the way families operate. (For more on this subject, the shocked/ fascinated/intrigued reader is referred to *A Family of Value* [Andrews McMeel Publishing, 1995], by yours truly.)

These three understandings, taken together, form what I call *the First Great Understanding. From this point on in our relationship, child, you will pay more attention to us than we, generally speaking, will pay to you, and you will do what we say because we say so.* His parents' success at communicating this Understanding enables the child's successful socialization, beginning with their success at *disciplining* him—again, at turning him into a *disciple.*

Assuming the parents in question *do* succeed (and there are many, even extremely well-intentioned parents who do *not*), the child:

- puts his parents at the center of his attention;
- looks to them for definitions of right and wrong;
- invests his sense of security (that he's being well taken care of) in the belief that his parents are capable of providing for and protecting him under any and all circumstances;
- seeks their approval (tries to please them);
- and derives his sense of identity from his member-ship, his role, within his family.

All this bears witness to the fact that the child has made the transition from *self-centeredness* to *parent-centeredness,* which means the parents have made the transition from *care-takers* to *authority figures.* Nothing in the parent-child relationship will ever again be the same.

Unfortunately, many American parents are not staying the course during this transition. Instead, they allow themselves to become diverted by the child's screaming. More specifi-cally, they take the child's screams to mean they are doing something wrong (when in fact the child is screaming because they are doing something *right*). As a consequence, they fail to take the child out of the center of attention and, in effect, continue to cater. They fail to apply the pressure needed to *force* the unwilling child out of infantile self-centeredness, thus allowing the child to wallow indefinitely in "psychological toddlerhood." That this has never happened before on such a culture-wide scale is undeniable. People my parents' ages (at this writing, mid-to-late seventies) and older consistently report that prior to around 1965, one rarely if ever heard of (much less saw) a child above the age of three (a) throwing a tantrum in a public place, (b) being openly defiant to his/her parents, (c) hitting a parent, or (d) using inappropriate language toward a parent or other authority figure—all of which have since become fairly commonplace occurrences. Thanks to the deconstructive good intentions of mental health professionals, American parents have allowed the "Pandora's Box" of childhood to burst open. As a result, a host of "psychological toddlers"—children above the age of three who have become hard-core narcissists—are terrorizing America's homes and schools with their antisocial outrages.

That's the bad news. The good news is parents who are willing to admit their children are "psychological toddlers" can go a long way toward correcting this problem *as long as the necessary steps are taken before the children in question hit the teen years*. More on this later.

The Big Picture, Part Three: *Early and Middle Childhood*

Again, parents who know what the "game plan" of the above transitional period is and carry it out resolutely establish themselves as *authority figures*. Their responsibilities

have expanded considerably. During infancy and early toddlerhood, they were responsible almost exclusively to their
children. Now, they are responsible to both their children and
the culture, as in *the rest of us*. Their task is to instill the es-
sentials of good character: self-control and moral virtue. Parents who do a good job (even a *reasonably* good job) during
the years between toddlerhood and early adolescence not
only teach their children how to behave properly but also im-
part to them a core set of cultural values which I term the
"Three Rs": respect, responsibility, and resourcefulness. The
"Three Rs" are the essence of good citizenship, and as
Grandma knew, good citizenship begins at home. (Note: For
the specifics of teaching the "Three Rs," the reader is again referred to *A Family of Value*, cited above.)

In the course of teaching the lessons of citizenship, a
child's parents utilize the tools of corrective discipline such
that by the time the child enters adolescence, he/she has
learned the Second Great Understanding, which also exists in
three parts:

1. *You, child, are completely responsible for the choices you
make.* You behave as you do *not* because of your genes, allergies, your father's alcoholism, our divorce, or the fact that
your father rarely sees you, but because of *choice,* also known
as *free will*.

2. *If you make bad choices, bad things will happen—not
always right away, mind you, but sooner or later.* As a Bud-
dhist might put it, "You cannot escape the karma of a bad decision." The consequences of having made a bad decision will
catch up to you eventually. Maybe not in this life, even, but
eventually. Or, to paraphrase a line from an old blues tune:
"You can run, but you can't hide."

3. *If you make good choices, bad things are less likely to*

happen. Fancy that! Good choices do not guarantee good results! This is what Rabbi Harold Kushner means with the title of his best-seller *When Bad Things Happen to Good People*. Furthermore, the fact that *no one deserves a reward for doing the right thing* (!) means it requires more effort—much more!—to be a good person than a bad one. This means, of course, that it is the responsibility of parents to teach children the value of making the effort.

It is worth noting that for thirty years, well-intentioned, but highly misguided mental health professionals have been telling parents to teach children as follows: If you do something good/right, *you deserve something good in return*. The well-intentioned translation of this lie into parenting behavior has produced more than a few children who cannot grasp the fundamentals of social responsibility, and who, moreover, are in danger of never grasping those fundamentals. For my readers, the questions become:

a. Are you willing to consider that the above description may apply to your child? If it does, remember, you are not to *blame*. You are a well-intentioned, responsible individual who was simply caught up in the child-rearing propaganda mental health professionals have been pushing at us for more than thirty years. No, you aren't to *blame*, but it's your responsibility to do whatever you can to set things as right as possible. Read on.

b. If you conclude that the above description *does* indeed apply, are you willing to begin making whatever effort may be necessary at this point to correct (as much as is possible) your child's fantasies concerning what he is owed by the rest of us?

c. Are you willing to begin the effort today? Starting right now?! Because in hesitation, all may be lost.

The First Great Understanding stabilizes the parent-child relationship, sets it right (as in *right side up*). The Second Great Understanding stabilizes the adolescent years. Another way of putting this:

- *The First Great Understanding enables the parents to effectively lead,* to assume their rightful authority;
- *The Second Great Understanding enables the youngster to effectively lead himself,* to assume responsible authority over himself!

A child who has not learned the Second Great Understanding by early adolescence is in imminent danger of becoming a "Loose Cannon"—a teen who, lacking a moral compass, begins to career unpredictably and self-destructively around the deck of life. In this regard, two points are material:

1. The First Great Understanding is prerequisite to the Second Great Understanding. In other words, parents who haven't taught the first set of rules cannot teach the second. However—and this is extremely important—*there is no guarantee that a child who learns the first set will learn the second, even if parents do a good job of teaching.*

2. The fact that a child learns both the First and Second Great Understandings greatly increases the likelihood of, but does not by any means guarantee, a stable adolescence. Good choices—in this case, on the part of parents—don't guarantee good results, remember (see *Put It in Perspective Principle Number Four*, page 12). In short, children share responsibility for both the course and the outcome of their own upbringings. Furthermore, their share of that responsibility increases as they get older, along with the risk they will engage in irresponsible behavior. To repeat myself, but not needlessly, *children have minds of their own.*

Once the Second Great Understanding has been learned by a child, the child's parents can, and should, begin transforming themselves into mentors. A mentor is *an authority figure who has no need to prove it.* In this case, we're talking about a parent who, having resolved authority issues with his/her child, has segued rather naturally into being a consultant, a guide, a guru. The mentor-parent stands in the background—not the foreground!—of the child's life. The child in question has developed a sufficient amount of self-control. He's taken over the greater share of his own discipline. But, as is the case with the first transition in parent job descriptions—from caretaker to authority figure, the previous job is not entirely over. In this case, parents must always stand ready during the teen years to exercise authority over the child when he lapses in his ability to discipline himself.

The teen who has learned the Second Great Understanding is respectful of parental authority (and, by extension, *all* legitimate adult authority). From this point on, therefore, the parent should have little, if any, need to demonstrate it. The teen has learned to accept responsibility and does so independently (without having to be told) in most instances. He's resourceful, meaning he carries a "hang tough" attitude into any challenging situation. His parents, therefore, don't need to go to any lengths to motivate him to always do his best. In short, he's a "good kid."

Ah, but here's a sobering fact: *You absolutely cannot make the transition from authority figure to mentor if authority issues between you and your child have not been completely resolved.* This is a simple matter of common sense: You cannot mentor someone who does not accept your authority, your competence, your ability to provide competent guidance.

Here's another sobering fact: *Today's parents, by and large, are not resolving authority issues with their children by the time those children become tweenagers.*

Why? Because today's parents, by and large, are trying to be their children's *friends*. Today's parents want their children to *like* them. All too often, today's parents never take their children out of the center of their attention during late toddlerhood. Today's parents are afraid to make their children even temporarily unhappy, for fear that they'll grow up with bitter memories of their childhoods as a result. Today's parents, largely because of thirty-plus years of "parent-babble" from mental health professionals, are reluctant to employ *powerful* disciplinary methods of the sort that nip misbehavior in the proverbial bud and, in so doing, *declare* (!!!) parental authority. (Don't misunderstand me on this point. I'm not necessarily talking about spankings, although I have no fundamental problem with them.) Today's parents have been brainwashed by so-called "helping" professionals into thinking they can talk their children into behaving properly. So, they talk, talk, talk, talk, talk themselves blue in the face. Their problem is, they talk so much they usually fail to *act*.

Because of all of the above, today's child is never fully confronted with the reality of his/her parents' authority. His parents never stand firm enough for long enough to allow the child to fully grasp and accept that reality. Therefore, authority issues in today's typical parent-child relationship aren't being resolved before adolescence. Unfortunately, for obvious reasons, it's significantly more difficult to resolve authority issues during the teen years than before.

The problem is, parents who haven't resolved authority issues by the time a child reaches adolescence usually panic. They realize they've "missed the boat," and they begin attempting desperate means of asserting their dominion over the child. This knee-jerk response is destined to fall flat on its face. Please read the next sentence very carefully. Then read it again.

If your child is a teen, and you realize you haven't resolved authority issues, the very worst thing you can do is begin making sudden, strenuous attempts to make your child accept your authority.

Those sudden, strenuous attempts to force the issue will lead you to become impatient and reckless. Under the circumstances, instead of solving anything, you may well precipitate a full-blown rebellion.

So, just what *should* a parent do under those less-than-desirable circumstances? Just throw in the towel? Actually, this problem has a paradoxical "solution." Read the next sentence carefully. Then read it again.

If you haven't resolved authority issues by the time your child becomes a young teen, then the best thing you can do is act like you've resolved them and move on.

That's right. Just cut your losses, put your chin up, and stay focused on the road ahead. If you try to go back in time and resolve authority issues now, then you will only compound one problem (having missed the boat) with another (trying to paddle upstream when you need to be concentrating on what's in front of you—upstream!).

The bad news is, many if not most of today's parents are failing—through no real "fault" of their own—to resolve authority issues by the time their children become young teens. The good news is the parent-child relationship is a very forgiving one. It better be, after all, because being human, parents *will* make mistakes. If *you* are one of the parents in question (and remember, you aren't alone!), you need to first, accept responsibility for it and second, resolve to not compound that mistake with yet another. Feeling guilty about it will only impair your ability to do what you need to do from this point forward. And by all means, from this point forward you need to be an on-your-toes, forward-looking, in-control-of-yourself parent because your mettle is about to be tested.

Remember the turmoil that accompanied the late toddlerhood transition? Well, you ain't seen nothin' yet! At this point, for a second time, but for entirely different reasons, the parent/child relationship is about to undergo major upheaval, and I do mean *major*.

The Big Picture, Part Four:
The "Terrible Tweens"
(or, That's Why God Made Boarding Schools)

Parents often tell me stories of children who, after twelve years or so of being sweet and lovable (the "terrible twos" notwithstanding), suddenly, as in overnight, became transformed into hateful little monsters—defiant, disrespectful, disobedient, discourteous, disingenuous, and other d-words—in brief, moody little wretches. Parents tend to attribute this sea-change in the young adolescent child's personality to hormones. But this explanation begs the question, "Why disrespect and defiance? Why not some other emotional extreme—chronic hysteria perhaps?" Hormone surges produce a boil-over of emotion, but not necessarily disrespect, defiance, etc. In this case, the *strength* and *irrationality* of the emotional reaction can be attributed to hormones, but not the emotions themselves. They have to do with something else.

That something else is peer group influence; or, more specifically, peer group *worship*. In effect, the peer group becomes a *religion*—more accurately, a *cult*—during the tween-age years. But please don't misunderstand me. It has been convenient of late to attribute every deviant act, large and small, committed by tweens and teens to peer group "influence" or "pressure" or what have you. And indeed, the adolescent peer group has significant influence and yes, peers apply pressure to one another, but this phenomenon is hardly unique to adolescence. After all, adults are influenced by and even pressured by their peers every day. In fact, I've observed that most adults are complete wimps when it comes to peer pressure! This business of peer pressure/influence, in other words, is nothing more than a fact of social life. Children become increasingly social as they get older; therefore, the peer group exerts increasing influence.

In the final analysis, however, the adolescent peer group is merely a catalyst. It is *not* the primary problem of "tweenagerness." The primary problem is that human beings, once they have control over something, are not wont to give up that control easily. In this case, the human beings in question are *parents*.

Around age twelve, it dawns on the preadolescent that he won't be living with his parents for the rest of his life; that his future lies not with them, but with members of his own generation. And so, he throws his lot—or most of it—in with his peers. In and of itself, this is nothing to fret over. It's not only inevitable, but also functional. After all, there is perhaps nothing more pitiful than a child who, for whatever reasons, cannot manage to begin cutting the proverbial apron strings during the teen years. I'm referring to the youngster who would rather spend a cozy night at home with his parents than go to the high school football game with classmates; who can't go on a weekend retreat with the church youth group because he has anxiety attacks when he's away from home overnight; who gets so homesick the first week of "big" college that he drops out to attend the local junior college. A nice kid, for sure, but one who desperately needs to grow up and get a life.

Sometime during the preteen or early teen years, the typical youth "unplugs" from his parents and "plugs into" his peers. Naturally, his parents become somewhat anxious about the kinds of friends the child chooses and will choose. But again, the primary problem is, *his parents feel themselves to be losing control of the parent-child relationship.* Ironically, what happens to the parent/child relationship during early adolescence is a mirror image of what occurred some ten years earlier, except that this time, the proverbial shoes are on the parents' feet.

When the child was a toddler and his parents rather suddenly changed the rules, thus asserting their authority, the child felt *himself* to be losing control of the relationship. He became, therefore, insecure and tried every conceivable means (i.e., tantrums, defiance, etc.) of keeping things the way they had been, of keeping himself at the center of his parents' attention. Now, however, it is *the child* who initiates the change in the "rules." For nine years, he has been *parent-centered.* Suddenly, he:

- puts his peers at the center of his attention;
- starts looking to them for cues as to how to act (in effect, for definitions of what is "right" and what is "wrong");
- begins acting as if peer approval is more important than parental approval;
- begins to derive primary security and, therefore, a sense of identity, from acceptance by his peers;
- acquires a sense of meaning, of importance, from his role within his peer group.

In so doing, he asserts his independence. And suddenly, it's his parents who are upended. When he was a toddler, his parents changed the rules, and *he* felt insecure. Now, *he* changes the rules, and *his parents* feel insecure. When he was a toddler, he reacted to what his parents had done—*their* revolution—by attempting desperate means of maintaining control, of maintaining himself at the center of their attention. Now, his parents are likely to react to what the child is doing—*his* revolution—by attempting desperate means of maintaining control, of maintaining *themselves* at the center of *his* attention. When *his parents* initiated the two-year-old revolution, *the child* screamed and yelled and banged his head against the wall. When *the child* initiates the "tweenage" revolution, *his parents* are likely to scream and yell and beat *their* heads against the proverbial brick wall. *He* didn't understand what was going on when he was a toddler, now it's *his parents* who are likely to lack understanding. No, the primary issue is not the peer group. Peers are truly peripheral to the crux of the matter, mere bit players in Act Four of the drama that's been unfolding since day one of the parent/child relationship. To review:

- In Act One (infancy and early toddlerhood), the protagonist was lulled into a sense of false omnipotence.
- In Act Two (late toddlerhood), he experienced his comeuppance, his fall from grace. He is expelled, if you will, from the Garden of Eden.
- During Act Three (ages three to twelve approximately), the child accepts parental authority, is fairly obedient, and all goes relatively well.
- As Act Four (the tween years) begins, we find the child reasserting control over his own destiny, thus throwing the aristocracy into a state of panic as his parents struggle to answer the question: *What is the meaning of being a parent if the person you're parenting doesn't want one?*

The fact is, the tweenager doesn't want, nor does he need, the parent(s) he's lived with for the last nine years or so. The requirements of parenting a teen demand change in the parent job description. Keep in mind, this is nothing new. The parent job description changed once before. During the transition that takes place between a child's second and third birthdays, it changed from caretaker to authority figure.

This time around, the parent job description needs to change from authority figure to mentor. Again, the parent who shifts into mentor-mode will still, on occasion, have to exercise corrective authority. He even does some occasional caretaking. But his/her primary function has changed. The difference between being an authority figure and a mentor can be summed up thusly: *An authority is explicit about the lessons he wants his student to learn, while a mentor guides the student toward learning those same lessons on his or her own.* For example:

An authority says: "Today, I'm going to teach you that two plus two equals four."

A mentor says (to himself): "I'm going to wait for my student to present me with a golden opportunity to help him learn that two plus two equals four. Not only that! I'm also going to help him learn *why* two plus two equals four!"

Likewise, during the time when he/she is functioning primarily as a teacher/authority figure, a parent says (to the child), "I'm going to set limits on your freedom." A mentor, on the other hand, says (to himself), "I'm going to help my child take control of his own life and learn the relationship between responsibility and freedom."

If you are proactive about changing your job description, then there's little your teenager can do that will throw you off balance. Will he upset you? Disappoint you? Amaze you? Yes to all of the foregoing, but a parent can be upset, disappointed, and amazed without being off balance. To be proactive about changing your job description, you must anticipate and be waiting for your child to initiate the parent-child revolution that commences true adolescence. If you know that the revolution is coming, and you are clear on what your new job description must be and have its essential elements "waiting in the wings," so to speak, then as soon as your child initiates the revolution, all you have to do is slip out of your old job description and into your new one. This is nothing more than parent-judo. If you try, as many parents do, to continue in the didactic role of authority figure (who controls the parent-child relationship)—a role which once served a good purpose but is no longer compatible with the demands of the parent-child relationship—you will become your own worst enemy. Your rigidity (refusal to change when change is demanded) will force your child into conflict with you.

To Continue . . .The young adolescent, once compliant, affectionate, and a source of great pride, becomes obstinate, even defiant, sullen, rude, disrespectful, and a source of great dismay. His parents, on the other hand, are at times angry, at other times confused; at times anxious and grasping, at other times depressed. The profound changes in the child's behavior and the equally profound loss of control his parents experience is likely to cause them to commit the Worst of Parenting Mistakes, one that has been the downfall of many a parent/teen relationship.

The Worst Mistake You Can Make with a Tweenager or, The Devil Is in the Details

In the corporate world, there are macromanagers and there are micromanagers. Let's take a close look at each:

Macromanagers do not believe it is their responsibility to always prevent employees from making mistakes. They understand, first of all, that irredeemable errors are extremely rare. They understand, second, that people learn best through trial and error, with an emphasis on the latter. Finally, they understand that people learn from their mistakes only if they take responsibility for them, and that *managers who try to prevent employees from making mistakes also prevent them from taking responsibility when mistakes are made*. Macromanagers let employees make mistakes, take responsibility for them, correct them, and learn from them.

A macromanagement style fosters employee growth, which facilitates promotions. When workplace prospects are this promising, employees become extremely loyal. The result is a win-win relationship between employee and employer. The employee feels competent, trusted, valued, and that he/she has an ever-improving future with the company. The employer, having fostered competence and responsibility and loyalty, is graced with an employee who is productive, creative, and isn't likely to look for a better job (because it isn't worth the effort to look!).

Macromanagers also don't believe it's their responsibility to drive productivity in the workplace. They realize that if they create a work environment that facilitates employee satisfaction, employees will produce, and produce, and produce. You don't need to stand over such employees. But note! Macromanagers eliminate the need to keep the proverbial eagle-eye on employees precisely because they *don't* keep an eagle-eye on employees! Their management style communicates trust, and employees respond by being trustworthy. Does this mean those employees never make mistakes? No, but it reduces mistake making to a minimum, which is all one can expect of imperfect beings.

Micromanagers, by contrast, are what in the vernacular are known as "control freaks." On a recent flight, I was seated next to two gentlemen who were obviously employed by the same company. I overheard them talking about a fellow manager whom one described as "wanting to inspect every single gizmo that comes off the line." He was talking figuratively, I concluded, because it quickly became apparent that the company in question was service-oriented.

The other responded, "Yeah, he's so responsible no one else can be."

"Well," the first gentleman said, "when he's lost his third assistant, maybe he'll wake up." They were obviously talking about a micromanager, someone who is obsessed with not just control, but detail as well. Actually, one goes hand-in-hand with the other. Micromanagers, in whatever context they are found, are anxious people who fear losing control. In a corporate setting, their tightfisted management style manifests in constant hovering over their staff (i.e., "wanting to inspect every gizmo that comes off the line"), ever vigilant for error. Clearly, the message they send their employees is "I don't trust you to do your work correctly, much less even *do your work*, unless I stand over you, making sure everything gets done, and done right."

A micromanagement style breeds not employee satisfaction, but resentment, anger, and avoidance. The employee, under these oppressive circumstances, is likely to make a habit of showing up late for work, and taking extended lunch "hours" and more sick days than is common. This "irresponsible" behavior, of course, is used by the micromanager to justify his vigilant hovering. Such an employee, under other circumstances, might be punctual, productive, and innovative—a positive example to his coworkers. But under the watchful eye of a micromanager, he is slack, unmotivated, and unwilling to go beyond the letter of his job description. He's there to get a paycheck, period—doing time until something better comes along.

Again, take note! Just as macromanagers eliminate the need to keep an eagle-eye on employees by *not* keeping an eagle-eye on them, micromanagers do just the opposite. The more of an eagle-eye they maintain, the more of one they have to maintain. Micromanagers, in short, are their own worst enemies. They not only make their employees' lives difficult but their own as well! Workplace studies have shown that micromanagement leads to four inevitable results:

1. communication problems (lack of, misunderstandings, and so on)
2. conflict (between manager and employee as well as between disgruntled, frustrated employees)
3. deceit (as employees try to cover their inevitable mistakes)
4. disloyalty (seeking to leave the company at the first possible opportunity)

For the purposes of the present discussion, it is important for parents to understand that micromanagement produces the same four results regardless of context. During my years as a family counselor, I came gradually to the following conclusion: *Many, if not most, of the problems parents (of the sort who will read this book) report having with teen children have more to do with parental micromanagement than the influence of the ubiquitous "wrong crowd."*

Indeed, the teens in my client-families were more often

than not associating with kids who were less than desirable, but I eventually realized that choosing the wrong friends was a predictable *consequence* of micromanagement. A child who, as a teen, abandons his parents' values and takes up with a group of kids who epitomize the antithesis of everything the child was taught concerning right and wrong, is being *disloyal*—and remember, disloyalty is one of the four inevitable consequences of being micromanaged. Interestingly, every single time—without exception!—a parent (or parents) came in to talk with me about a rebellious teen, I quickly discovered that the parent(s) was a micromanager. (Some of these parents had been micromanagers for many years; some had only recently begun to micromanage. The difference, where parenting teens is concerned, is irrelevant.) And sure enough, the problems the parent described fit into four categories: communication problems, conflict, deceit, and disloyalty.

Understand, please, that the only type of parent who is willing to spend seventy-five or more dollars for forty-five minutes of counseling with another imperfect, sinful human being is responsible, committed, hardworking, concerned, and all the things good parents should be. Lazy, irresponsible parents don't micromanage. They don't manage at all! Nor do they read parenting books. Responsible parents read parenting books. (Note: It does not, however, follow that a parent who *doesn't* read parenting books is irresponsible.) Likewise, highly conscientious parents—that means you, dear reader!—tend to become micromanagers during the teen years, if not before.

These parents who came to see me with stories of teens gone astray always had hearts that were in the right place; nevertheless, they'd lost control of their relationships with their children. Why? Because they were micromanaging, or *trying to,* at least. Why were they micromanaging? Because when their children became "tweens" and began doing typical "tweenage" stuff, they felt themselves losing control of their relationships with their children. Ironic, eh? Losing control made them hyper-anxious. Their hyper-anxiety drove desperate attempts to maintain control. Their children responded by trying to "escape"—trying to establish as much distance as possible between themselves and their micromanaging parents. Their overbearing parents responded by turning up their attempts at micromanagement and . . . You get the picture, I'm sure. The descriptive term is *vicious cycle*.

Here's a fact: *Teenagers will not allow parents to micromanage.*

Read that again, please. You see, an employee who's being micromanaged has two rational options (assuming he needs income): either (a) grin and bear it until a better job opportunity presents itself or (b) resign in good grace and find a new job. The employee cannot, however, begin cursing at his supervisor or flat out refuse to do what he's told or turn his back on his supervisor when his supervisor is talking to him. Not unless he wants to be fired, that is, and no one who's thinking clearly *wants* to be fired. But a teenager *can* exercise options of the latter sort because no matter how disrespectfully, how belligerently, how rebelliously he behaves, he knows he's not going to be "terminated." So whereas an employee who's being micromanaged can't defy his supervisor and keep his job, a teenager who's being micromanaged can indeed defy his parents and still live at home and enjoy a good standard of living. His parents may eventually get to the point where they throw up their hands and (a) commit him to an adolescent treatment center, (b) send him to live with a relative, or (c) send him to a military school or boarding school. Meanwhile, however, they keep making matters worse by constantly pumping up their desperate attempts to micromanage.

When I began asking questions pertaining to the history of

the problems in question, these parents described kids who did well in school and were reasonably well behaved until adolescence. Then all perdition broke loose. The parents would usually attribute the child's wayward veer to hormones and bad peer influences, or a combination thereof. Between the lines of their version of the story, however, was another story that went as follows:

Phase One: As the child approached his teen years, he began asserting his independence in typically immature ways. He talked back, ignored his parents when they spoke to him, defied them, and the like. His parents described him as having a "bad attitude."

Phase Two: As he "unplugged" from his parents and "plugged into" his peer group, his grades dropped and some of his choices of friends were less than desirable.

Phase Three: His parents became anxious and their anxiety caused them to begin trying to control things they either couldn't control or shouldn't even try to control. They wanted to know his every move. They wanted him to introduce them to each and every one of his friends. They wanted to check every homework paper. They searched his room for evidence of wrongdoing (and found it!). They told him he couldn't wear certain items of clothing to school. In other words, they began micromanaging. They forbade association with certain kids (which simply drove the relationships underground), insisted he make better grades or suffer being grounded (in which case the child accepted the dare and, if the parents actually *did* ground him, he walked out of the house when he felt like it), etc., etc.

Phase Four: Things went rapidly downhill. The child began doing exactly what his parents told him not to do. His grades went from bad to awful, and he didn't seem to care. His friends went from bad to awful and his parents suspected he was experimenting with alcohol and/or drugs. Likewise, his behavior went from bad to awful and no punishment worked. He lied, he stole money from his parents, he left the house without permission, he stayed gone for days at a time, he talked back, he physically threatened his parents, and so on.

As things went from bad to worse and then to the very pits, his parents, bless 'em, not only kept right on trying to micromanage, they tried that much *harder* to micromanage. They persuaded the well-intentioned junior high school counselor to circulate, on every Friday, a form among the youngster's teachers on which they were to report on his grades and behavior for the week. When he got home, they tried to talk about the teachers' reports with him. They told him he couldn't go out the front door with a friend, not even onto the front porch, unless he first introduced them to the friend (whom they would then interrogate as to his parents' jobs, what church they attended, their ancestry, whether he'd ever been drug-tested, and so on). When he went out to, say, a movie with a group of friends, his parents would be lurking in the parking lot when the movie got out, making sure he'd actually gone where he had told them he was going. At home, they reprimanded and corrected his every move.

"Don't use that tone of voice with me, young man!" his father would say.

"Can't you just answer my question without putting a sour expression on your face?" his mother would complain.

"Why do you insist on wearing the same two shirts all the time?" they would ask.

"You're not leaving the house without tying your sneakers and tucking in your shirt," they'd order.

"Look at me when I talk to you!"

"Stop chewing your food so loudly!"

"Who is this friend of yours anyway? Who are his parents? What kind of grades does he make?"

And the more the parents tried to micromanage, the worse the child's behavior became. Until finally, they'd be sitting in my office, all three of them. The child would be stone-faced, sullen, uncommunicative. The father would be angry, almost visibly shaking. The mother would be in tears. The parents would almost always make the same request of me:

"Please," they'd implore, "find out what's bothering him."

Hah! They couldn't see their own noses! To put it in teenage terms, the parents *didn't have a clue.* They did not see how their own responses to their ever-wayward youngster had contributed to the problem. Now don't get me wrong. I'm not, by any stretch, justifying a child who lies, steals, talks back, becomes a slouch in school, takes drugs, etc. I'm simply saying that in many of these cases, the fact that the child's behavior eventually became a self-destructive snowball rolling downhill was due more to parental good intentions than anything else.

Control Freaks Are Never in Control!

Parents who micromanage are attempting the impossible: They are trying to control their children. Yes, you read me right, and I want you to read the next sentence very slowly, out loud, and then read it again.

Parents cannot control their children!

I know. You've heard, many times I'm sure, parenting "experts" advise parents to maintain control of their children. *Don't lose control of your kids!* they say. The parenting "experts" in question are also well intentioned; nonetheless, they are reinforcing a fundamental misunderstanding, one that often proves calamitous. The fact is, *parents cannot control their children.* For proof of what I'm saying, please turn to Genesis, Chapter 3. There you will find God, and behold!

> *God cannot control His children!*
> *He cannot make them obey!*

He created them, no less, and He can't stop them from doing what they feel like doing. He tells Adam and Eve not to eat of the fruit of the tree of knowledge of good and evil, and as soon as His back is turned, they eat the fruit. Let's face it, people, if God can't control His children, if He can't make us obey, then none of us puny packages of foible and flaw is going to be able, no matter how strenuous the attempt, to control one of God's children either. And if you think about it, it's the height of absurdity to even try. So what's a parent to do? Is it hopeless? Are we, as parents, just supposed to cross our fingers concerning our children and cast their/our fate to the proverbial winds? No, it's not hopeless, and no, we can do a lot more than just cross and toss. But before I get into that, I need to get a bit deeper into this matter of *control.* There are, you see, three kinds of parents:

- Control Freaks: *Parents who try to control their children.* These parents—commonly called *authoritarian, dictatorial,* or *overcontrolling,* are usually nothing more, as we've already seen, than well-intentioned micromanagers. In the course of trying to control their kids—of attempting the impossible, remember?—they force their children to rebel. These parents respond to the rebellion by attempting ever more desperate means of control. Their children respond with more rebellion. As this vicious cycle spirals downward, their children eventually begin leaning dangerously in the direction of self-destructive behavior. Without realizing it, in their constant attempts to be so doggone responsible, Control Freak Parents prevent their children from ever taking full responsibility for the decisions they make, the things they do.

- Wimps: *Parents who let their children control the parent/child relationship.* These parents are typically called permissive, but I call 'em wimps. My wife and myself were wimps once. Our kids whined and complained, or—if that didn't work—screamed bloody murder and we gave in. This sort of parent/child relationship has its own vicious cycle: The more the child whines, complains, and/or screams, the more the parents give in, and the more the child whines, complains, and/or screams. Deep down inside, as Willie and I know all too well, Wimp Parents feel deeply insecure within the parent/child relationship. They feel comfortable in their "parent-skin" only when their children are pleased with them. Permissive Wimp Parents, without realizing it, allow the parent/child relationship to become inverted. Simply put, the wrong people end up doing the pleasing. Their children—like the children of control freaks, but for different reasons—are also prevented from learning to take responsibility for their behavior.

- Mentors: *Parents who realize that, indeed, they have to be in control, but also realize that they can only control the parent-child relationship; they* cannot *control the child.* Mentors understand their limitations. They establish rules (but not too many!) and stand ready to enforce those rules such that their children learn they are completely responsible for their own behavior. They parent according to the *Long Rope Principle,* which I'll come back to shortly.

Going back to the story of man's descent into sinfulness as portrayed in Genesis, God is a shining example of a mentor. He's not a micromanager, that's for sure. After He tells Adam and Eve what the rules are, He does not stand next to the tree of knowledge of good and evil, saying things like, "Now, remember what I told you about this tree" and "Hey! Eve! You're getting a bit too close to the forbidden fruit! Find something else to be interested in, okay?" and "Don't talk to that serpent! He's a bad influence, mark my words!" Nope. Genesis tells us that after God handed down the rules, He wandered off somewhere, in the cool of His garden. Later, still just wandering around, He notices that Adam and Eve are wearing fig leaves. They're trying to hide something! God starts asking pointed questions, and quickly gets to the truth. Then, with great disappointment and regret, he lets His children (forevermore!) know that when they break His law, there will be unpleasant consequences. In so doing, He assigns responsibility for His children's behavior squarely to them. He doesn't wail, as do so many parents when their children misbehave, "What have *I* done wrong!" Rather, He tells Adam and Eve *they* did wrong and metes out their punishment. (Note, God pays no attention to Adam's claim that Eve "made me do it," nor to Eve's claim that the serpent "made me do it.") Does God punish His first children with glee, with relish? No, he does so because he *must*, in order to teach them that disobedience is not free. Ever!

The Long Rope Principle

My stepfather, Julius, was fond of saying to me, "I knew if I gave you a long enough rope, you'd eventually hang yourself."

It goes without saying that he said this when I'd done something wrong and gotten into deep trouble as a consequence. Interestingly enough, he always said it with great glee, which I did not begin to understand until my children were teenagers. Then it dawned on me that Julius was doing nothing more than telling me I was responsible for the choices I made, and that bad choices caused bad things to happen. Furthermore, his reference to the "long rope" was the very crux of macromanagement. Julius always gave me lots of freedom, yet he was not by any means permissive. He simply wanted me to learn that with choices come consequences. If he tried to make the choices—in the manner of overcontrolling/micromanaging Control Freak Parents—I would not make the connection. If he let me make the choices, but was reluctant to enforce consequences (for fear of making me unhappy with him)—in the manner of anxious/permissive Wimp Parents—I would not make the connection. I made the connection (albeit belatedly) because Julius let me make lots of choices, yet stood ever-ready to "lower the boom" whenever I made a bad one (of which I made quite a few). He understood that like all children, I was destined to learn certain things courtesy of the "hard way." In order to bring the "hard way" into play in my life, Julius had to parent according to the Long Rope Principle. Did I, as a consequence of being given a lot of freedom as a teenager, make bad choices? You bet! I'll tell you about some of the really bad ones later. Did he, in retrospect, regret having given me the freedom in question? Not a bit. He was actually glad I made bad choices because it gave him the golden opportunity of teaching me, if someone or something else (a teacher, my principal, the juvenile court system) hadn't already done so, that *bad choices result in bad consequences.* So, he let me hang around with whomever I wanted to hang with, no matter their reputation. When I got into trouble, which was inevitable, he yanked the rug of my freedom out from under me quicker than you can read this sentence. And there I sat, on my rear end, left to ponder what had happened to cause such an ignominious downfall. After a period of no freedom, he'd let me start over again. He'd fling wide the gates of freedom, sweet freedom, I'd rush forth, and sooner or later, I'd do something wrong. And once again Julius would say, "I knew if I gave you a long enough rope, you'd eventually hang yourself." And once again, I'd have no freedom.

Did I learn the lessons I needed to learn? Not, unfortunately, until I was well into adulthood. Through my teen and young adult years, I got into one mess of hot water after another. Finally, I figured it out, long after the typical person of my generation had done so. Does the fact that I made one mistake after another mean that Julius was wrong to give me a lot of freedom? Absolutely not!

"I don't get it," some of you are saying. "Julius gave you freedom, you abused his trust. He continued to give you freedom, and you continued to abuse his trust. Of course he was mistaken!"

No, he was right to do what he did. Julius was a good teacher. I was a slow learner. He did the right thing. I did the wrong things. He did not try to control me because he knew he couldn't. He controlled his *relationship* with me, and as part of that, he controlled the *consequences* of the choices I made, nothing more. *I controlled the choices!* The next thing I'm going to say is extremely important, dear reader, so listen up!

Good parenting does not guarantee that a child will make good choices.

That should sound familiar. It's nothing more than a variation on Rule Three of the second set of understandings/rules (page 28).

In Summary . . .

1. A child comes into the world carrying with him a certain temperamental makeup. During the first two years of the child's life, parents wait on the child hand and foot.

2. Around the child's second birthday, the parents begin communicating the first set of three understandings. The child wants things to remain the same, so he screams and thrashes about on the floor and bites himself and does precisely what his parents tell him not to do.

3. His parents, however, stay the course. They do not allow the child's reaction to the "new regime" to knock them off track. By the time the child is three, he has accepted the First Great Understanding (pages 24–26).

4. Parental influence dominates over the next nine years, approximately, during which time the parents are communicating the Second Great Understanding (pages 28–29). (Note that the parents don't wait until the child is twelve to begin communicating them; rather, as soon as the First is in place, they begin communicating the Second.) The child, during this time, seeks his parents' approval, absorbs their values, and is, as a consequence, secure as to their unconditional love.

5. At around age twelve, give or take a year or two, the peer group assumes dominance. The child wants more freedom, namely the freedom to choose his own friends. At this point, the child begins to value peer approval more than parental approval. He begins to look to the peer group for definitions of what is "cool" (right) versus "uncool" (wrong), and he derives security from success at establishing peer relations.

6. Parents respond to this revolution by:
   a. attempting to micromanage; trying to control the child's every move (Control Freaking).

b. giving the child lots of freedom, not because they want to, but because they are afraid that if they don't, the child won't like them (Wimping).

c. giving the child lots of freedom, but using every opportunity to remind the child of the immutable truth contained within the second set of three understandings (Mentoring).

To repeat, because it deserves repeating: Control Freak Parents attempt what not even God could do: They try to control their children. Wimp Parents let their children control the parent/child relationship. Mentors conduct themselves according to the Long Rope Principle.

The rest of this book was written to help you become an effective mentor. To accomplish this, I'm going to focus your attention on the six issues that are key to successfully managing a teenager: curfew, cash, car, the child's choice of cohorts, conflict, and consequences.

I'm going to share with you . . .

- the not-so-secret secrets of teaching your teen that he is completely responsible for the decisions he makes and that when he makes bad decisions, bad things will happen;
- how to stay completely out of arguments with your teenager (and yes, I do mean *completely*);
- and the secret (and this one is truly a secret!) to dealing effectively with your teen's inevitable misbehavior—even "in your face" challenges to your authority.

At this point, the reader has every right to say, "A teenager who doesn't argue and obeys sounds too good to be true, John."

Ah! But I didn't say your teen wouldn't argue and would always obey. I said I'm going to teach you how to refuse the invitation to argument and handle misbehavior effectively. Even if you become a Perfect Master of Teen Parenting, your child will still try to invite you to argue and will still disobey. Remember, you are not God, but your child is a direct descendant of Adam and Eve; therefore, no matter how good a parent you become, how effective you become at handling him, he will still misbehave. So? What's new?

Believe me, this is going to be fun.

SECTION TWO:

The Plan!

CHAPTER THREE

◆

Everything Is Possible, But Nothing Is Free!

(SIX C-WORDS OF CONSIDERABLE CONTEMPORARY CONSEQUENCE)

Sigmund Freud revealed his bewilderment concerning females by asking, "What do women *really* want?" He wasn't asking what women want for their birthdays, but rather what motivates them. To Freud, their behavior was a mystery. His labyrinthine thinking on the subject drove him to attribute a host of absurd psychological flaws and powers to women. According to this brilliant but terribly confused man, women envied men because men had penises, women caused their male children to develop "Oedipus complexes," and women were fundamentally neurotic. Because Freud could never think about them in clear, simple terms, he remained essentially "clueless" where women were concerned. Accordingly, "happy" does not describe his relationships with them.

Today's parents are bewildered by teens. They want to know what teenagers *really* want—what motivates them to do the things they do. Like Freud on women, today's parents are generally confused where teens are concerned. They attribute to teens exaggerated flaws and powers. They think teens are more susceptible to "peer pressure" than adults, when the susceptibilities are approximately equal. They think the typical teen is but one parental mistake away from abusing drugs and/or alcohol, running away, or committing suicide when the fact is, the typical teen is never close to doing any of the above. (Granted, the typical teen drinks alcoholic beverages on occasion and may even experiment with pot, but drug/alcohol *abuse* is and always has been atypical.) Some parents even talk as if it's impossible to prevent a teen from doing what he wants to do and equally impossible to effectively discipline him when he does. Because so many of today's parents cannot seem to think about teens in clear, simple terms, they end up having relationships with their teenage children which can hardly be described as "happy."

The "flight or fight" principle is a psychological construct which asserts that a person, when threatened by something, will try to either put distance between himself and the threat by fleeing or lessen it by trying to suppress/subdue it. Let's face it, the typical parent is threatened by the mere thought of trying to cope with a teenage child. As the "flight or fight" principle predicts, parents of teens tend to separate into two distinct groups:

1. Some parents deal with their anxieties by running away from conflict with their teens. They adopt an "it's hopeless/ if you can't beat 'em, join 'em" stance concerning issues that harbor the potential for great conflict. They let their teenage children drink alcoholic beverages at home or at adult-supervised parties, allow teenage children to have coed sleepovers and supply condoms for "safety's sake," and even smoke pot with them. The standard explanation: "They're going to do it anyway. Better they do it under supervision than where they could get in trouble." This reflects a very strange, not to mention irresponsible, thought process.

2. In the second group are found parents who deal with their anxieties by employing vainly aggressive management strategies. They try to keep tabs on their teens' every moves, tell their teens who they can and can't associate with, force participation in certain activities, and mandate certain grades. Their standard explanation: "I'm not about to let my teenager do something self-destructive."

The first group comprises wimps; the second, control freaks. Wimps are afraid of exercising power in their relationships with their teens; control freaks are afraid of what will happen if they ease up on the power even a little bit.

In my experience, wimps are extremely difficult to reach. Most of them are in such a deep state of denial that they won't even recognize themselves in the first description above. Over the years, I've come to the conclusion that I'm probably not going to persuade fundamentally lazy people who have no common sense to begin with that they're acting like unmitigated idiots. To stop acting like an idiot, one must be able to first recognize one's behavior for what it is. In most cases, the wimp will not recognize himself/herself until his/her child is in deep trouble.

Control freaks, on the other hand, are receptive to the idea that what they're doing is well intentioned, but counterproductive. After all, we're talking here about people who are genuinely concerned about their teenage children and want to do the very best job they can do. Best of all, control freaks possess the ability to laugh at themselves and the absurd things they do to control that which cannot be *controlled* by parents—a child's behavior. Unlike wimps, they are not in denial; therefore, they have no problem recognizing themselves. Unlike wimps, they do not accept that teens are "going to do it anyway." Unlike wimps, most control freaks have good common sense. If shown a better way of handling the problems potential to the teen years, they will recognize it for what it is—a better idea.

For those reasons, I'm going to address myself primarily to control freaks. If you, dear reader, are the rare wimp who can be shaken out of his/her self-deception, then you'll wake up and smell the coffee sometime between here and the end of this book. If not, well, good luck to you. If you're a control freak, I've probably already succeeded in helping you recognize yourself. The rest of this book is devoted to helping you, silly control freak, become a mentor to your teen.

I promised earlier that this book would not be theoretical. It would be based on Real Life. In fact, it's based on the Very Real Life of the Rosemond Family during the Rosemond children's teenage years. After Willie and I developed and implemented the concrete, down-to-earth, practical—not to mention brilliantly creative (just kidding, sort of)—management style described in this chapter, I further refined it during my private practice years (1979–91), most of which were spent working with parents and their teenage children. That backlog of personal and professional experience enables me to confidently assert,

"This Stuff Works!!!"

That's not to say it's going to work for you. Even putting the Plan into letter-perfect practice doesn't guarantee trouble-free teen years because of Putting It Into Perspective Principle Number Four, which says *You can do the right thing, and things may still go wrong* (see page 12). No parenting plan is fail-safe. But the parenting plan that follows significantly reduces the chance of failure. Another way of saying the same thing: You are not and will never be *omnipotent,* but you can always be *competent* regardless of whether your teen makes good decisions or bad ones.

Let's get started: Willie and I realized that above all else, we could not afford to get carried away with anxiety and begin micromanaging Eric and (later) Amy during their teen years. We decided that our best strategy was first, to distinguish those issues which were "wheat" from those which were "chaff." We reflected back on our own teen years and came up with the following six:

1. Curfew
2. Cash
3. Car
4. Cohorts
5. Conflict
6. Consequences

For an obvious reason, I call them the Six C's Parents of Teens Most Need to Keep in the Fronts of Their Minds so as to Prevent, as Much as Is Possible, Problems, Frustrations, and Downright Broken Hearts. Teens want freedom, which is closely tied to the issues of Curfew, Cash, and Cars. They want parents to stay out of their choices of Cohorts. Because teens generally want more freedom than they can handle and parents are generally unwilling to give them the freedom they need, parent-child Conflict tends to escalate—often dramatically—during the teen years. Finally, because all teens will flirt with misbehavior—some compulsively, some only now and then—there's the matter of what Consequences are most appropriate when such misbehavior occurs. Willie and I determined:

1. These six critical parent-teen issues need to be addressed *proactively* as opposed to *reactively*. We had already

learned that crossing any given "bridge" in the parent-child relationship before one comes to it is far preferable to waiting until the last minute—not to mention after the fact!—to decide one's manner of crossing.

2. Each issue should be handled such that the child in question learns to manage himself competently. The reward for doing so is freedom, sweet freedom! This requires, yes, that parents establish initial disciplinary structures concerning each issue—clear understandings as to the "rules." It also requires that parents allow the teenager the trial and error needed to assume his own discipline.

3. In order to develop self-management skills, the teen must "tote" as much responsibility as possible (and reasonable) concerning each issue, thereby learning that freedom and responsibility are two sides of the same coin—the coin of autonomy.

Taking each "C" in turn, here's what Willie and I did:

No More Curfew Cops!

To determine which child among them is the "luckiest," elementary-age children compare bedtimes. They envy the child who can stay up the latest, and his/her bedtime becomes the standard to which the other children refer when petitioning their parents for more evening privilege.

Years pass and these children become teens, at which time curfew replaces bedtime as the ultimate symbol of privilege. Just as eight-year-olds dream of being able to stay up until ten o'clock, so fourteen-year-olds dream of being able to stay out until midnight. Unfortunately, just as curfew represents *free-*

dom to teens, it represents *control* to their parents. I say *unfortunately* because the parent who tries to control curfew is:

    a.   missing an ideal opportunity to help his/her teen develop a stronger sense of responsibility.

    b.   likely to provoke power struggles over the issue of curfew.

    c.   likely to push the "rebellion button," albeit unwittingly.

    d.   micromanaging; therefore, likely to precipitate all of the problems appertaining thereto (conflict, communication problems, deceit, disloyalty).

    e.   probably going to experience a lot of unnecessary heartache.

    f.   often going to go to bed angry.

    g.   often going to have difficulty falling asleep.

    h.   going to eventually suffer from chronic sleep deprivation.

    i.   all of the above.

The issue of curfew provides parents with an ideal way of promoting self-discipline, restraint, goal-setting, good decision-making, delay of gratification, responsibility, and trust. To do so, however, means that parents *must avoid (like the plague!) the tendency to micromanage this important issue.*

Shortly after Eric (our "experimental" child) turned thirteen, Willie and I made an astonishing announcement. We told him, "We really don't want to be your parents anymore."

He just looked at us, but I'm sure he was thinking, "We agree on *one* thing."

By "we don't want to be your parents anymore," Willie and I meant we no longer wanted to reprimand, scold, restrict, or exercise the power of "office" in any sort of punitive, controlling manner. We went on to say, "You know the rules, and you're well aware of the consequences of violating those rules. You're also an intelligent and responsible individual, capable of keeping yourself out of trouble, which is what we expect. What we're trying to say, Eric, is that if you act responsibly during your teenage years, Mom and Dad will not only stay off your back but also give you a lot of freedom. But with freedom comes responsibility. If you act responsibly, your freedom will grow. If you break the rules, if you act irresponsibly, if you fail to put your priorities in a fairly proper order, then we're going to have to be your parents—we're going to have to step in and do things you won't like. In short, whether your freedom grows, shrinks, or stays the same is *completely* up to you."

Having secured his undivided attention, we popped the Big Q: "How would you like to be setting your own curfew when you're sixteen?"

"That would be cool," he said, feigning nonchalance.

Here's a point-by-point description of what we proposed:

1. At that point in time, Eric's curfew on non-school nights was nine. We told him that if for six months he did not violate that curfew, his curfew would be extended to nine-thirty. Every violation-free six months thereafter, his curfew would increase by thirty minutes.

2. Curfew was determined by the digital clock on the microwave which, except when the microwave was on, did not mark seconds. (Clocks with hands and clocks that mark seconds leave the precise moment of violation open to question.)

3. A violation consisted of walking into the house after the designated curfew had lapsed on the "curfew clock." (For example, if his curfew was nine-thirty, and Eric walked in the door at nine thirty-one, he was in violation.) In the event of a violation, the current six-month period would begin anew.

4. In the event of a violation, no excuses would be accepted, even if we were certain Eric was telling the truth. It was his responsibility to be in before his curfew lapsed, *no matter what.*

5. When he had earned a midnight curfew and had not violated it for six months, he would be able to set his own curfew on a night-by-night basis. No strings attached! If he said he was coming in at four in the morning, we would accept that without argument. (Note: This arrangement applied to non-school nights only. Eric's curfew on school nights was flexible, but had to be agreed upon beforehand.)

"There are three things that you need to understand," we told Eric. "First, when you are setting your own curfew, you must still keep us informed as to where you are and who you are with. Second, if you say you are going to be in by two o'clock, we expect you in at two o'clock, and not a minute later. If you violate a curfew you set for yourself, then we go back to midnight for six months. In other words, Eric, being eventually able to set your own curfew means freedom, but it also means commitment and responsibility and, most of all perhaps, trust. Third, and perhaps most important, agreeing to this deal means that when you turn sixteen, you may be able to set your own curfew or your curfew may still be nine o'clock. Is it a deal?"

"It's a deal!" he said, without hesitation.

Two months into this arrangement, Eric came in fifteen minutes late. He gave us a song and dance about not knowing what time it was and how he'd forgotten to wear his watch and his friend's grandmother's second cousin's anaconda got sick and they had to take it to the vet, and we simply listened and shook our heads and said, "See, now we have to be your parents again." His six-month period started over from there.

Eric figured out the system quickly. In fact, that was the only violation he ever incurred. Six months later, his curfew became nine-thirty, and he was on his way. Shortly after he turned sixteen, he earned his "wings" and was setting his own curfew!

The principle at work here is a simple one; to wit: *A child will take responsibility not for things that are handed to him on a silver platter, but for things he must earn.* I never cease to be amazed at parents who give their children nearly everything they want and then wonder why their children (a) don't take care of their belongings, (b) take their parents' benevolence for granted, (c) behave irresponsibly and even dangerously, or (d) all of the above. By the time a child becomes a teen, a parent ought to know better. Give a five-year-old ten toys and no more, and the child will take good care of all ten toys. Give that same five-year-old two hundred toys (the number of toys, by the way, the average American child has received by age five) and the child will take care of none of them. In the latter instance, it's not that the child is destructive, it's that his parents have given him no reason to take care of any of his possessions.

The fundamental problem is that today's parents, all too often, try to both (a) please their children and (b) be pleasing to them. Consequently, they avoid doing anything that will make their children unhappy. And should one such parent do something that causes a child unhappiness, he/she feels compelled to correct it, thus making the child happy once again.

Willie and I dedicated ourselves *not* to making Eric and Amy happy, but rather to helping them develop the qualities and skills they needed to create their own happiness. Nor did we feel compelled to please and be pleasing. Rather, we made it perfectly clear that it was *their* responsibility to please and be pleasing to us!

This, by the way, is the crux of the difference between *psychological parenting* and *scriptural parenting*. The Psychological Parent feels his primary responsibility is to help the child develop a nebulous psychic ether mental health professionals call "self esteem." By definition, this requires that the parent do everything in his power to make the child "feel good about himself," which is accomplished—or so mental health professionals have told us for going on forty years—by paying lots of attention to the child and, more generally, being constantly busy, busy, busy in the child's life. This busyness is the Psychological Parent's way of demonstrating his commitment to his child. In short, the Psychological Parent focuses on the child—not just during infancy and toddlerhood, which is absolutely necessary, but forever and always, amen—and, furthermore, most of the obligation in the parent-child relationship is shouldered by the parent. The Scriptural Parent, on the other hand, once the incubation period of infancy and toddlerhood is over, understands that it is in the child's ultimate interest that he/she:

1. learn to focus on the parent.
2. learn that he/she has obligations to the parent which, as he/she gets older, become increasingly weighty.
3. be pleasing to the parent.

The story of God's relationship with Man is, at one level, a parenting story. In this story, as it is recorded in Judeo-Christian scripture, we find God trying over and over again, in one way after another, to help mankind understand that:

1. It is in the ultimate interest of His children that they focus on Him—that we pay more attention to Him than He, ultimately, pays to us.
2. The obligation in the relationship is borne primarily by us.
3. We are expected to be pleasing to Him.

The parent-child relationship is intended to be a model for the child's eventual understanding of his proper relationship to God and the obligations that relationship impose upon him. In short, parents who sincerely desire to help their children grow toward God (as opposed to the far greater number of parents who give lip service to this idea, but are unwilling, when it comes right down to it, to "walk their talk") have a responsibility to God and their children to make it clear that the pleasing in the parent-child relationship is to be done by children.

In this same vein, note that God obligates His children but also gives them the ultimate freedom—the right to think for themselves! God knows from the beginning that His children are going to abuse this privilege—that they're going to disappoint Him—but he gives it to them anyway. Likewise, every human parent needs to strike a balance between the assignment of obligation and the extension of freedom. And every human parent needs to do so with eyes open, knowing that to give a child freedom means the child is likely to abuse it. The solution to this is simple, and again, scriptural. When Man abuses the freedom God has given him, God punishes. He doesn't threaten, explain himself, attempt to reason with us, give second chances. He makes us pay a price. So, when a child abuses the freedom given by a parent, it is the parent's obligation—to God, the child, and the rest of us—to punish. Not threaten, explain, equivocate, or talk, talk, talk until blue in the face but simply, quickly, and effectively *punish*. We will come back to this idea in the section on consequences.

With the curfew system described above, Willie and I extended to our children the opportunity to earn a lot of freedom. To earn this freedom, Eric and Amy had to be responsible. We said, in effect, "Whether you have freedom or not—in this case, whether you can stay out as late as you want or have to come in early—is not up to us; rather, it's completely up to you!" When one of them violated curfew—abused the freedom we had extended—the punishment was built into the system. They knew in advance what the consequences were going to be.

This relieved us of the hassle of having to be Curfew Cops. The payoff, in other words, was twofold: First, the children obtained nearly all the freedom they wanted. Second, so did Willie and I.

Epilogue

At a talk in Iowa in the early 1990s, I related the story of How Eric (and later Amy) Earned the Right to Set His Own Curfew to an audience in Iowa, suggesting that nearly all teens should be given the same opportunity. A fairly irate parent (it so happened she had made the mistake of bringing her sixteen-year-old son to my presentation) stood up and protested that if the typical teen was allowed this sort of freedom, he'd get into "nothing but trouble."

What an unfortunate—not to mention counterproductive—belief! The facts:

1. Relatively few teenagers ever get into serious trouble. Granted, nearly all teens make mistakes, but very few make big mistakes and of those, even fewer keep on making them.

2. Read the following very slowly: *It isn't early curfews that keep teens out of trouble; rather, it's a strong sense of responsibility combined with proper respect for one's parents and family.* In other words, the only parents who truly need to worry about what their teens are doing under the cover of darkness are those who haven't succeeded at (a) helping their children develop responsibility and (b) commanding their children's respect. If you respect your parents, you will try not

to disappoint them. You will try to please them. It's as simple as that.

3. It's been my experience that teens who are allowed to set their own curfews actually set quite reasonable ones. This was certainly the case with Eric. More often than not, this highly social, strong-willed, risk-taking youngster (to give the reader some appreciation for this, Eric was piloting corporate jets at the age of twenty-six) set an earlier curfew for himself than his mother and I would have set for him. Furthermore, the latest curfew he ever set for himself was 1 A.M. There were times, in fact, when we would encourage Eric to stay out later than when he'd told us he'd be home! Nonetheless, he never, ever, walked in the house later than 1 A.M.!

The above irate parent, who can't see further in front of herself, unfortunately, than to the tip of her own nose (and she is by no means alone in this regard), typifies the micromanaging parent. I'd bet my life savings that when it comes to her son's curfew, the "conversation" goes something like this:

MAGNIFICENTLY MICROMANAGING MOM (3M): You want to what? Stay out until ten-thirty?!! Absolutely not, young man! There is nothing for a sixteen-year-old to do in this town after ten other than things he shouldn't be doing! You will be in at ten, as usual, and that's that!

SON: But, Mom, I just . . .

3M: You'll just nothing! Now I don't want to hear even one more word on this subject!

SON: Mom, please. I'm not . . .

3M: Not another word, I said!

SON: . . . going to . . .

3M: Did you hear me?!!

SON: . . . do anything wrong.

3M: All right! That's it! I've had enough of your back talk! Furthermore, I obviously can't trust you, so you're staying home tonight, young man, and that's final!

SON: (under his breath) Just you wait.

Magnificently Micromanaging Mom is the epitome of overcontrol, and she is probably proud as a plum of how successfully she puts down her son's "rebellion." But in the final analysis, she is her own worst enemy. The problem is, when her son has had enough of her heavy-handedness and really *does* rebel, 3M won't be able to see that she, in effect, *drove* him to do foolish things because she was so unwilling to let up on the reins. This scenario is a prime example of what I've already said twice before in these pages: *It's certainly true, most teens want more freedom than they can handle or should have. On the other hand, most (responsible) parents are not as willing as they should be to give their teenage children the freedom they need.* The consequent tension drives a wedge into the parent-child relationship—precipitating conflict, communication problems, deceit, and disloyalty—at the very time children need the most skillful guidance from their parents.

Fact: You can't help a teen learn to control himself if you're doing all the controlling.

Fact: If you don't extend to your teenager the opportunity to experience lots of freedom along with an equal measure of responsibility, your teenager will, in all likelihood, find ways to be free. (Note the use of "in all likelihood." In some rare cases, teenage children cooperate with parental micromanagement. My sense is that these rare cases usually involve teens who are fundamentally shy and retiring. They don't desire a lot of social freedom; therefore, not getting it is not a problem.)

Fact: You can't effectively guide/mentor your teenager if you're fighting with him almost all of the time.

Fact: Whether the parent-child relationship is tension-filled or relatively relaxed during the child's teen years depends primarily on the parent.

Fact: The Fact immediately above is something parents don't want to even hear, much less admit is true.

Fact: The very parent who doesn't want to hear that particular Fact is the parent who most needs to hear it.

Coda

Shortly after writing an article on the teenage curfew issue for *Better Homes and Gardens* magazine, I received a letter from Bethany Hahn, an eighteen-year-old freshman at Stetson University. She wrote: "My parents trusted me to decide my own curfew. Anytime I wanted to go out, we would sit down and discuss what time I should be home. . . . They almost always let me come home when I wanted. . . . I didn't want to do anything to break their trust so I was always home on time. . . . This trust also led to a very healthy relationship with my parents. Unfortunately, the same was not true for many of my friends. Their parents were very strict when it came to curfew, so many of my friends would lie to their parents about their whereabouts. I think if parents treated their children the way mine did, families would get along much better."

Well said, Bethany! Please, dear reader, pay attention to what this young lady is saying: *From a teenager's point of view, if his/her parents mistrust him/her, then there's no future in trying to be trustworthy.*

"But, John!" a parent might rejoin, "I gave my teenager freedom and he abused it! What do you say about that?"

Excellent question! to which I have several things to say:

1. If all you did was *give* your teenager freedom, then I'm not surprised he abused it. Teens aren't likely to take good care of freedom that's simply given; they take care of freedom that's balanced with an equal measure of responsibility.

2. If you did, in fact, couple freedom and responsibility, and your teen abused the privilege, that doesn't mean you did the wrong thing; nor does it mean you can't ever trust your teenager. Eric occasionally (albeit rarely) "abused" a privilege. On those occasions, Willie and I curtailed his freedom (temporarily), talked with him, or just let him know we were disappointed. Then, we tried again.

3. With most teens, as with Eric, this business of learning to take responsible control of their lives is going to be a trial and error proposition. Error on the part of a teen—even Big Error (freedom abuse)—doesn't necessarily mean his parents allowed too much freedom. More often than not, it simply means the child is human. To err is human, remember? Also remember that if children did not err more than adults, they would not need parents! More often than not, when a child errs, the parents should simply stay calm, talk to the child about what went wrong, apply some mild restrictions for a while (maybe), and then—as Willie and I did when Eric messed up—try again. Believe it or not, the overwhelming majority of them "get it" fairly quickly, and in the final analysis, their missteps have few, if any, permanent effects.

Concessions Concerning Cash

As a child, whenever the subject of money came up between my parents and me, I could always count on my stepfather saying, "Money's not important." It was one of his favorite pronouncements, and I quickly tired of hearing it. Besides, there were the contradictions. If money wasn't important, why was he so tightfisted? Why, every time we went to the store, did he complain about the cost of nearly everything he bought? But he was consistent in one respect—he virtually refused to discuss money matters of any sort with me. I suppose he was trying, in his own way, to instill in me an appreciation for the truly valuable things in life. Notwithstanding, he succeeded in raising a stepson who had to learn to manage money the hard way, making a good number of expensive mistakes in the process.

Willie and I resolved to emancipate Eric and Amy with as thorough a working knowledge of money management as we could possibly pass along. There are, after all, few skills that are as essential to one's peace of mind and overall well-being. So, when Eric was fourteen and beginning to ask for more money more often to (a) pay for social activities and (b) buy the latest "thing" in clothing fads so as to project a sufficient amount of "cool" within his peer group, Willie and I hit upon a plan for teaching him fiscal responsibility. To be completely honest, we were growing weary of his frequent requests for money and the unproductive conversations that would often ensue.

"Why do you feel you need a new pair of sneakers, Eric?"

"Dad, I've told you they're not 'sneakers.' They're athletic shoes, and the pair I have hurt my feet."

"We just bought them for you a month ago."

"I know, but they're not comfortable."

"But you insisted that no other sneakers, I mean *athletic shoes,* would do."

"I know, but they're not comfortable and besides, all the guys are wearing these new ones that just came out."

"Ah! So they're more socially uncomfortable than physically uncomfortable."

"What do you mean?"

"I mean you don't need a new pair of sneakers."

"Athletic shoes, Dad, and Dad, okay, I want the new ones that just came out because that's what everyone's getting."

"Everyone?"

"Dad! No, not every single person, but almost everyone."

You get the picture. Now, here's a test for you, the reader:

Question: What fundamental parental mistake is reflected in the above exchange?

Hint: It's the single most unproductive thing parents of teens can do.

Answer: You got it! Micromanagement!

Willie and I finally realized these conversations or litigations or adversarial exchanges or what-have-you were a big waste of time and energy. Either we got upset or Eric got upset or we all got upset. Furthermore, because we were micromanaging the issue of money, we were failing to teach him anything except that if he badgered us long enough, he just might wear us down and get what he wanted. Not always, mind you, but often enough to keep on trying to wear us down.

The Plan, Part One

We opened a checking account for him through our bank. (All three of us were listed on the checks, and Willie and I agreed [of course] to take responsibility for overdrafts.) On the first of every month, we deposited $100.00 into this account. This was Eric's monthly allowance. Yes, you read that right. No, the decimal point was not shifted one space to the right, but just to confirm, the amount in question was one hundred American dollars and no cents.

Short aside: When I recount this story to one of my audiences, I sometimes ask, "How many of you think this is entirely too much money to be giving a fourteen-year-old?"

Almost everyone raises a hand and there is general murmuring to the effect that the Rosemonds must have suffered temporary insanity when Eric was a young teen. (Many parents, after all, do; and some, furthermore, never recover full soundness of mind.) I ask the same question when I've finished the story. Interestingly enough, very few hands go up to the second asking. I think you'll understand why. But first, I'll take a question from the well-dressed fellow in the second row.

Q: *How'd you arrive at one hundred dollars?*

A: We estimated we were giving Eric approximately that amount monthly to fund recreation and discretionary clothing, *and we were being fairly conservative concerning how much money we gave him per request.*

Q: *Still, that sounds like a lot. Besides, my wife and I can't afford more than fifty dollars a month, if that. Is there some magic to one hundred dollars?*

A: Not at all. The amount is not the critical factor. The idea, as you'll see, is to help the child learn to set sensible fiscal priorities. This is something not a lot of today's parents are doing. Most talk a lot about teaching children the "value of a dollar," but when I ask, "So how are you going about doing this?" the general reaction is something highly nebulous, along the lines of, "Well, we try to, uh, help our teenager understand that money doesn't grow on trees." That's all fine and good as a general concept, but the critical question remains: *"By what mechanism* are you teaching your child that money doesn't grow on trees?" Unfortunately, in spite of good intentions, the typical parent is doing nothing more than *hoping* his teen is learning—by some mysterious process—the value of money. The plan Willie and I hit upon and used with Eric and Amy is, as I'm confident you'll see, several giant steps past hoping. Anyway, to answer the question, if you can't afford more than fifty dollars, or you feel fifty dollars is enough, try fifty dollars. Keep in mind, however, that as time passes and teens get bigger, both clothing and recreational costs tend to naturally escalate.

Q: *So did you give Eric periodic raises?*
A: Never. Read on.

Q: *Did you require him to earn the money, or was it just given?*
A: He and his sister did, in fact, have to clean my office once a week, but that wasn't the crux of the plan, either. Now, stop asking so many questions and just read on.

The Plan, Part Two

Out of his allowance, Eric had to pay for all nonessential clothing and any recreation (movies, amusement parks, concerts, etc.) that did not include at least one other family member.

Concerning clothing: We continued to purchase such things as socks, underwear, and any item of clothing that needed replacement. But let's say Eric needed a new winter jacket, and we found a thirty-dollar jacket that was perfectly suitable, but he wanted the fifty-dollar jacket that had the stainless steel chicken logo on the left sleeve. We wouldn't argue (which we otherwise would have done). We'd simply give him thirty dollars and tell him to use it as he saw fit. In other words—staying with this example—if he wanted the logo jacket badly enough, he'd have to come up with twenty dollars.

Concerning social activities/recreation: If Eric wanted to go to the movies with his buddies, he had to pay his own way.

If, however, he was willing to take his sister along, then we would pay for both tickets and give each of them money for snacks. (Can you believe it?!! Eric never took us up on the take-Amy offer!)

The Plan, Part Three

Eric had to figure out how to get his money to last through the month because we absolutely, unequivocally, refused to ever, ever advance him money against the next month's allowance. Why? Because children don't pay their debts, that's why, and Willie and I were not, under any circumstances, going to get into the collection business concerning our kids.

It wasn't a year before Eric was telling us that a hundred dollars just wasn't enough. He correctly pointed out that he had outgrown children's clothes and was now shopping in the men's department where clothes were more expensive. Also, his recreational choices were more expensive than they had generally been a year or so before. Again, correct.

"So," Eric said, "I'm asking for an increase in my allowance."

"We're *never* going to give you a raise, Eric."

"What!!? That doesn't make any sense! What am I supposed to do—wear clothes that are too small?"

"The solution, kiddo, is for you to find ways of earning more money. And not from us, either, but from other sources. You're not yet old enough to get a regular job, but you could mow lawns in the summer, house-sit for people when they go on vacation, baby-sit, wash cars, and so on. In short, if you want more money, you're gonna have to hustle, kid, 'cause you're not getting any more from us."

(We had the same basic conversations with Amy, by the way, but it's far less complicated—and, therefore, confusing—to couch the description of each "C" in terms of one child—in this case, the older one.)

One weekend, shortly after he'd entered college, Eric came home and told us there was "no way" one hundred dollars a month would take care of extracurricular college costs.

"Hey, Eric, you've heard this song before. It's by Smokey Robinson and the Miracles: Get a Job."

"Dad! Mom! How am I supposed to keep my grades up if I have to work?"

"Eric! We figured it out when we were in college. You have our genes; therefore, you can figure it out, too!"

"Uh!" (That was the sound both of our kids made when they were absolutely disgusted with us. I understand it's universal.)

As you might imagine, Eric got a job and learned by trial and error to manage his time such that his job did not interfere with his studies. In fact, at one point, he held down two part-time jobs, took a full class load, and still maintained a "B" average. Add the following together and see what you come up with: time management (a.k.a. setting effective priorities), self-reliance, accepting increasing amounts of responsibility, and resourcefulness.

The answer, of course, is *responsible adulthood!* I hope I don't need to point out that shepherding our children to responsible adulthoods is what parenting is all about. But I will anyway, because it's worth repeating: Shepherding our children to responsible adulthoods is what parenting is all about.

Questions?

Q: *Our two children have been required to help with housework for the last five years. They are now in their early teens and are capable of doing just about anything around the house, including washing and ironing their own clothes* *and cooking simple meals. We have never paid them for chores, nor have we ever given them allowances. Recently, however, they threatened to "strike" if we don't begin paying them for the work they do around here. Should we?*

A: Absolutely not! Children should not be paid for helping with housework. They should, from an early age, be conscripted into "family service," which is the keystone of "family citizenship." By doing chores without compensation, children learn the service ethic, which is essential to preserving a democracy. It sounds as if you've done a good job to this point of instilling both the service ethic and a sense of responsibility in your children. Unfortunately, too many of today's hyper-busy parents fail to realize that in the course of striving to keep their children happy and racing them from one after-school activity to another (staying busy in their lives), they're neglecting the fundamentals of good citizenship, which begin in the home. In the final analysis, being a "star" in one's own family is infinitely more character-building than being a star on the soccer team.

Like your children, Eric and Amy were expected to perform a daily routine of chores around the home. By the time they were in their early teens, Eric and Amy were doing most of the housework. For all this we paid them absolutely nothing. As a result, their acts of contribution took on the kind of value one can never measure in dollars and cents. The children took pride in what they did for the family, began to understand the basics of good citizenship, and became ever more independent in the process.

At this point, I'd suggest you implement the allowance plan described above, but make it clear to your children that their allowances are not being given in return for the work they do around the house. The two issues, in other words, are completely separate. Keep 'em that way. Oh, and the next time they bring up the "strike" thing, just say, "You make your decisions, I'll make mine" and walk away. See the section below on Consequences for what to do next.

Q: *Once a child begins earning his or her own money, can parents rightfully place certain restrictions on how the child spends it?*

A: Indeed! Parents can, and should, place limits on how a child spends both (a) his allowance and (b) money he's earned himself, but they'd better choose their battles carefully. It's reasonable to restrict purchases that put the child in danger (i.e., a motorcycle) or are in direct conflict with the values of the family (satanic paraphernalia, pornography). It's going to cause more problems than it solves, however, to try to enforce restrictions that are, in the final analysis, arbitrary and capricious. I'm thinking of such things as a youngster's tastes in music and clothing. Most attempts to restrict purchases of this sort qualify as micromanagement. As such, they're likely to fail and create predictable problems in the parent-child relationship to boot. Ask yourself, "Is forcing a confrontation over an article of clothing that I simply don't like (but which is not clearly inappropriate—i.e., sexually provocative) worth the conflict, communication problems, and even deceit that are likely to result?" Having lived with two teenagers, I would advise parents to save their strength for more important issues. Here's a helpful policy for the teen with an outside job: "For the most part, you can spend money you earn as you choose; however, if the item you want to purchase costs more than fifty dollars, you must first discuss it with us."

Q: *Should parents require teens to put some of their allowance in savings?*

A: While this is a laudable idea and should certainly be suggested, I'd caution parents against trying to enforce any specific guidelines in this area, as such enforcement attempts amount to micromanagement. The allowance plan described above, when managed properly, teaches a child the value of savings, even if the child never puts a dime in the bank.

My Final Word on the Subject

This generation of parents has done a wonderful job of sharing their standard of living with their children, but a miserable job of endowing those same children with the skills they'll need to achieve that standard on their own. As a result, too many children are growing up believing it's someone else's responsibility to take care of their needs and wants. Never having learned to accept responsibility for their own well-being, they are likely to go through life expecting other people to make them happy and blaming anything and everything that goes wrong on someone or something else. Unfortunately, as we all know, a person who fails to take full responsibility for his or her own happiness will never be fully happy. The paradox is this: The more parents try to make their children happy, the more they guarantee that their children will someday be miserable.

Car Wars

"Dad! I've decided what kind of car I want to get when I'm sixteen. Look at this!"

"Eric," I said, brushing away a copy of *Car Trader* he'd stuck in my face, "I've told you a hundred times, I'm not buying you a car when you turn sixteen. Read my lips! I'm . . . not . . . buying . . . you . . . a . . . car . . . when . . . you . . . turn . . . sixteen."

"Why not?!"

"I've told you why not."

"Yeah, but why not?"

"Because of the reason I gave you before."

"But can we talk about it?"

"We talked about it before."

"But, Dad, can we talk about it today?"

"No."

"Why not?!"

Eric simply would not give up. He started in on me when he was fourteen and kept it up relentlessly for two and a half years. I mean every day. And everyday I told him he wasn't getting a car.

"Why not?!"

"Because you won't need a car of your own, Eric. We have two cars. You'll be able to use one of them."

"Right! The station wagon! Forget it! I won't drive a station wagon!"

"Nerd mobile, eh?"

"Right!"

"Well, Eric, nerd sort of runs in the family. I was a nerd, you know. It's probably genetic, so you'll be a nerd, too, sooner or later. If driving a station wagon doesn't do it, wearing glasses will."

"I don't wear glasses!"

"Then you have to drive a station wagon. It's either one or the other. We nerds don't have a lot of options."

"Dad?"

"Yes, son."

"Seriously, will you buy me a car when I'm sixteen?"

"No."

"Why not?!"

My reasons for refusing to even consider buying Eric a car when he turned sixteen were:

- philosophical (Giving a sixteen-year-old a car served only to reinforce that something could be had for nothing.)
- ideological (Parents who bought cars for their teenagers were indulging their children's capitalist/materialist/bourgeois leanings.)
- psychological (Buying a teen a car was a way of avoiding spending quality time with the child.)
- Last but not least, I had practical objections, firmly rooted in reality (A car costs a lot of money.)

Then, sixteen came and so did the driver's license, and Eric started driving my car. (He was true to his word—he *wouldn't* drive the station wagon.) On a fairly regular basis, I was without a car. And it was irritating to get in my car after he'd driven it to find the seat pulled up under the steering wheel and the rearview mirror aimed at the floor and the gas gauge on empty. And Eric was unable to get a job because he didn't have reliable transportation, which meant I had to pay for his gas and insurance.

I expressed my frustration to Willie, who said, "We should buy him a car."

So we bought Eric a car. Women rule.

Actually, when we got down to talking about it, Willie and I decided the car would be a mixed blessing for Eric. It would be less a gift than a responsibility. The plan unfolded thusly:

1. We bought him a moderately priced new car and put the title in his name. "This car is yours, Eric," we said, "lock, stock, and barrel."

2. We toted all expenses—monthly payment, insurance, gas, maintenance, and repairs—for three months.

3. From month four on, Eric was required to pay his own insurance, gas, maintenance, and repairs. We would continue

to tote the note on the car loan, however. (After all, his having a car of his own was of great benefit to us, something we were willing to pay for.)

4. Since his monthly allowance (see Concessions Concerning Cash, page 75) was insufficient to pay for clothing, recreation, *and* car expenses, he had to find a part-time job. Our only stipulation was that his job could not require him to be out later than ten at night on weekdays, and even then no more than two nights per week.

5. In consideration of the adjustment that would attend getting a job, we would, we told him, allow his grades to drop slightly during the first grading period (nine weeks) thereafter. After that, however, we expected him to adjust his priorities such that his grades returned to where they had been previously.

6. If his grades dropped but did not improve within one grading period, he'd go on probation, meaning he would only be able to use the car to get to school and work. Probation would last one more grading period.

7. If, at the end of his probation, his grades still had not returned to previous levels, he would have to quit his job.

8. If, after quitting his job, he was unable to fund his insurance and other car expenses, then his car would be put up for sale.

9. "And you should know, Eric," we finished, "that this is the last car we're ever, ever going to buy you."

So, the first thing Eric did with his car was find a job stocking the shelves in a drugstore. And lo and behold! his grades didn't drop a whit! In fact, they improved, which only goes to show, responsibility begets responsibility. Because he was financially responsible for his car, Eric took immaculate care of it. Seven years later, when it was sold, it still looked brand new.

When Amy turned sixteen, we bought her a car and rolled out the same policies. She promptly got a job working in a frozen yogurt shop. In both cases, after paying for their insurance, the kids had slightly more than half their paychecks left to do with as they pleased. Adults should be so lucky!

By linking grades, job, and driving privileges together, Willie and I created circumstances that began to approximate adult realities. This age child needs experiences of that sort, ones that prepare him or her for dealing with the complexities of independent living. I call it *SOOP* training: *Standing on One's Own Pedestals*. That's what it's all about, remember? As I've said before, the purpose of being a parent is to help your children get out of your life and into successful lives of their own.

The plan forced Eric to take care of his car, further refine his money-management skills, set more effective priorities where time and activities were concerned. As he learned to better manage his life—to balance responsibility and fun—he felt more and more competent and self-assured. As I said, his grades actually improved during his last two years of high school, meaning he was able to upgrade his college prospects. Last but not least, at age twenty-nine (at this writing), Eric still has a clean driving record.

Note that our modus operandi where a car was concerned paralleled our approach to the issues of curfews and cash. In all three instances:

- The child is given a tremendous amount of freedom (determine your own curfew; determine how you spend your money; a car).
- The child is assigned new responsibilities.
- The child's ability to enjoy his new freedom depends on his ability to properly manage the associated responsibilities.

- In the process of discovering that one is only as free as he or she is willing to accept responsibility, Eric (and later Amy) learned lessons that could not have been learned as effectively in any other fashion.

To Bring You, the Reader, Up to Date . . .

At this point in the story, Eric is sixteen years old. He has more freedom than any one of his friends. In fact, the only kids he knows with more freedom are those whose parents are lazy, irresponsible, good-for-nothings (and some of them very well-to-do, highly respected good-for-nothings). Besides, the "freedom" those children "enjoy" isn't really freedom at all. Because it's *free*—in other words, devoid of responsibility or obligation—it's fraught with chaos and imminent danger. In the final analysis, it's not freedom at all, but anarchy—unstable, frightening (although the child in question must never allow his/her fright to show in front of his/her peers), and ultimately unsatisfying. Eric's freedoms (and later Amy's), on the other hand, have either been earned (curfew) or come with a price tag (allowance, car). The likelihood that he will act irresponsibly is minimal because in no way has he gotten something for nothing. The difference is that what a child—in this case, Eric—earns, he almost certainly will take care of, while a child who has not earned his freedoms, but has been handed them on the proverbial silver platter (or has appropriated them by default) has nothing at all to take care of. Therefore, he does not take care of anything, much less himself.

The proof, after all is said and done, is in the pudding. Once he earned the right to set his own curfew, Eric never came in later than one o'clock in the morning—and even that was rare. He never asked us for an advance on his allowance, albeit he did, on the two occasions described above, ask for a raise. He kept his car in mint condition all the way through college. For his college graduation, we were so proud of him (he'd graduated with a degree in economics *and* a commercial pilot's license—no small accomplishment), we bought him a new car. I know, we had told him the high school car was the last car he'd ever get from us. What can I say? We lied.

Questions?

Q: *When you bought Eric his first car, did you say anything at all to him about drinking and driving?*

A: Yes, we did. We said, "Eric, m'boy, if you ever give us good reason to suspect you've been drinking—even one beer!—and either driving your own car or riding with someone else—*suspect*, mind you, meaning we don't need proof—we'll take your car and sell it. Immediately. You won't pass GO, and you won't collect two hundred dollars. The same goes for letting someone who's drunk ride in your car as a passenger. We are not going to fool around with drinking and driving, son. You got it?" He must have taken us seriously, because it never happened.

Q: *You mean he never drank an alcoholic beverage as a teenager?*

A: Oh no. We were hardly so naive. As a matter of fact, at the same time we made it clear that while we did not approve of under-age drinking, we told him if he ever had something to drink, all he had to do was call us and we'd come get him, no questions asked. Under no circumstances, however, was he allowed to ride with someone who'd been drinking—again, even one beer—or drink something and then ride in someone else's car (even if the driver hadn't been drinking). If he broke either of the above rules, his car would be for sale the next morning.

Q: *Didn't this policy give him certain permission to drink?*
A: It gave him permission to do what we knew he was going to do anyway. We're talking about a highly gregarious, fun-loving, risk-taking youngster who ran with equally gregarious, etc., friends. We weren't about to try and forbid something we couldn't forbid. Instead, we acted strategically (instead of trying to micromanage) so as to put some reasonable limits on any drinking he did. Please note that he could be aboveboard with us about drinking without fear of consequences. In fact, on at least two occasions he called and requested that one of us come get him. When he got in the car (and on neither occasion was he sloppy drunk), we were true to our word and never asked him anything. If you'll read the above rules/understandings again, I think you'll agree that we made it easy for Eric to tell us the truth and unprofitable for him to conceal the truth from us.

Q: *I'm sorry, but I don't feel at all comfortable telling my sixteen-year-old that he can drink alcoholic beverages and call home for a ride. I've told him that if I ever find out he's had anything to drink, he'll be in big trouble.*
A: I understand. If you don't feel comfortable with it, then don't do it. Let me warn you, however, about this "big trouble" stuff. In the first place, whether a teen is or isn't going to drink has nothing to do with threats. Notice we didn't tell Eric he couldn't drink (albeit we made it clear we didn't approve and would be disappointed if he did); only that he *couldn't drink and drive* or ride as a passenger when he'd been drinking. Your "big trouble" statement clearly amounts to a threat, and a teen is all too likely to take a threat as a challenge to try and do the forbidden something and not get caught. In short,

threats make it more, not less, likely that the forbidden something will happen. For that reason, we opted not to forbid, but to build some safeguards around something Eric was going to do anyway. The difference is between being *idealistic* and *realistic*. Ideally, I didn't want Eric to drink alcohol. Realistically, I knew he was going to experiment to some degree. If I acted according to my ideals, I would surely have caused him to be deceitful, if nothing else. So, I acted realistically. Parenting sometimes requires compromises, folks. You can't have it all your way, and the earlier in the game parents accept that, the less heartache they're likely to experience.

Q: *Well, you may be the child-rearing expert, but I'm the expert on my child, and I don't want him drinking, period. I intend to talk to him about the dangers of drinking and let him know, in no uncertain terms, that he's forbidden to ever even touch the mouth of a beer bottle to his lips.*

A: Aren't you the stubborn one! If your son's anything like you, you'd do well to take another tack on this issue. I suggest you reread the section in Chapter Two on the pitfalls of micromanagement (page 40), because that's exactly the type of parenting style you're moving toward, if you aren't there already. Your son is likely to react to your attempts to control his every waking minute by being deceitful, to say the least. In that event, you will have driven underground something that might otherwise have been aboveboard between you. Believe me, when a parent drives something underground, the something in question just gets worse and worse—in this case, the child in question is likely to drink *rebelliously,* which raises the specter of danger to self and others. Your intentions are laudable, but your strategy leaves much to be desired. If you persist in this foolish, cut-off-your-nose-to-spite-your-face course, then all I have to say is good luck.

You've had the floor long enough, buddy, so sit down and let someone talk who doesn't want to argue. Yes sir? That's right, you there in the purple pompadour and sequined Elvis jumpsuit.

Q: *With the start of the school year upon us, and with a child about to turn sixteen, my wife and I were wondering what your feelings were about high school kids having jobs during the school year. Our daughter, who has always been a fairly good student, says she wants to get a job. We're not sure it's a good idea. Do you think we should let her, and if so, what kinds of rules should there be?*

A: I think you should let her. Your daughter's initiative and willingness to accept obligations outside of home and school, especially one that will allow her less time with her peers, should definitely be encouraged. At the very least, she'll find out that she really isn't ready for a job. Either way, it will be a tremendously valuable learning experience, one she shouldn't be denied.

Now, if she wasn't already a fairly good student, I would advise you to tell her she could get a job when her grades come up. As she showed improvement in her grades, you would allow her to work a certain number of hours per week. As her grades improved, you'd let her increase her hours, and so on, and so forth. In that case, I'd point out that her desire to work presents you with "leverage"—a chance to turn her motivation for doing one thing (getting a job) into motivation for something else (better grades). In the long run, seizing upon this sort of opportunity benefits the child more than the parent, although it may take the child a while to figure that out.

Compadres (a.k.a Colleagues, Cohorts, Comrades, Co-Conspirators)

Every week, it seems, I hear another horror story about a teenager who's gone "off the deep end." In many cases, these are kids whose parents are involved and responsible, and who themselves were well behaved, nice kids until they hit the teen years.
The questions to be asked:

1. Is the "wrong crowd" more of a problem today than it was thirty-something years ago when I was a teenager?
2. Is there something parents can do *proactively* that will help children resist negative peer pressure during their teen years?

To the first question, I am indeed convinced that the "wrong crowd" is considerably more of a problem today than it was thirty-something years ago. Part of the problem is it can be difficult to tell which teens are bad news and which aren't. When I was a teenager, the kids in the wrong crowd generally stood out like sore thumbs, and they weren't "cool" in anyone's eyes but their own. Today, however, the wrong crowd is composed of kids from all walks of life, and a "bad reputation" is no longer necessarily bad in the eyes of other teens.
This assessment is supported by the facts. Over the past thirty years, every indicator of positive mental health in teenagers has been going in the wrong direction. Another way of saying the same thing: The incidence of self-destructive, antisocial behaviors on the part of teens has increased dramatically over the last generation. Drug and alcohol use, teen pregnancy, teen suicide, and delinquency have all tripled, and

across the demographic spectrum. There's no doubt about it: Today's teenager is more prone to serious problems than was the typical teen in generations past.

Television, a general weakening of parental discipline (as well as discipline in schools), the proliferation of father-absent families, and the assignment of child care responsibilities to various "proxies" have all contributed to this sorry state of affairs. Perhaps the most insidious contributing factor, however, has been the good intentions of today's parents. In the course of giving their children entirely too much and expecting entirely too little in return, well-intentioned parents often fail to instill in their children an adequate sense of family loyalty and obligation. In generations past, parents expected a lot of children. They expected them to keep themselves occupied, do their own homework, make decent grades, demonstrate respect for adult authority, and perform chores around the home.

Many of today's parents, by contrast, tend to expect a lot of *themselves* and relatively little of their children. They believe it's *their job* to keep their children occupied, help with their homework (if not do it for them), and see to it they make good grades. They undermine respect for adults by defending their kids when they get in trouble. They assign no chores, then complain that their children "won't lift a finger around the house."

Many of today's parents act as if the only person in the parent-child relationship who has obligations is the parent. Under these circumstances it's no wonder so many children seem to develop little sense of responsibility toward their families; and thus no strong defenses against negative peer pressure. The fact is, and listen up, dear reader: *Family obligations engender family loyalty, which is the best preventive of negative peer pressure.* The child who doesn't want to disappoint his/her parents is the child least likely to fall in with the "wrong crowd."

In short, parents who want to "immunize" their children against the epidemic of problems inherent in today's American teen culture would do well to stop acting so obligated, and begin obligating their children.

They could begin by saying "no" more than they say "yes." At least three times more, in fact. They could stop paying so much attention to their children and expect instead that their children pay attention to them. They could get their children off "family welfare" and put them into "family workfare." They could stop trying to be so darned pleasing to their children and expect instead that their children please them. They could stop trying to be their children's friends and start acting like leaders. (Note: Good leaders, while they are friendly, don't befriend the people they're supposed to lead.) If the above foundations/expectations are established before the teen years, the likelihood the child will become a rebel without a cause is minimal. (But remember, there are no guarantees.)

When to Do Something, What to Do, and When to Do Nothing

No question about it, the peer group exerts great influence on teenagers. (Remember, however, the peer group is *not* the primary problem during the teen years!) From the way teens dress to the way they carry their books, the stamp of peer pressure is upon them. If the influence is positive, parents can breathe easy. But what if the influence isn't so positive? What should parents do in that case? This poses a dilemma: On the one hand, parents are supposed to make sure children don't do anything that could put their overall well-being in jeopardy. On the other, teens are touchier about their friendships than anything else. Any parental intervention is likely to be seen as interference and met with cries of "You're trying to choose my friends for me!"

Just knowing when to intervene in your child's social life is hard enough because many of the variables are intangible. There are the concrete facts, and then there are your intuitions, your biases, and your protectiveness, not to mention your ego. Sound confusing? It is!

First, here are four rules of thumb concerning the peer group issue:

1. Be willing to let your teenager make mistakes. Don't forget children can't grow up unless parents let go. Adolescence is a time of social experimentation. As such, we must accept that our children may not make the social choices we would make for them. Keep in mind, however, that slightly flawed and even disastrous friendships can teach a child a lesson. In some cases, there may even be merit to letting a child make some social decisions you *know* aren't going to turn out well. There's a lot of truth to the idea that the most valuable lessons in life are those learned the hard way.

2. Hold your child responsible for his or her own behavior. Don't even begin to think your child can do wrong only as a result of someone else's bad influence. Children won't accept responsibility for their behavior unless parents hold them responsible, regardless of who or what may have influenced them.

3. Don't ever force or manipulate a child toward choosing certain companions. This almost always ends in disaster (see Shakespeare's *Romeo and Juliet* for a historical perspective on this issue). The danger is that the youngster will rebel and take his friendships "underground." At that point, communication and trust will begin to deteriorate.

4. Don't pull rank unless you must in order to protect your child's safety and well-being. Given a little time, some potentially bad situations work *themselves* out.

With those rules of thumb in mind, here are some guidelines for determining when and how to draw the line where a teenager's choice of running mates is concerned:

You should do nothing about your teenager's choice of friends when your disapproval is based solely on stereotypes, personal tastes, or opinions you may have of a friend's parents. These aren't valid reasons for doing anything other than keeping your opinions to yourselves.

- Example: You react negatively to one of your teen's friends because he's from the "wrong side of the tracks," or because of racial, religious, or ethnic differences.
- Example: You don't like a friend's dress, haircut, or manner of speech (The friend greets you with "What's up?" instead of "I'm pleased to meet you.")
- Example: You don't like the youngster's parents. Maybe the father tried to take advantage of you in a business deal or insulted you at a party.
- Example: You don't like the child's personality— he/she is "too quiet" or "too boastful" or "too vain."

You should express your feelings and keep a close watch on things when there are signs of potential problems, but none of actual trouble.

- Example: The friend occasionally associates with known troublemakers, but has never been personally involved in any wrongdoing.

- Example: The friend has been in trouble before, but seems to have "cleaned up his act."
- Example: The friend's parents don't supervise as well as you think they should, or they give freedoms you're not yet willing to give your child (e.g., going to unchaperoned parties).

Under circumstances such as these, tell your teen how you feel: "I'm probably just an old worrywart, but I have to tell you I'm not completely comfortable with the friendship you've formed with so-and-so." Explain the reason behind your discomfort and state your expectations: "I'm going to keep closer tabs on this friendship than I normally would. You can prevent me from intervening by acting responsibly and staying out of trouble."

You should set some definite limits on the relationship in question when your teen's friend has a habit of getting into trouble, but only in certain, select situations; or, if your teen and the friend get into some minor trouble together. These are "marginal cases," so the line is a bit blurry.

- Example: The friend has a bad driving record.
- Example: The friend has been arrested for shoplifting.
- Example: Your child and the friend skipped school together.

Situations such as these demand that you put some sensible restrictions on the relationship. For instance, if the friend's driving record is poor, don't let your teen ride with him. If the friend has been arrested for shoplifting, don't let them go to a shopping center together unless an adult is present to supervise. If they skipped school, put the relationship "on notice," as in: "For the time being, I'm only going to put some controls on your friendship with so-and-so. If problems occur, I may have to put a complete freeze on things. It's all up to the two of you—mostly *you*."

You should prohibit the association altogether when the friend is a proven, habitual troublemaker, or your child and his/her friend make major mischief together.

- Example: The friend is a known drug user.
- Example: The friend has a history of juvenile delinquency.
- Example:Your teen and his/her friend burglarized someone's home.

These guidelines can help you decide your first response to friendships that make you uncomfortable. At first, adopt the most liberal position possible. If problems begin to develop, go to the next most appropriate step. As well as is possible, this approach balances the teen's growing need for independence with the continuing necessity of parental supervision. A tight-wire act, if ever there was one!

Questions?

Q: *What should teenagers be doing with their spare time?*
A: A variety of things. It's not a healthy sign when a teenager seems obsessed with doing only one thing, whether the thing is listening to rock music, sitting at a computer terminal, hanging out at the mall, or doing homework. Ideally, a teenager's free time should be fairly equally distributed among:

a. activities that are organized and adult-directed (clubs, sports teams, Scouts, church youth groups);

b. those that involve only peers (going to movies, parties, ball games);

c. those that are family oriented, and;

d. those that are solitary (listening to music, reading, working at a computer).

Q: *Is it all right for parents to sometimes require a teenager to participate in a certain activity, such as a church youth group?*

A: There's nothing inherently wrong with parents mandating a certain activity, as long as the mandate is the exception rather than the rule. It's generally better, however, to encourage participation in an activity rather than insist upon it. Nonetheless, parents can, and should, provide direction when they feel direction is needed. Oftentimes, a teen's reluctance to get involved in something is based on inadequate information or the fear of not "fitting in." If parents see a gap that's begging to be filled, they have every right to take steps to fill it. If, however, the push comes from parents, the teen may dig his or her heels in that much more. For that reason, I recommend that parents discreetly ask another teen who's already involved in the activity to extend the invitation.

Q: *Two of our friends have told us that teens are going to drink, no matter what, and that we're being unrealistic to tell our sixteen-year-old daughter that she may not, under any circumstances, consume alcoholic beverages until she is of legal age. Are we?*

A: Your friends' words bespeak of a "look the other way" attitude toward teen drinking. That's the sort of attitude taken by parents who will do anything to avoid conflict with their teens—parents, in other words, who are certified wimps.

Under the circumstances, it's all but inevitable that the teen in question is going to drink, and in a high-risk fashion. Now, one might contend that any and all teenage drinking is high risk. I disagree. There is, indeed, always risk involved when a teenager consumes an alcoholic beverage, but the risk does not have to be high. The risk is held to a minimum by parents who:

a.   do not attempt to control that which they cannot control (micromanage);

b.   clearly communicate their disapproval of teen drinking;

c.   establish policies concerning alcohol consumption which allow the teen in question to be forthright and honest.

The only person who can set limits on a teenager's drinking is the teen. Parents can only manage this issue such that the youngster has absolutely no reason to be rebellious and every reason to be honest where alcohol consumption is concerned. This is exactly what Willie and I attempted to do with Eric and Amy, and there was/is every indication that our alcohol policies successfully contained something that might have gotten out of hand had we either looked the other way or tried to control the uncontrollable. In that regard, you might want to rethink telling your daughter that she may not, under any circumstances, consume alcoholic beverages. Better, I think, to tell her you don't approve, but are willing to reluctantly accept it if, and only if, she is willing to be honest.

Q: *My husband and I enjoy an occasional alcoholic beverage, and have seen nothing wrong with doing this in full view of our kids. Our best friends tell us we're being hypocritical to tell our fifteen-year-old son he's not allowed to drink. Do you agree?*

A: Not at all. If you were both drunks, this would certainly be a problem. Parents who enjoy an occasional drink, however, can legitimately tell a teenager they don't approve of his/her drinking. You and your husband sleep together, don't you? Is it hypocritical to tell your teenage son he can't have his girlfriend over to spend the night?

Look, folks, I know that nearly everyone reading this book is consumed with anxiety over the possibility their teen either is or might get involved with alcohol and drugs, but hear me loud and clear:

If, because of anxiety, you make these issues the focus of your parenting during the teen years, you will be asking for major troubles!!! Instead, focus on the Six C's, thus letting your teenager know that everything is possible, but nothing is free. A management style that promotes responsibility and honesty on the part of a teen is the best preventive of self-destructive behavior.

I can't say any more than I've already said concerning alcohol/drugs. Those of you who want me to say more aren't getting it. I suggest you reread my answers to the previous two questions again (as well as my comments concerning the issue of drinking in the section on "Cars" above). And again. Until you get it. Please!!! For your sake and your child's!!!

Q: *How can parents tell if a teenage child is doing things he shouldn't be doing?*

A: Parents who are interested in what their children are doing and maintain proper supervision concerning their comings and gongs will usually be able to sense when something is amiss. They may not know the details, but they will know nonetheless. The test for trouble: Ask yourself, "How often do I have a feeling of discomfort concerning what my child is doing or says he's doing with his time?" If your answer is once a month or more, then you'd better take a closer look. Some of the more definite danger signals include (1) dramatic changes in behavior, friends, or attitude toward school; (2) secretiveness concerning whereabouts; (3) outright lying, often concerning unimportant things; (4) refusing to participate in family activities; and (5) prolonged periods of self-imposed isolation when home.

Q: *What should parents do if they suspect problems?*

A: They should first share—not *accuse*, mind you—their observations and feelings with the child and try to engage the child in a discussion of the problem. As a general rule, the more defensive a youngster becomes when parents share concerns, the more on target the parents probably are. If talking things through doesn't work, parents should consider seeking professional help. Beware, however! Choose your professional counselor with utmost care, because some of these well-intentioned folks can actually make parent-child problems worse instead of better. Before committing to a particular counselor, go and talk with him to find out what his parenting philosophy is and where he stands with respect to the issues in question. If he's at all evasive, go find someone else.

Q: *Our fifteen-year-old daughter's room is a pigsty. Whenever we mention it to her, she tells us it's her room and she has a right to keep it a mess if she wants. Do you agree?*

A: It's not "her" room in the sense of it being a personal possession. It's a room you've given over to her use until she is emancipated. It's perfectly reasonable of you to expect her to maintain her quarters according to the housekeeping standards you establish. On the other hand, engaging in a power struggle over this issue will only create more problems. I recommend that you deal with this issue strategically, as opposed to heavy-handedly. Simply tell your daughter that if she won't keep her room neat and clean, you will. Anytime her room is a mess, you'll gladly go in and put everything in order, including her dresser drawers, the shelves in her closet, her cabinets, and any other place where she might store personal items. This was the understanding in the Rosemond household, by the way, and we only had to "clean" each child's room once and miracle of miracles, neither of their rooms were ever a mess again. This strategy simply forces a teenager to choose what's more important: privacy or a messy room? Believe me, privacy will win the day.

Q: *When should teens be allowed to date?*

A: Personally, I see no problem with girls and boys as young as fourteen going out as a group to a movie or the skating rink, as long as adults provide the transportation. At first, it's wise to limit dating to daytime and early evening hours. Dating gives parents another opportunity to teach that when children take care of privileges, their privileges expand. If a young teen handles those initial experiments with dating in a responsible manner, then by age sixteen, I think it's reasonable to begin to allow single-dating. In the final analysis, questions along these lines can be answered only by considering the child in question, not the calendar.

The teen years have a reputation for being "the best of times, the worst of times" for parents. We all need to remember, however, that this may possibly be the best and worst of times for our children as well. The fact that we've already walked this path means we can understand teenagers better than they can sometimes understand themselves. And a little understanding can go an awfully long way.

Conflict Relief (How to Defang Your Teenager)

At a speaking engagement, I will ask the audience, "How many of you have argumentative children?" In an audience of five hundred, at least three hundred and fifty will raise a hand.

At this point, I say, "I have good news, or bad news, depending on how you look at it: *None of you has an argumentative child.* In fact, there is no such thing, and none of you will ever get a grip on the arguing that takes place between you and your supposedly argumentative child as long as you persist in the belief that these arguments originate with the child."

If you find yourself engaging in numerous arguments with a teenager—or a child of any age, for that matter—putting an end to the arguing requires somewhat the same thing required of people in twelve-step programs. You must admit to yourself, "I am completely responsible for these arguments. My child has nothing to do with them whatsoever. He is only taking advantage of an opportunity which I continue extending." That may sound discouraging, but it actually means that *since you are in complete control of whether arguments take place or not, you can stop them, and permanently so, whenever you decide to do so.*

At this point, I always hear some people making noises of disbelief, so I prove that what I'm proposing is within their grasp. "How many of you," I ask, "grew up with parents who absolutely, completely refused to argue with you, ever?"

Close to half of the people in the audience raise their hands. "See?" I say. "Your parents knew that they were in total control of whether you argued or not. And they would not allow it! And you can do the same, whenever you'd like! You can stop giving your child opportunities to argue. The next time your child disagrees with a decision you've made, or an explanation you've offered for a decision he didn't like, just look at him and say, 'Yes, well, I'd feel the same way if I were your age. No problem.' And at that critical point—the point of "'nuff said," turn around with a shrug of the shoulders and walk away!

I call it "pulling the plug on the power struggle"! There's only one person who can pull the plug, and that's the parent! Pulling the plug will not guarantee compliance, but it increases its likelihood significantly.

Give 'Em the Last Word!

There was a look of desperation, of last resort, in this prematurely gray-haired mother's eyes. "What can I do," she asked, pleadingly, "with a twelve-year-old daughter who always wants the last word?"

"Oh, give it to her, by all means. Always."

She blinked, taken aback. "You've gotta be kidding."

Not at all. You have a child who wants the last word? So, what's new? All of God's children want the last word. You do, I do, our kids do. Such is the nature of being human. The fact that adults generally "refuse" (Ha!) to let children have the last word causes nothing but trouble. It is our very undoing, the virus of parental self-destruction.

The power struggle over who gets the last word begins when a parent makes a decision a child doesn't like. The child responds with loud complaint, demanding reasons. The parent begins to explain. The child denounces the explanation as "stupid." The parent insists upon respect. The child, sensing that the parent is on the defensive, becomes more provocative. The parent begins to threaten. The child mocks the parent's exasperation. The parent . . . Does this sound familiar?

The end result? Nothing is accomplished except that the stage is set for further power struggles. The level of stress in the family steadily escalates. The child, determined to assert autonomy, but denied the right to do so, becomes ever more disrespectful, ever more "mouthy" and rebellious. Resentment builds, conflict in the family spreads from relationship to relationship like a perpetual brushfire, the child's rebellion takes on risk, and the parents become angrier and angrier, all the while backing themselves further and further into the proverbial corner.

When my son, Eric, the quintessential "strong-willed child," was in his early teens, I belatedly discovered the strategic advantage that could be gained by always giving him the last word. I realized that my anger at his determination to have the all-important last word stemmed from the fact that—revelation!—I wanted it, too. The last word was the prize for which we both vied in any disagreement. It occurred to me that letting him have the prize would pull the plug on his "disrespect," let the air out of the potential power struggle, and contain his rebellion.

From that point on, whenever I would make a decision that provoked his ire, I'd let him express himself, then I'd say something along the lines of "Eric, if I was your age, I wouldn't agree with me either, but I've made my decision. Right now, you're angry, and I don't blame you, but anger and good communication don't mix. When you calm down, if you want to talk, I'll talk. Not argue, but talk. Meanwhile, the decision stands, and I trust that you'll abide by it, whether you agree with it or not."

"Well, I think it's stupid," he'd say, or something similarly "insolent," and I'd say, "I understand." Then I'd walk away, leaving him to—as my stepfather used to put it—*stew in his own juices*.

Sometimes, Eric would come back later and want to talk.

We'd start to talk, he'd begin getting upset, and again, I'd let him have the last word and walk away, suggesting that he try again later. Sometimes he'd stew for hours, making non-verbal displays of disgust. But the amazing thing was, he never disobeyed. He did what he was told, albeit with a "bad attitude," about which I ask, "Who cares?"

Most important, I retained my authority, which, I realized in retrospect, I had abandoned each and every time I had foolishly engaged in the game of "Who Gets The Last Word?"

You want respect from your children? Then retain your authority. It's that simple. Give them the last word, and get more than you ever insisted upon in return.

Parent Judo, Part One

Eric came to me one day when he was fifteen. "Dad," he said, "I want to talk about getting a motorcycle."

"For *me,* son?"

"No, Dad! For me!"

"Eric, m'boy," I said, "this is going to be the shortest conversation we've ever had."

"Why?"

"Because you will never get a motorcycle from your mother and me. In fact, just to be completely clear concerning this matter, you can't even—at some future date—buy a motor-cycle for yourself and continue to live here."

"But, Dad!" he pleaded. "All my friends are getting them!"

"Then, Eric," I answered, "you're going to be the most spe-cial kid in your peer group!"

His shoulders went back, his chin jutted forward, and he leaned forward so as to lend more emphasis to his protest: "Dad! I hate it when you talk like this! I wanta know why you won't buy me a motorcycle!"

"Because," I said, "motorcycles are dangerous and you are not old enough to appreciate the danger; nor will you be for many years to come."

He loosened up a bit and said, "Now, Dad, I knew you were going to say that, and I know motorcycles are danger-ous, and I promise, I'll be careful."

"Eric," I said, "let me explain something. If I was your age, I'd want a motorcycle. And if I asked my parents for one, they'd say the same thing to me I just said to you. And believe it or not, I'd say the same thing to them you just said to me. Furthermore, there'll come the day when you'll be standing in my shoes, saying pretty much the same thing to your fifteen-year-old." And without further ado I turned around and began walking away, pulling the plug on the power struggle.

"Dad!" he cried, "where are you going? Dad? I wanta talk about this some more! Hey! We're not done, Dad!"

I paused, turned around, and said, "Oh, I guess I forgot to tell you something, Eric."

"What?"

"We're done." And just like that, I was gone.

Now, will someone who thinks teenagers can be reasoned with please tell me what I could have said to Eric that would have caused him to agree with me, as in, "Well, Dad, now that you put it that way, I see the error of my thinking on this mat-ter. I'm sorry I brought it up."

The silence you hear is because there is absolutely *nothing* I could have said to Eric that would have caused him to agree with me. In his mind, he, Eric the Invincible, was not going to get hurt on a motorcycle, and that was that.

And as for my walking away from him instead of trying to resolve the issue with him in some compromising win-win manner: Where, I ask, is the compromise between a naive fifteen-year-old who wants a motorcycle and a thirty-something parent who thinks that's insane? A motorcycle poster? A black leather jacket? A video of Evel Knievel jumping the Atlantic Ocean?

How about: "Eric, here are a few playing cards and some clothespins. If you clip the cards to the back tire of your bicycle, they'll make a sound like a Harley-Davidson!"

In short, there was no way for me to compromise with him on this matter of motorcycles, not without doing something I didn't want to do. So, with nothing more to say, I walked away. If I had stuck around and tried to get him to understand, he would only have gotten more angry, and so would I. The kindest thing to do was walk away. He didn't think so, of course. He was mad at me for several days. In fact, he wouldn't speak to me. It was sort of a blessing, actually.

You can't reason with a teenager. You can either say yes or no, just like with any other age child. A teenager will understand his parents when he *needs* to understand them. No sooner.

Q: *When is that?*
A: When the child is a parent.

So, when Eric is forty-one and Jack, his first child, is fifteen and asks for something outrageous, Eric will understand why I did what I did way back when. But then, you can reason with a forty-one-year-old. Most of the time.

A Brief Pause for Review Along With Some Advice Concerning the "Bad Attitude" Thing

Giving a teen (or any age child, for that matter) the "last word" is how a parent can stay out of power struggles. Instead of engaging in a nonproductive verbal "shoot-out," the parent simply

1. Says what he has to say;

2. Allows the child complete freedom to disagree, even giving the child latitude as to how the disagreement is expressed;

3. Acknowledges that the child's disagreement and attitude are understandable, as in, "If I were you, I'd feel the same way right now" or, "If I were twelve, I'd think the same thing";

4. Walks away (pulling the plug on the power struggle), trusting that despite the child's dissatisfaction, he will obey the rules.

And while I'm at it, let me say a few words about the "bad attitude" issue. You know, grumbling under the breath, the disgusted scowl, the sassy tone of voice, the impudent posture, and other examples of seemingly rebellious body language. Once a parent begins harping on the "bad attitude" issue, it will quickly become a stumbling block in the parent-child relationship. The child's attitude will definitely get worse, the parent will get angrier and angrier, and matters will go from bad to worse.

Fact: If you want obedience with a good attitude, you will get very little obedience, and you will get a really bad attitude.

Fact: If you want obedience, and you don't care what the child's attitude is, then—not right away, but within a relatively short order—you will start getting more obedience and a better attitude. This may sound hard to believe, but it's true. You'll just have to discover it for yourself.

In the early states of my parenthood, I—like most parents—wanted my children to not only be compliant but have a "good attitude" about what I told them to do as well. I belatedly realized that this was like wanting to have my cake and eat it, too! At this point, I began letting go of my insistence that they like my rules. Lo and behold! I quickly discovered that the freer they were to express their feelings about my instructions, the more likely they were to comply with them.

Parent Judo, Part Two

One evening as we finished dinner, I pointed out to Amy—then sixteen—that since her brother was gone, it would fall to her to clear the table and do the dishes on her own.

"I can't, Daddy," she said, "I have too much homework."

"Oh, I'm sure you can do the dishes and still have plenty of time left for homework, Amy," I replied.

"No, Daddy, I have a test to study for."

I thought about this for a moment, and said, "Then you'd better waste no time in doing the dishes, Amy."

She glared at me for several seconds, and then said, "I'm not going to do the dishes, Daddy! I've given you a good enough reason why I shouldn't have to, *and that's my final word on the subject!*"

Willie and I exchanged smiles, then rose from the table.

"Amy, you may certainly have the last word," I said. And with that, Willie and I exited the dining room as Amy continued to say that, no, she wasn't going to do the dishes, not tonight, and that was final.

Willie and I retired to the living room and awaited the verdict. Several minutes later, we heard the dishwasher pop open and dishes begin rattling around. Then a cabinet door slammed shut and more dishes rattled. Remember I didn't say Amy had to do the dishes with a *good attitude;* I just said she had to do them.

If I had never discovered the advantages of letting children have the last word, I would actually have tried to intimidate

Amy into doing the dishes! And I might have succeeded, but at great cost to our relationship. Under the pressure of a strong enough threat, Amy would have complied, but she would not have respected me, and for good reason; namely, a child cannot respect an adult who uses threats to secure cooperation. I would have won the battle, but lost the war.

As it was, Amy finished the dishes, stalked off to her room, did her homework, studied for her test, and gave me the silent treatment for the rest of the evening. Ah, but I'll trade a few hours of her not liking me for a lifetime of her not respecting me, any day.

Q: *What would you and your wife have done if Amy had gone to her room, leaving the dinner dishes on the table?*

A: Oh, I'd have done the dishes without a word of complaint.

Q: *What?!! Teaching Amy that there were no consequences for disobedience?*

A: No, I'd have done the dishes and . . . well, I'm not going to tell you right now what would have happened next. You'll just have to wait until later in this chapter to find out. But bear with me. I won't keep you in suspense for long.

Parent Judo, Part Three

A single mother in Dayton, Ohio, tells me that she quite accidentally stumbled upon the advantages of giving a child the last word several years ago, during her daughter's early teen years. True to form, this child had taken to expressing loud, rude contempt for any maternal decision which was not to her liking, meaning nearly all maternal decisions.

The more Mom tried to explain herself, the louder and more contemptuous the daughter became. Mom finally realized that attempts to make her daughter understand the reasons behind her decisions were fruitless.

"It dawned on me," she told me, "that even if Shelly listened quietly to every word I said, she still would not understand me. She would understand me when she was my age and had a daughter her age, and not a moment sooner."

Having been touched by the god of common sense, Mom began simply telling Shelly what she could do, couldn't do, and had to do. If, as was almost inevitable, Shelly protested, Mom said something along the lines of "Oh, I understand. If I was your age, I'd feel the same way, sweetheart, no doubt about it. Nonetheless, I've made my decision, and it's not open for discussion." And Shelly would yell something disrespectful and, getting no response from Mom, something even more insolent. Still getting no response, she'd pout. But, her mother went on to say, if simply left to "stew in her own juices," Shelly would eventually do as she'd been told.

"Needless to say," Mom adds, "Shelly still doesn't like the fact that she isn't yet free to do as she pleases. But we haven't had an argument in more than two years, and outside of getting the silent treatment from her when she's unhappy with me, we get along a lot better. I mean a whole lot better. The constant stress and tension just aren't there anymore."

Just recently, before Mom left for her second job one Saturday morning, she told Shelly to mow the grass. No way, was the reply.

"Well, Shelly," Mom said, "I have company coming over this evening, so you can either mow the grass or vacuum the house and clean the bathrooms. Whichever chore you don't do, I'll do when I get home."

Shelly stood firm. She wasn't going to do either the grass or the vacuuming. She'd done enough work around the house that week, she said. She was tired of being treated like a "slave" and had decided to take the day off.

"I understand, Shelly, I'd probably feel the same way if I were you, but I still need you to either mow the grass or clean the house."

Shelly reiterated that she wasn't gong to do either, and even challenged, "Make me!"

But Mom didn't take the bait. "I've got to go to work, Shelly," she said in parting. "Thanks for doing either the grass or the vacuuming and the bathroom."

As Mom walked to her car, Shelly stood on the front steps, letting fly with not only the last word, but many last words, trying to goad her mother into a confrontation. But Mom simply got in the car and drove off.

Guess what? Arriving home later that afternoon, Mom discovered that the yard had been mowed! And upon coming inside, she discovered that the house had been vacuumed and the bathroom had been cleaned!

Not a bad deal, eh? Shelly gets the last word, while Mom gets a manicured lawn and a clean house. And they both enjoy a far better relationship than if Mom, like many unfortunate parents, was determined to have her cake and eat it, too.

Questions Anyone?

Q: *Our twelve-year-old son has a way of drawing us into conflict with him, and it's driving us close to crazy. The "game" generally begins with him refusing to do something— go to his piano lesson, do a chore. We become upset, and he stands his ground until we levy a threat meaningful enough* and believable enough to convince him we mean business. At this point, he will comply, albeit with a great show of displeasure. Even though we always win these battles, the frequency of them is wearing us out. Do you have any idea why he's doing this and suggestions for what we can do, if anything, to stop it?*

A: Your tweenager is playing this "game" with you because you so willingly play it with him. He throws down the gauntlet and you pick it right up. In the exchange that follows, he has absolutely nothing to lose. So, he pushes the confrontation to the limit. Meanwhile, you bluster and threaten, but in the final analysis, you do absolutely nothing! Your son has learned, therefore, that refusing to do what he's told is inconsequential—to him, that is. You, on the other hand, suffer all manner of emotional consequences as a result of the power struggles that ensue.

A child—regardless of age—feels most secure with parents who demonstrate that they are perfectly clear on where they stand and where they want the child to stand. A youngster will not always be happy with the decisions his parents make, but in the final analysis, he will always feel more secure with parents who are resolute when it comes to making decisions. And a secure child is a happier child. It's as simple as that. The moment a parent steps into a power struggle with a child, however, the parent loses all power. The child wins. Period. Even if you're ultimately successful at getting the child to do what you want, he's won by virtue of the fact that he succeeded in pulling you down to his level, however temporarily.

Breaking this pattern is going to require that you give your son the last word. As it stands, you're trying to have the last word, and you ultimately prevail, but at great cost to yourself emotionally and in terms of the steady erosion of your authority. One of these days, if you don't pull yourself out of this quicksand rather quickly, you're going to find yourself faced with a son who's no longer fazed by your threats. Then what?

The next time he refuses to go to his piano lesson or do a chore, simply say, with a shrug of your shoulders, "Oh well, I guess that's up to you." And walk away. If he persists in trying to draw you into a struggle, simply repeat that the decision to obey or not is his. There's a chance he may, after some posturing, do what you've told him to do. On the other hand, he may not comply. In that event, later that day (or even the next), when he asks if he can watch television or go outside with his friends, tell him that no, he can't. When he demands to know why not, say, "Well, you see, whether or not you go to your piano lesson is up to you, but whether or not you go outside is up to me. So, you can't go outside." If no other opportunity presents itself, send him to bed early with "When you go to bed is up to me."

From that point on, every time he refuses to do something, just say, "It's up to you." In no time at all, your son will figure out that those four words mean that if he doesn't do what you've told him to do, something evil and unfair is in store for him. He'll be much more cooperative, I assure you, but the best thing is, he'll be much more secure, and therefore much happier. Everyone wins!

Q: *Every time my fourteen-year-old daughter gets upset with me—which is every few days it seems—she tells me she "hates" me. When I try to talk with her about this and explain to her that I'm only doing what I think is best, she refuses to talk. What should I do?*

A: You should stop letting her "hate" bother you, and you should stop trying to explain yourself to her. In the first place, if a decision you make upsets her, the likelihood is the decision is in her best interest. In the second place, she cannot possibly understand this at her age, and no amount of explanation is going to drive this understanding home. She will understand you when she has children. In the third place, children aren't supposed to like their parents that much anyway. They are supposed to *want* to leave home.

I once asked the five-hundred-plus people in a Nashville audience, "How many of you—when you were teenagers— truly liked your parents?"

Maybe ten hands went up, which didn't surprise me, because I didn't like my parents either when I was a teen. They annoyed me, inconvenienced me, and made me angry on a fairly regular basis. I couldn't wait to leave home, which simply means they did a good job of convincing me I could make a better life for myself than they were willing to make for me.

Today's parents, by all accounts, are not doing a very good job of convincing their children of this. When I was twenty, I was married and on my own. The average age of economic emancipation in my generation was, in fact, twenty-two. Today, the average age is approaching twenty-six. In my time, for a child to live at home well into his or her twenties was considered indication of something very odd in the parent-child relationship. Today, it is considered normal.

And, by the by, lest you think this is because it's far more difficult for today's young person to get out on his own, it's not. The researchers who discovered this trend were unable to explain it in terms of economics or the availability of jobs. They said, "The children of this generation have been given too much by parents who have been generally guilty of self-induced nearsightedness," or words to that very damning effect.

When a teenager says "I hate you!" to a parent, it's a sure bet the youngster means exactly that. No, she hasn't thought it through, but she means it nonetheless. In this regard, it's important for parents to understand several things:

First, teenagers don't generally experience emotions in moderation. If a parent makes a decision a teen doesn't like, she's not going to say she's merely "annoyed" or "disappointed." She's likely to act as if her world is coming to an end. She'll wail piteously, stomp her feet, say something insolent, scream she "hates" you, stomp her feet, scream she "hates" you, or all of the above. This is not the sign of a moderate heart.

Second, these episodes of really and truly hating one's parents don't last long because within hours, a couple of days at most, the teen in question must come back to her parents and ask them for something else. And in order to elevate the likelihood that they will look favorably upon her request, she's got to pretend she likes them again! Such is the roller-coaster ride that is parenthood.

Third, anytime your daughter screams that you've been "unfair" or she "hates" you, there's a 99.999 percent likelihood you've just done the right thing.

Lastly, none of this is to be taken seriously. "I hate you!" in all of its manifestations is nothing more than an example of the foolishness inherent in children, as spoken of in Proverbs 22:15. Such outbursts don't merit feeling anxiety, guilt, or anger. They are laughable, although I am not recommending that one actually laugh. The most appropriate, honest, respectful, accepting, authoritative, and loving response one can give a child (regardless of age) when the child tells you he hates you is, "I understand. If I were you, I'd hate me right now, too." Then, walk away, leaving the child to stew in his or her own juices.

Talking to the child about how he really doesn't hate you, that hate is a very serious thing to say to someone and shouldn't, therefore, ever be said in haste, and that he may be angry with you but he doesn't hate you, not really, and even if he does, you still love him, no matter what, is completely, totally, ridiculously unnecessary. That sort of heartfelt response, although certainly sincere, only adds fuel to the fire.

Anger, as in, "You're not going to talk to me like that, you filthy-mouthed little brat! You're going to show me the respect I deserve, or I'll beat the living daylights out of you!!" is more childish than "I hate you!" Besides, one cannot *demand* respect. One can only *command* it, and one does not effectively command by going ballistic.

Q: *A communication problem has recently developed with our thirteen-year-old son. He's always been an affectionate child who would tell us what was going on in his life and talk to us if he had a problem. That all changed shortly after he started school (seventh grade) this year. He's more distant, seems uncomfortable when we show affection toward him, and is no longer open with us about what he's doing in school or with his friends. If we try to engage him in conversation, he gives us one-word replies. According to his teachers, he's well liked by his classmates, but his grades are starting to slip. What would you suggest?*

A: This is probably nothing more complicated than early adolescence (tweenagerness), in which case you would do well to stop "bugging" your son to talk and emote. He'll come around when he's ready, not before.

The tweenage years begin around age eleven and last two, maybe three years. Before this important transitional stage, the child's security is invested primarily in his relationship with his parents, he seeks parental approval, and he looks to his parents for a definition of right versus wrong.

The "task" during the tween years is to find a secure niche within the peer group. This requires that the youngster put some distance between himself and his parents. And so, around age eleven, the child begins withdrawing (from one degree or another) from the family and investing in peer relationships. Increasingly, he seeks peer approval and looks to his peers for a definition of right (cool) versus wrong (uncool, nerdy).

As you can imagine—and probably remember—this metamorphosis generates its share of anxiety and insecurity, which explains why the young teen often looks worried and troubled. But to whom can he talk? Not to his friends, because to do so would be a tacit admission of weakness. Not to his parents, either, because that would be an admission of continued dependence. The tweenager is having to make a lot of adjustments and—outside being understanding, patient, and supportive—there's probably little that parents can do that will significantly ease the process.

Although he may at times act as though he wants nothing to do with you, your son is actually trying to figure out how he can develop a place for himself among his peers and still keep you "on his team." Without realizing it, you're doing half his job for him. Every expression of concern on your part affirms the security of his relationship with you. And so, he seizes the opportunity to turn the tables on you a bit. You pursue, and he plays hard to get.

I'd suggest you back off a bit and let him begin assuming a greater share of responsibility for the relationship. You might issue an open invitation of the "if you want to talk, you know where to find us" sort. As far as his grades are concerned, a slight slip is no cause for alarm, but if they continue to deteriorate, you might consider reading my book, *Ending the Homework Hassle* (Andrews McMeel Publishing, 1990).

Creative Consequences (Where the Fun Begins!)

It's now time to go back to the story of Amy and the dinner dishes. To recap: The Rosemond family, sans Eric, was finishing dinner when I informed sixteen-year-old Amy that she was going to have to clean the kitchen and do the dishes on her own. She told me she couldn't; she had too much homework. I told her she was going to have to do her homework *and* the dishes. She said she couldn't; she had a major test to study for. I said, "If you have a test, you'd better get on the dishes right away." She bristled, as I fully expected, and told me, in no uncertain terms, she wasn't going to do the dishes, and that was her "final word on the subject." Willie and I told her she could have the final word, excused ourselves, and left the dining room. Amy did the dishes.

The Logical Question: "What would you have done if Amy had not done the dishes, instead going to her room to study?"

Answer: "I would have cleared the table, done the dishes, and cleaned the kitchen, and it would not have bothered me one iota."

The Logical Exclamation: "You'd have let her get away with it?"

Answer: "Not at all. I'd have simply done the dishes, etc., taken a deep breath, and waited for what I call a 'strategic opportunity,' generally defined as *a consequence which is appropriate to a certain misbehavior, but one which is delayed hours, if not days.*"

The Logical Challenge: "I've heard several psychologists say that in order for a child to make the connection between a misbehavior and its consequence, the consequence must be immediate."

That's what psychologists and other mental health professionals have told today's parents, all right, and it simply isn't true. Well, I take that back. It's true for a child younger than three years of age, for whom consequences must be immediate because long-term memory has not yet formed. Between thirty-six and forty-two months (three and three and a half years), however, long-term memory comes into play. When it does (and its emergence is obvious) parents can, whenever they choose, delay consequences—wait for a "strategic opportunity"—when the child misbehaves.

Here's a fact: *Eight out of every ten times a child misbehaves, effective consequences are not immediately available.*

If an effective consequence is immediately available (please take careful note: effective and immediate), it will spring to mind immediately. If, on the other hand, an effective consequence is not immediately available, you will begin to suffer immediate brain strain. You will, in other words, start to get upset. Getting upset, you see, is a sure-fire indication there's nothing you can do about the misbehavior right then and there. So, if a child misbehaves and you begin to get upset, just take a deep breath and wait for a "strategic opportunity." Good things come to those who wait.

Illustration: Your five-year-old daughter refuses to pick up her toys. Fine, you say. You just send her to her room for a while. But what if you've told her to pick up her toys in advance of leaving the house for a dental appointment? Fine, you say, you send her to her room when you get home and/or send her to bed early. But what if, after the dental appointment, you've promised to drop in on a sick friend, and you're probably not going to get home until thirty minutes before your child's regular bedtime? Obviously, there's nothing immediate you can do about her disobedience. There's not anything you can do about it for the rest of the day! What do you do then?

"Well, John," you might reply, "I'd tell her she won't be able to do something she's looking forward to doing the following day, like spending the night with a friend."

"That's fine and good, but allow me to play the devil's advocate: What if, that same evening, your husband comes home and informs you that the two of you have been invited to dinner at his boss's house the next night?"

"I'd get a sitter."

"And what if you quickly discover that all your 'regulars' have commitments?"

"Well, I'd, uh, I'd, let's see . . . I'd, uh."

"Allow me to assist. You'd have to let your daughter go to her friend's house to spend the night."

"Okay, you're right."

"My point, dear reader, is that when it comes to the consequences of a child's misbehavior, you shouldn't try to predict the future, because you don't know what the future may hold."

"So, then, I do nothing?"

"No, no. To repeat: If a child misbehaves and an effective consequence is not immediately available—which will be the case eighty percent of the time!—don't get frazzled, and don't try to predict the future. Instead, just wait! Wait for a 'strategic consequence.' You might have to wait only an hour or two. Then again, you might have to wait days. But sooner or later, a consequence that is appropriate to the 'crime' in question will present itself, at which point you say to your child, 'Do you remember two days ago when I told you to pick up your toys and you refused? Well, I didn't do anything about it then, but I'm going to do something about it now. Because of refusing to do what I told you to do, you can't [insert something the child has just asked permission to do, like go with a friend and her parents to the movies].'"

"That doesn't seem fair, John."

"To tell you the truth, I don't know what fair means, unless it means something a child doesn't like. I do know this, however: In the real world, the 'price' one has to pay for inappropriate behavior does not always come due immediately. It is often delayed."

"For example?"

"For example, you misbehave on the job, and your supervisor says nothing to you until your annual review, which takes place four months later. At your review, you learn that your misbehavior is costing you that promotion you anticipated."

"Okay, I think I get it."

Okay! So, if Amy had refused to clean up after dinner, I'd have cleaned up myself, without a word of complaint. What could I have done? Send her to her room? She was on her way to her room as it was. Send her to bed early? She was sixteen years old at the time. Trying to get a sixteen-year-old in bed early seems rather silly. Tell her she was grounded that weekend? What if Willie and I decide we want to have two quiet nights at home with no kids? In other words, if I tell Amy she's grounded for the weekend, I might have to take it back, which is the potential cost of trying to predict the future. So, I do the dishes, clean up the kitchen, and wait.

You see, I'm certain the reason Amy did the dishes was because of something that had happened some three months before, when . . .

Good Things Come to Those Who Wait

Willie and I were leaving the house one Saturday afternoon and I told Amy, age sixteen, we needed her help.

"We're having a dinner party tonight, Amy, and we've got some errands to run. Please vacuum downstairs and clean the downstairs bathroom while we're gone."

"Every time there's an extra chore around here," she said, "you give it to me! You never give anything extra to Eric!"

"He says the same thing."

"Well, I don't care! I'm telling it like it is!"

"Okay, we love Eric more, or whatever it is you're trying to tell us. In any case, we need you to vacuum and clean the bathroom."

"Get Eric to do it."

"Amy," I said, "you don't delegate around here. We do."

"Well, delegate to someone else, because I'm not going to do anything today. I'm taking the day off."

(Please note that my children could be as insolent, each in his/her own way, as anyone else's children, which only goes to prove: Perfect parenting does not result in perfect children.)

I thought about this for a moment. "Okay, Amos," I said, "if you don't do the vacuuming and the bathroom, then when we get home, I'll do them. No problem." And we left.

When we came home, nothing had been done, so I did the vacuuming and Willie did the bathroom. Furthermore, we were not the least bit upset. As I vacuumed, I did not scream up the stairs, "Hey! Amy! Do you hear the vacuum running?!!! It's not running on its own, you know!!!! Guess who's running it because you wouldn't?!!!!!!!" Nah. I just took a deep breath and vacuumed. And Amy went out for the evening, and we had our dinner party, and everyone was happy.

What, I ask, could I have done about Amy's flagrant insubordination? Keep her home that evening? No way! The last thing I want during a dinner party is a hotheaded sixteen-year-old stomping around upstairs, trying to let everyone know how upset she is. If I try to predict the future, I may not be able to follow through on my "promise." So, I did nothing. I took the path of least resistance, and waited.

Sunday, Monday, Tuesday, Wednesday, Thursday, Friday.

Friday! I come home from the office to find Amy and her best friend, Angie, in the kitchen, talking animatedly.

"What's up, girls?" I ask.

"Oh, Daddy," Amy blurted, "tonight is going to be the best!

We're going to the game, then we're getting together with our friends at Smokey Joe's, then we're going over to Allison's and having a dance party!"

"Oh, my gosh," I said, "I almost forgot."

"Forgot what?" Amy asked.

"Oh, goodness, Amy, you can't go out tonight."

"What?!!!!!!"

"Gosh, Amos, I'm so sorry to be the bearer of bad tidings, but it's not possible for you to go out tonight."

"But I've had these plans for three days, Daddy!"

"I know, I know, but it's just not possible."

"But why?!!! I mean, I deserve a reason!!!!"

"And so you do. Do you want me to tell you in front of Angie?"

"Yes! She's my best friend!"

"Well, Angie, I'll just tell you then. Last Saturday, Mrs. Rosemond and I were leaving the house and we told Amy we needed her to vacuum and clean the bathroom because of a dinner party we were having that evening . . ."

(Cut to Amy, who has an incredulous/outraged look on her face—mouth open, eyes wide, body leaning slightly forward.)

". . . and Amy stood up in my face and told me she wasn't going to do anything we asked her to do, and she didn't."

I turned to Amy, whose eyes were blazing with impending pyrotechnics. "Amy, you obviously still don't get it."

"Get what?!!" she snarled.

"You still don't understand that disobedience isn't free. When you defy someone with legitimate authority—in this case, your mother and I—there is always a price to be paid, sooner or later. The price for your disobedience, young lady, has just come due. You aren't going out tonight because of what happened last Saturday."

KAAAAAAAAAABOOOOOOOOOOM!!!!!!!!!!!

Amy went ballistic. To tell the truth, I couldn't make out a word she said, but the imaginative reader will have no problem filling in the blanks. In the midst of her ranting and raving, as Angie shrank back out of the line of the explosion, I turned and started walking out of the room. Suddenly, you could have heard the proverbial pin drop.

"I'm leaving anyway!!!!!!!"

I stopped. I turned, slooooowly. I looked Amy in the eye. I shrugged my shoulders. "A girl's gotta do what a girl's gotta do, Amy," I said, and with that, I turned and left the room.

A reader exclaims: "You're just gonna let her leave?"

Yep. I'm just gonna let her leave. Here are the alternatives:

1. I could turn and snarl, "Just try it, young lady! You walk outa this house and, and, and . . ." And issue some threat, any variation of which will cause her to prove what we are taught in Genesis 2–3, to wit: Obedience is always a choice! Remember! Not even God could/can make His children obey! He couldn't make them obey His rules in the Garden of Eden, and He can't make us obey today. Obedience is and always has been a choice, no matter how powerful the authority! Please, dear reader, listen to the voice of experience here. You do not ever want to force a child to prove to you that you can't make him/her obey! Which is exactly what you force a child to prove when you issue a threat, especially when the child isn't thinking straight, as was the case with Amy at that moment.

2. Try and stop her from leaving the house. Now, isn't that a charming picture? John Rosemond and his sixteen year-old daughter battling it out in the back hall for the World Championship of Dysfunctional Family Wrestling!!!!

3. She stomps out of the house, gets in her car, and leaves. I race from the house, jump in my car, and Amy leads me on a high-speed chase through town. Fat chance of that!!! I'm

John Rosemond, for gosh sakes! I've got a reputation to pre-serve!!! This would definitely not look good on the ten o'clock news: Good evening. This is Diane LaGorgeous speaking live from Gastonia, North Carolina, where a police roadblock has just brought an abrupt end to a high-speed chase through this normally sleepy Southern town. In one car, nationally known parenting expert John Rosemond. In the other—the pur-sued—his teenage daughter, Amy. Police report that the two cars reached speeds of over one hundred miles an hour be-fore city, county, and state police, aided by helicopters carry-ing a special antiterrorist FBI SWAT team, were able to slow and finally stop the vehicles. After their arrest, it is reported that Rosemond and his daughter, although handcuffed, began kicking and trying to bite each other. Our viewers may know Rosemond as the author of numerous books on healthy par-enting. More at eleven.

You see? I had no rational choice but to let her leave, and I pride myself on being rational.

So, to continue, Amy puts on her jacket and storms out of the house, Angie in hot pursuit. I go upstairs where Willie is reading. I crack the blinds in our bedroom so as to watch the action in the driveway.

"Tell me what happens," Willie asks, nonchalantly.

"Amy is stomping around in the driveway. I can't hear her, but I can tell she's yelling. Oh! She's making gestures toward the house now."

"What kind of gestures?"

"Oh, just gestures. Mostly one. Angie looks like she's pleading with her. Amy's getting in her car. Angie's talking to her through the driver's side window. Amy's getting out of her car and slamming the door. She's gesturing again."

And so it went, for fifteen or twenty minutes after which Amy stormed back in the house, slammed the door, stormed upstairs to her room, slammed the door, and wasn't seen until early the next afternoon, when she came downstairs, looked at me and said, "I hate you for life!" and left, slamming the door as she exited. Oh well. So it goes. She stayed mad for several days. Then, needing to ask my permission to do something, she became all sweetness and charm.

I figured out, by the way, what Angie was saying to her in the driveway. She was saying, "Amy, if your dad is grounding you tonight for something you did six days ago, just think of what he's going to do if you leave! And you won't know when he's going to do it!!!"

A reader asks: "So, John, what would you have done if Amy had actually left?"

Realizing there was absolutely nothing effective I could have done at that moment, I would have taken a deep breath and waited for a "strategic opportunity." Actually, as I was standing at the upstairs window, watching Amy storm around in the drive, I decided upon my course of action. It would have played out as follows:

Monday morning, three days later: Amy comes running back into the house at seven forty-five, announcing, "Daddy! My car won't start!"

"I know," I say, with nonchalance.

"No, Daddy, really, my car won't even turn over!"

"Daddy knows, sweetheart. A car won't start without an alternator."

"What do you mean?"

"I mean that last night, after you were asleep, I took the alternator out of your car. And before you say anything, I'd suggest you hear me out.

"The fact is, Amos," I continue, "Mom and I have decided that because you left the house without permission on Friday night, you will be without a car for one month. You're not on any sort of restriction, but you won't be able to use a car—

yours or one of ours. When the month is up, I'll put the alter-nator back in your car if, and only if, you have been the per-fect child during that time—meaning, no back talk, no disobedience of any sort, no displays of temper, no 'gestures,' if you know what I mean. If there's an incident during the month, then we'll have to do this another month, and if there's an incident during the second month, then we're just going to sell your car, because we're not going to do this for more than two months. And by the by, if we end up selling your car, the next car you drive will be one you buy for your-self. Oh, and one more thing, before you say anything at all, please understand that your month begins (as I look at my watch) right . . . now!"

That's an example of what I call a "Checkmate Move"—a consequence so powerful, so awesome, so momentous, so critical, that there's absolutely nothing the child in question can do but say "Uncle!" (or, to be politically correct about it, "Sibling of a parent!"), however reluctantly. Whether they realize it or not, parents always have the power to put a child in checkmate. The keys to the proper use of a Checkmate Move are:

a.   Use a Checkmate Move neither prematurely or belat-edly—neither too early nor too late. In either case, its effec-tiveness is considerably diminished. As with comedy, timing is everything.

b.   Use a Checkmate Move only once in a blue moon. The more Checkmate Moves are used, the less "potent" any given employment will be. As with comedy, don't deliver the same "punch line" over and over.

A Checkmate Move is a consequence that takes a child completely by surprise. It is not rashly delivered, but well thought out. Most of all, there's absolutely nothing a child can do about it. Relative to the wimpy disciplinary methods mental health professionals typically recommend, a Checkmate Move is *outrageous*. By this I mean any consequence that serves to prove to a child, once and for all, that his or her parents mean business—permanently.

You see, a child who walks the proverbial "straight and narrow" needs only a slight nudge when he steers off the proper path. But a thousand slight nudges will not suffice to move a child who's careening rapidly out of control back on track. Using nudges (reprimands, short periods of grounding, taking away a privilege for a brief period of time, and so on) to deal with the "outrageous" child is like trying to stop a charging elephant with a fly swatter. The fact is, the outrageous requires the equally outrageous, and by no means am I referring to discipline that is hateful, cruel, or sadistic. Just *memorable*. To illustrate, here are four real-life examples of memorably outrageous Checkmate Moves, beginning with one with which I am intimately familiar:

1. *Indisposed!* Thomas Sowell—author, columnist, economist, and brilliant social analyst—says that the problem with America's social policy is the replacement, in one generation, of what worked (and still will!) with what sounds good. Nowhere is that more true than concerning the rearing and education of children, where we have substituted the "sounds good" of self-esteem rhetoric for the lessons of character development, most of which can be learned only the old-fashioned "hard way."

Syndicated columnist William Raspberry once wrote a column in which he proposed that the nouveau attempt to *understand* social problems (i.e., crime, poverty, illegitimacy) has provided certain individuals with the perfect excuse to continue behaving in antisocial ways. The same could be said of the nouveau attempt to understand why certain children seem determined to behave in self-defeating ways.

Thirty-eight years ago, when I was in the seventh grade, adults did not lack compassion for problem children. Nonetheless, the emphasis was on *solution,* not understanding. I am an authority on this subject because in 1960, I was a problem child. I was, in fact, more of a thorn in the sides of my teachers than any other child then enrolled in my suburban-Chicago elementary school. Although able to make straight A's without much study, I was inattentive, irresponsible, disruptive, distractible, immature, and infuriating. Come to think of it, I was probably worse than that.

My teachers tried everything—sitting me in the hall, keeping me in during recess and after school, making me write sentences—but nothing worked. My parents tried everything—taking away privileges, making me do extra chores, grounding me for weeks at a time, lecturing—but nothing worked.

One February day, my parents (mother and stepfather) went to the school for a conference with my teachers. They came home two hours later and summoned me into the living room, where there occurred a "conversation" I will never forget.

My stepfather spoke: "This will be short. The agreement reached at the conference was that if you are reprimanded by any one of your teachers even one time between now and the end of this school year, you will repeat the seventh grade. In fact, your mother and I didn't agree to this; rather, we suggested it, and your principal and teachers gladly agreed. Any questions?"'

My only question was, "You're kidding, right?" to which my parents said simply, "No, but you are free to find that out for yourself."

Today, it is likely that a team of helping professionals would descend on a similarly incorrigible child, seeking to divine the "why" of the child's problems. They would propose boredom (which is another way of claiming a child is gifted), or attention-deficit disorder, or low self-esteem due to his parents' divorce, or a neurotic need for approval from his peers due to inadequate reinforcement of positive behaviors by his parents. They would investigate, speculate, theorize, temporize, label, and sublabel. Meanwhile, everyone would dance around the problem while handling the child with kid gloves and, in the process, providing the child with one or more tailor-made excuses for continuing to misbehave.

In my case, courtesy of my parents' and teachers' joint determination to simply solve the problem, my attention-deficit disorder with massive boredom and divorce-related loss of self-esteem resulting in immature social behavior was cured in but one day. For the remainder of the school year, I faced forward, locked eyes with the teacher, and said not a word unless called upon. And I passed the seventh grade.

Were my parents kidding? I asked them several years ago. They said, "You'll never know. But it worked, didn't it!"

2. *Deposed!* A certain young man was a major behavior problem both in school and at home. He was disruptive, disrespectful, and disobedient. At conferences with his seventh-grade teachers, principal, counselor, et al., it was repeatedly suggested that the young man had attention-deficit disorder (ADD). The parents were reassured that ADD is genetic; therefore, his behavior wasn't their fault. He needed medication to help him control his impulses, they were told. The parents resisted this well-intentioned hogwash for months.

"Finally," the mother told me, "we reached the limit of our tolerance for his shenanigans. He came home from school one day to discover a padlock on the door to his bedroom, which houses his television, computer, video game unit, sports equipment, models, and so on. We told him he'd be allowed in his room for ten minutes in the morning to dress for school and another ten minutes in the evening to get ready for bed, which was going to be seven-thirty every night, seven nights a week. His bed was going to be the sofa in the living room—most comfortable, if you ask me."

The boy was stunned, to say the least. When he threatened to report his parents for child abuse, they reminded him that he would be properly fed, properly protected from the elements, and sleep in a bed that was much safer than his own. After all, he could only roll out of one side of it!

"But please!" his parents said. "Tell whomever you like how abused you are."

This austere state of affairs would last a minimum of six weeks, they told him. During this time, he would not be allowed to participate in any after-school activity, have friends over, use the phone, watch television, or go anywhere except to accompany his parents. Furthermore, every single incident of misbehavior at school or home would add a week to his "exile," and no amount of good behavior would shorten it.

"It was amazing," his mother continued. "His counselor called us several days later to tell us he'd become a completely different child. She'd never seen so much improvement so quickly. He became a model child at home as well—polite, cooperative, talkative, a general pleasure to be around."

Six weeks later, the padlock was removed from his door with assurances that it would be reattached at the first hint of relapse. It's been almost a year, and the youngster has yet to fall off the wagon.

If more parents were like that, the makers of anti-ADD drugs might have to go into the sleeper-sofa business.

3. *Exposed!* The young lady, age fourteen, liked spending

time in her room. In fact, her parents rarely saw her for all the time she spent there. She'd come out, albeit reluctantly, for family meals, which she would sit through sullenly, and after which she would retire to her room. Furthermore, when she went into her room, she'd shut the door and "click!"

If her parents wanted to speak with her, they'd have to knock on her door and wait for her to answer. Sometimes, getting an "answer" took knocking several times, after which the young lady would growl, "What?"

"Darling sweet love child of ours," the parent(s) would say, "I/we need to talk to you, if you would so kindly deign."

"About what?" the daughter would demand.

"Well . . ." and the parents would explain themselves through the door and maybe the young lady would come to the door and unlock it. She wouldn't open it, mind you, just unlock it. The parents would open it to find her sitting on her bed, reading something perhaps.

"What is it?" the young lady who-would-be-Queen-of-the-Universe would snap, not looking up, and so it went.

If the parents tried to talk with her about her "attitude," it would only get worse. She was not, by the way, a "bad" kid by any stretch of the imagination. In fact, her teachers used words like "charming" and "delightful" to describe her, much to the parents' surprise. Obviously, she was a World Class Creep only when around her own family, which had done nothing to deserve her rude, sassy, insolent, petulant, bratty, obnoxious, creepy behavior.

One day, during the family meal, the parents were talking about something they'd done the night before, trying to ignore the Creep, who was stuffing her long face with food they'd bought and prepared, while leaning her elbows on their table, which stood in a room they'd furnished in a house they were paying for in a subdivision they'd chosen because it was in a good school system, and so on.

The father said something that made his wife laugh and suddenly, amazingly, the Creep spoke.

"You guys are such jerks," she said, and went back to stuffing her face.

The parents just looked at one another, stunned beyond words. What had they done to deserve this? they asked themselves. Nothing!!! Absolutely, positively nothing!!! They finished the meal in silence.

That night, after the Creep was asleep (at least, there was no light coming from the crack at the bottom of her bedroom door), the parents talked. The next day, the Creep came home from school to discover that her room—her very own private domain, her refuge, her shelter from the storms she imagined (in the grip of supremely narcissistic fantasies) were pummeling her life—had no door!!!!!!

"Hey!!!!" she screamed, and came running downstairs to the living room where her parents were seated, talking to one another about next summer's vacation plans.

"What is it, dear?" her mom asked.

"You know what!!!" the Creep snarled. "I want my door back!!!!"

"Oh, sweetness," her dad said, "we're such jerks, you know, that we took your door and gave it to Habitat for Humanity to use when they build a house for some appreciative person who is an actual human."

"Well, then," the Creep yelled, "you're just going to take me to the store and let me pick out a new door!!!! Today!!!"

"No, light of our lives," the father said, "we're not. In fact, you will not have a door for a month. At the end of the month, at three-thirty that afternoon [looking at his watch], your mother and I will hold a conference with you for the purpose of reviewing your behavior. If, during the month, you've been able to keep Satan from possessing you, we'll allow you to use your own money, if you have saved enough during that time, to buy yourself a new door. If, however, you've allowed your personality to be taken over by Satan on even one occasion while in our presence, then you'll have to wait another month for another conference. Now, just to show you how fair we are, in light of the fact that you may need to vent about this for a while, your month begins in sixty minutes. Until then, sugar-sweet love child, you have complete permission to demonstrate your feelings about this turn of events in any way you choose. But in exactly one hour, your month begins, at which point we would strongly advise that you put Satan out of your life forever."

"You can't do this to me!!!" the love child screamed. "It's not fair!!! That's *my* room!!! That's *my* door!!! I deserve my privacy!!!"

And so it went for sixty minutes, at which time the parents said, "Your month begins right now, charming one, but please, continue your tirade if you'd so prefer." And they walked off, leaving the light of their lives to stew and steam in the perfect silence that accompanies proper, timely use of a Checkmate Move.

During the next month, the parents saw no evidence whatsoever of satanic possession. In fact, their daughter was polite, talkative, helpful, and many other good things. So, at the end of the month, when they had their conference, the parents said, "You've been charming and delightful during the last month! An absolute joy to live with! How much money do you have?"

"Uh," their daughter replied, "about twenty dollars."

"That won't buy a door," her father said. "You must not have been planning ahead. A door will cost fifty dollars, sweetheart."

"You're not really going to make me buy my own door, are you?" she said, beginning to get a bit testy.

"Oh, you bet!" her mother said. "That was part of the original deal, sweetie, and we're not going to go back on our word."

"You're kidding!!!" the daughter said, really testy this time.

"No, and until you save enough money, we would strongly suggest that you be the charming person you were during the last month, because if you aren't, then when you save fifty bucks, you still won't be able to buy a door. The deal, sweetheart, has always involved two conditions: One, you are sweet and charming during every moment of time spent with us; and two, you have saved enough money to buy a door. You've been a joy to live with, to be sure, but you haven't fulfilled condition two."

"But I didn't know a door was going to cost fifty dollars!"

"That's your problem, honey-buns," her mother said. "At any time during the last month you could have asked and we'd have told you."

The girl steamed, but she said nothing. Later that day, at the family meal, she was all smiles and charm. And that's the way it went for another month, during which she did lots of extra work around the house and saved her money, meaning she didn't do much at all with her friends. At the end of the month, at the second conference, she was told she could buy a door if she wanted. They all went to the store, bought a suitable door, and then went out to dinner to celebrate. The daughter celebrated her door. The parents celebrated having their daughter back. And they all lived happily ever after.

4. *Decomposed!* Billy was so very, very cool. He was sixteen and his parents had bought him a car—a new car!

"Take care of this car," his parents said.

"I will," said Billy.

"There are rules, you know," his parents said.

"What?"

"Very simple, actually. No drinking, no drugs, keep your grades up, and go with us to church every Sunday."

"No problem," said Billy.

For the next six months, Billy kept his grades up, went to church, and showed no signs of drinking or drug use. Then, quite suddenly, he began bringing home scruffy-looking people he called "my friends." When his parents expressed concern about their appearance—long hair (dyed in various shades of Day-Glo), earrings, nose rings, tattoos, sloppy dress—Billy explained that they "had" to look that way because they were in a band.

"The Beatles were a band," his mother said, "but at their scruffiest, they looked like stockbrokers compared to your friends."

"Very funny, Mom," said Billy.

"We don't feel good about you hanging out with these boys," said Billy's father.

"Dad!" Billy cried, "you can't choose my friends for me."

"No, Billy," his father answered, "we're not even trying to choose your friends. Just expressing our concerns, that's all. For all we know, your friends may be very nice boys who have good values. We've seen no evidence of that, but it very well may be. If not, however, we only want to say two words: Be careful."

"What do you mean by that?" asked Billy, an edge to his voice.

"We mean be careful, that's all. Don't forget who you are."

"Yeah, right," Billy huffed.

And life went on. Billy's grades began to slowly slip from straight A's to A's and B's, and then B's, and then B's and C's. When his parents expressed concern, Billy told them his courses were getting harder.

"Billy?" his father said.

"What?"

"Be careful."

"Yeah, right."

One day, Billy announced he'd been invited to join his friends' band. His parents looked at one another.

"What?!" asked/cried Billy, in a most challenging tone.

"Be careful," his father said.

Billy started spending more and more time with his scruffy friends—"Practicing," he said. The more time he spent with them, the less he spoke to his parents, even when he was around them. Later, his parents would say that he started "pulling away." He stopped going to church every Sunday, usually with the excuse that the band had practiced late the night before trying to get ready for a "big gig" and he was too tired. All the while, his hair was getting longer and longer and his clothes were getting scruffier and scruffier and his grades were getting slippery-er and slippery-er. When his parents tried to talk with him about their concerns, he'd get testy and accuse them of "copping 'tudes" and other descriptors they couldn't find in the dictionary. Billy also started wearing sunglasses all the time, even at night.

"Do you wear them when you drive?" his father asked.

"Oh, man!" Billy exclaimed. "You are too much!" And he laughed, never answering his father's question.

One day, his father asked Billy if he could use his car to run an errand, as his own car was in the shop and Billy's mother was out somewhere with hers.

"Sure, man," Billy said, not looking up from his guitar.

His father went out and got in Billy's car. There was a strange, smoky-sweet smell permeating the upholstery. It was the same odor he and his wife smelled on Billy's clothing, which Billy explained was the smell of the incense the band burned while they practiced. Billy's father thought it was strange that Billy would burn incense in his car. He opened the ashtray and found the source of the smell. It was a thin, yellowed paper cylinder, the diameter of a pencil and less than an inch long. One end was charred, the other squeezed almost shut. Billy's father fished it out of the ashtray. He took it in the house and knocked on Billy's door.

"What?" Billy shouted.

"May I come in?" his father asked.

"For what?" Billy shouted.

"I want to show you something."

"Sure, man, c'mon in," Billy said.

Billy's father opened the door, walked over to Billy, who was sitting on his bed, and held out the yellowed paper cylinder, charred on one end.

"I found this in your car, Billy," his father said, handing it to Billy. The look on Billy's face, his father would later say, was "priceless."

Without another word, Billy's father turned and left. He got in Billy's car and ran his errand. When his wife came home, they went into their bedroom and talked. That evening, during dinner, no mention was made of the yellow paper cylinder. In fact, Billy's parents chatted with one another and with Billy as though nothing was wrong.

The next morning, when Billy got up to go to school, he couldn't find his car keys. He asked his parents if they'd seen them. They had. In fact, they told him, they had Billy's car keys—both sets.

"Check out your car, dude," his father said.

Billy looked out the kitchen window into the driveway. His car wasn't where he usually parked it. He turned around to find his father pointing at the living room window. He hurried over and looked out. His car was parked on the grass in the front yard. It had a sign on the windshield. Billy didn't even have to read the sign to know what it said.

He turned around and looked at his parents. "You're kidding, right?" he asked.

"Not a chance, dude," his father said.

"You're selling my car?!!" Billy shouted.

Billy's father turned to Billy's mother. "I think the dude's copping a 'tude, Mother," he said.

"It looks that way," Mother said.

"What's going on?!!" Billy shouted.

"What's going on, Billy, my man," his father said, "is we're selling your car, which is the only car we're ever going to buy for you, and you won't ever, under any circumstances, be allowed to drive one of ours, by the way."

"But why?!!" Billy shouted.

"You know why, Billy," his father said. "We're not even going to discuss it with you, young man. In fact, all I'm going to say is you have only yourself to blame for this. You didn't take our advice."

"What advice?!!" Billy shouted.

"We told you all we needed to tell you, in two words: Be careful."

"Oh, man, if you're talking about that joint you found in my car, man, I can explain," Billy started, only to be cut off by his father.

"I'm sure you can come up with a very creative explanation, Billy, but I'd advise you not to waste your breath. Besides, anything you say can be held against you in a court of law. You do realize, don't you, that marijuana is against the law?"

"Man! That wasn't my smoke, man!" Billy shouted, indignantly.

"Oh, that's exactly what we expected you to say, and we believe you, but Billy, maybe you haven't heard," his father said.

"Heard what?"

"Possession is nine points of the law. The joint was in your car; therefore, it was in your possession; therefore, you were breaking state and federal laws."

"But it wasn't mine!!!" Billy screamed.

"We know, Billy, we know," his father said. "But, Billy, listen, you've put us in a very bad position here, son. Now that we know you were transporting drugs in your car, we should report you to the authorities. If we don't, we're accomplices to a crime. But if we *do* report you, they'll impound your car and sell it at auction, which means the money we spent on the car is down the drain. So you see, we're in a real bind here. But Mom and I are smart, so we've come up with a solution. First, we're not going to report you. But you have to have some punishment for your crime, so we're going to sell your car and get our money out of it. See? That solves everything!"

"What?!!" Billy howled. "That solves everything?!! How so?!!"

"Well," his father replied, "you get punished by no longer having a car, so we don't feel like accomplices. The state and federal authorities never get involved, which means you don't have to go to trial and maybe jail, and we get our money out of your car instead of having to watch it be towed away by the feds. What could be better?!"

Billy begged, pleaded, and tried to make deals. He even confessed, thinking if he did, maybe his parents would change their minds.

"You mean the marijuana was actually *yours?*" his mother asked, feigning incredulity.

"Okay! Yes! It was!" Billy said.

"Then that's even worse," his mother said, looking at her husband with great concern.

"What do you mean, *worse?!!*" Billy shouted.

"I mean," said his mother, "that you might need to go to a treatment center for drug addiction."

"I'm not an addict!!!" Billy screamed.

"Prove it," his father said.

"How?!!" Billy yelled.

"By showing us you can change your recently acquired bad habits and start making good choices again, young man," his father answered, the very picture of the *cool* to which Billy was only a rank pretender.

"Meaning?" Billy asked.

"Meaning get your act together," his father said. "And we're going to let you figure out how to do that, son, because a person who's not an addict, and who's really sincere will be able to do exactly that."

"And if I change my ways, will you reconsider selling my car?"

"Oh no, son," his father answered. "This is something we have to do in consideration of the crime you've already committed. We just hope you don't commit any more. Like we said, be careful. We have a suggestion, however."

"What?" Billy snarled.

"Quit the band and get a real job," his father said. "It's just a suggestion, mind you, but if you get a job and save enough money, we'll consider letting you buy yourself a car, if, like, your grades are up and you're looking and acting normal again."

"So, you're basically telling me I can't hang with my buddies anymore," Billy said.

"Oh no, Billy," his father said. "You can hang with any buddies you like. You're not on any sort of restriction, kiddo. We figure having no car is consequence enough for what you've done. Just remember what we've said to you all along."

"I know, I know," Billy said, looking not just resigned but downright dejected, "be careful."

And he was. He quit the band (which was headed for world fame, don't you know), cut his hair, got rid of his three earrings, got a real job, pulled his grades back up, and within a year saved enough money to buy himself a nice used car—not nearly as nice as the wheels his parents had bought him when he was sixteen, but considering the circumstances, nice enough. And beggars, as they say, can't be "choosers."

Billy graduated high school, went to college, and is today a straight-A student in a premed program. When asked (as I have), he says that what his parents did when he was seventeen was "the best thing that ever happened to me."

I'm sure great things are in store for Billy.

The Long Rope, Redux

The above story of Billy, his parents, and the yellowed paper cylinder is an example of not only a Checkmate Move but also the Long Rope Principle referred to in Chapter Two. Billy's parents, as you might have guessed, knew all along that Billy was probably smoking pot with his newfound "friends." They simply chose to sit back and wait for the most opportune moment to do something about it. Something final, as opposed to temporary.

The problem with many parents of teenagers—most, in truth—is that the moment they smell the proverbial "rat," they go into a killing frenzy. Because they're panicked and rash, they fail to take careful aim at the problem in question, and the "rat" winds up escaping—wounded perhaps, but still very much alive and, worse, that much more determined.

So, whereas Billy's parents were very, very concerned about his new friends, his new look, and his new grades, they chose to just observe, waiting for the right moment to act. From an outsider's perspective, they might have seemed oblivious to Billy's slow, steady deterioration. Someone who knew the family might have said they were "ignoring the problem." A mental health professional might have said they were "in denial." Far from it! They were giving Billy a rope long enough to guarantee he would hang himself.

In a situation of this sort, if a teenager's parents let their anxieties drive premature action, the teen's problems will probably abate—temporarily. The youngster, having been alerted to his parents' knowledge of his self-destructive doings, will take the problem "underground," making it that much more difficult to do something about in the future. In effect, by acting prematurely, parents almost inevitably do nothing but shoot themselves in their own feet.

Therefore, the "long rope."

An illustration: Two weeks into Eric's fifth-grade year (during which he turned eleven, thus qualifying as a "tween-ager"—Willie and I received a call from one of his teachers. She told us that Eric was a delightful student in most respects—likable, conversational, inquisitive—but he wasn't doing his work. He had discovered, it seems, the secrets of peer group popularity and was socializing a lot in class. He wasn't disruptive, just, well, negligent. Would we please have a serious talk with Eric? she requested.

Willie and I pondered our options, then sat down with Mr. Personality. We told him about the phone call, told him that neglecting his responsibilities was unacceptable, and that he was charged with going to school and clearing up the problem.

"Your report card comes out in seven weeks, Eric," I said, "and it will tell the story of whether you've taken care of this situation or not. To help you take care of it, we're going to stay completely off your back. During the next seven weeks, we're not going to ask you any questions at all about school. We're not going to ask if you have homework, if you've finished your homework, if you have any grades you want to share with us, or even whether you had a good day. If your report card says you've solved the problem, fine and good. If not, well, then Mom and I are going to have to get involved in this problem, and all we can say is, you would hope that we don't have to get involved."

"What do you mean?" he asked.

"I have no idea," I said. "We'll cross that bridge if and when we come to it."

Seven weeks went by during which Willie and I asked Eric not one question about school.

At this point, I'm going to pause in the story to make a few comments: *The approach Willie and I took to this problem was highly unorthodox, to say the least. Most parents, after receiving a call such as we'd received from Eric's teacher, would shift immediately into full micromanage mode. They'd begin monitoring homework, phoning the teacher(s) on a regular basis for updated progress reports, and asking questions, questions, and more questions. Our experience with such knee-jerk approaches to behavior and academic problems had led us to conclude that they made matters worse instead of better. In the face of parental micromanagement, a child is likely to become deceptive, which promotes ever more micromanagement, which leads to conflict and communication problems, which promotes ever more micro-management, which leads to . . . well, you get the picture, I'm sure. Instead of taking responsibility for solving a problem that only Eric could solve, we gave him a "long rope," hoping he'd solve it, but fully accepting that he might not. If he didn't, seven weeks was not going to make the difference between Eric going to college and being a lifelong bum.*

So, after seven weeks, Eric's report card came home. On it were two D's and an F (and I'm absolutely certain that one of the D's was a gift). Willie and I went to the school for a conference with all three of his teachers. They told us he'd improved slightly after the phone call, but quickly regressed. Since then, they'd been taking a "wait and see" attitude.

"That's fine," I said. "So have we."

Not surprisingly, they suggested that Eric be required to make a list of all homework assignments (including unfin-

ished classwork) at the end of each school day. He would
bring the list to his homeroom teacher, who would check
with his other teachers to make sure the list was accurate. If
it wasn't, she would add to it and/or correct it. Then she'd
sign it and send it home with Eric. We'd use the list to make
sure Eric did all of his homework, meaning we'd have to
check his work every night to make sure it was done and
done properly.

The teachers' suggested approach to Eric's problem can be
summed up in one word: *Micromanagement!*

We thanked Eric's well-intentioned, very concerned teachers and told them, as diplomatically as possible, that we were
going to try a slightly different approach. We scheduled a
follow-up conference to take place a month hence and asked
that they not contact us in the meantime unless there was an
emergency. Likewise, we weren't going to communicate with
them. Naturally, they thought our request was rather strange,
but they agreed to it.

Willie and I went home and sat down with Eric. We told
him we were highly disappointed that he hadn't solved the
problem, and that we were now going to have to get involved. We told him about the follow-up conference and assured him that during the intervening month we were going
to ask him no questions about school. None! No questions
about homework, grades, or even whether he had a good day
or not.

"If you want to tell us something about school, Eric," I said,
"please feel free, but we're not going to ask for any school-
related information.

"At the end of a month," I continued, "Mom and I are going
to have that conference with your teachers. We're going to
walk into the conference room, sit down and ask, 'So, how's
Eric doing?' All three teachers, Eric, must tell us that you're
having no problems at all. For even one teacher to say you're

having more good days than bad, or that you're doing better, or that you have a better attitude will not be good for you. All three teachers must say, 'Oh, Mr. and Mrs. Rosemond, thanks for dropping by, but there's nothing to discuss because Eric is having no problems at all.' If three teachers say exactly that, Eric, then you'll be allowed to come out of your room."

His eyes popped wide open, his jaw dropped to his chest, and he shouted, "*What?!!!*"

"You heard me," I answered.

"*But what do you mean, I'll be able to come out of my room?!!*"

"We mean, Eric, that for the next month, on school days you'll get up, do your chores, and go to school. Socialize as much as you can there, son, because that's the only place you'll be seeing other kids your age. After school, you'll come home, do your chores, and go to your room. You can come out to use the bathroom, do chores, eat dinner with us, and go places with us as a family. Oh, and Eric, on school nights your bedtime will be seven o'clock, lights out, whether your homework is done or not."

As you might imagine, the incredulous look on Eric's face was becoming more and more incredulous with every word.

"On non-school days, you'll get up, do your chores, and go back to your room. You can come out for the same reasons. And, Eric, if there's no school the following day, then you can stay up until eight o'clock, at which point you'll be in bed, and your lights will be out.

"In a month, at the conference, if one teacher says something like you're having more good days than bad, then we'll do this another month, and who knows how many months we'll have to do this? I know one thing, Eric. You have seven years left to live with us. If, during the next seven years, you choose to stay in your room, that will be no skin off our backs. We'll put heat in your room in winter, air-condition it in the summer, take you everywhere we go as a family, including church, feed you well, provide you with excellent medical care, and so on. The next seven years is your call, son. Completely. Any questions?"

He just sat there, looking back and forth between Willie and me. "I didn't know you were going to do this," he said, finally, and with utter dismay.

"Welcome to the real world, son," I said, "which is, as you need to learn sooner or later, full of surprises."

A month later, Willie and I walked into a conference room in which Eric's teachers were already seated, waiting. They were smiling broadly.

"So," Willie asked, "how's Eric doing?"

"Oh, it was next to amazing," his homeroom teacher said, speaking for the group. "The day after our last conference, Eric was a completely changed child. In fact, I'd have to say that for the last month, he's been the best student I've ever had!"

The other teachers agreed. And that was that.

Well, sort of. Shortly after Eric got into high school, we received a mid-term report that indicated some minor, but annoying conduct problems.

"Um, Eric," I asked, after putting the report down, "do you happen to remember the fifth grade?"

A startled look flashed across his handsome face. "Uh, yeah, sort of," he answered.

"Good," I said, and walked out of the room. That was the last we heard of conduct problems—or any other sorts of problems, for that matter—from any of Eric's high school teachers. One well-placed Checkmate Move, you see, used after the "long rope" has played out sufficiently, prevents forever the use of another Checkmate Move. The first such move creates a permanent memory that only needs scratching every once in a while for the child in question to straighten up and fly right.

A second illustration: One fine summer day when Eric was fifteen, I got a call from a friend of mine who happened to be a psychiatrist. He was calling, he said, because he was concerned about the boys Eric was hanging around with and knew I'd want to do something about it before Eric got into trouble. The boys in question, all from relatively well-to-do families, had become a pack of vandals/petty thieves. When people—their neighbors, if you can believe it!—were away on vacation, these young hooligans would break windows, set fires (none of which did much damage, thankfully), sink boats, and steal things. The boys' parents, according to my friend, refused to believe their children were capable of such things and became highly defensive when someone made an accusation.

I thanked my friend for his concern, and Willie and I talked. Later, we sat down with Eric and told him about the phone call (without identifying our benefactor). Predictably, he started defending his friends and painting a picture of them as misunderstood innocents. He was anticipating, no doubt, that we were going to forbid the relationship. Most parents, in the same situation, would have done exactly that. Not Willie and me. Oh no. We weren't about to act prematurely and drive his relationship with these boys underground. Much to Eric's surprise, we told him we wanted him to spend as much time with these boys as he possibly could.

"We'd suggest, Eric," I said, "that you use every possible opportunity to be with them. In fact, if you ever need a ride to one of their houses, please let us know and one of us will gladly drive you."

He looked at us disbelievingly.

"Now, Eric, here's the deal," I continued. "If we ever hear

that these boys have been involved in an act of vandalism or theft or whatever, and you weren't home at the time of the incident, we are simply going to assume that you were with them. Unless you have absolute concrete proof that you were elsewhere, we will take you over to the victims' home, sit down with them, and obtain a full report of the damages. You, and only you, will compensate the victims, not only for their damages but also for their heartache. And until you are able to make full compensation, you will be under house arrest.

"Let us make ourselves perfectly clear: Let's say you're with four of these boys when they break a one-thousand-dollar stained-glass window [as they had done in the past]. And let's say that by some miracle, the parents of the other four boys agree to cough up for their share of the damages. You, Eric Rosemond, will still have to compensate the victims to the tune of one thousand dollars. And if that takes the rest of your high school days, then you'll be under house arrest until you graduate from high school. But please, Mom and I sincerely want you to hang around with these boys as much as possible."

I describe Eric's look as confused, and understandably so. That's the last thing he expected to hear from us. He expected to hear that he couldn't associate with the boys, under any circumstances, and that we'd be checking with the counselor at school to see that he wasn't sitting with them in the cafeteria and attempting in various other self-defeating ways to micromanage, micromanage, micromanage. And the game of cat-and-mouse would have immediately begun. Instead, we handed him a long piece of rope and said, in effect, "Here. Go hang yourself."

For the next month, Eric spent a good amount of time with the rat pack. One day, I was out in the front yard when I heard someone calling "Dad! Dad!" in the distance. I looked up to see Eric racing down the cul-de-sac on his bicycle, looking all bent out of shape. He skidded into the driveway, dropped his bike to the ground, and ran over to me.

Breathlessly, he blurted out that he'd been with his buddies when they began hatching a plan to commit some act of vandalism. He'd told them he had to go home and go somewhere with the family, and he'd left, trying to put as much distance between himself and them as he could, as quickly as he could.

"Dad," he said, "if they went ahead and did it, and you hear about it, Dad, I wasn't there, Dad, I swear it! Please, Dad, you've gotta believe me!"

I told him I believed him, went in the house and made a phone call, hoping to preempt their crime. Then, Willie and I sat down with Eric and asked him what his plans were for the future.

"I'm going to find new friends," he said.

"You don't have to, you know," Willie said.

"I know, but I'm going to anyway. Those guys are bad news, Mom and Dad! I'm not going to have anything to do with them, ever again."

"Well," Willie said, "we think that's a good idea, but the deal is still the same, you understand."

"Don't worry," Eric said, "it's over. I've learned my lesson."

Today, Eric is a good husband, a good father, a good citizen, a good pilot, and a good friend. I haven't been able to keep up with all of Eric's former friends, but Eric told me recently that one of them has already spent time in prison for selling drugs. As I told Eric, if you want to dance, then sooner or later, you're going to have to pay the band.

A reader asks: "Do you have any stories about using the 'long rope' or Checkmate Moves with your daughter Amy?"

I answer: "No, I sure don't. Amy benefited from being able to sit back, at three and a half years' distance, and watch what happened to Eric when he stepped out of line. She took it all in, believe me, and used it to her best advantage. She gave us occasional problems, to be sure, but we never had to do anything out of the ordinary, so to speak, with Amy. Sorry to disappoint you."

"I Hate You!"

Someone reading this book is having a problem. I just know it. In fact, I even know what the problem is. The person in question is having great trepidation as regards my recommendations concerning discipline. She's afraid if she follows my advice, her child will:

a.   resent her for life;

b.   require weekly therapy sessions as an adult in order to "resolve" childhood issues that pertain to authority;

c.   run away from home;

d.   become an even worse statistic in a category that she dare not even name;

e.   all of the above, by some miracle.

What can I say except some adults take children and the childish things they do entirely too seriously. Take, for example, a child who because he doesn't get his way, screams things like "You're stupid!" or "I hate you!" or "I wish you weren't my mother [father]!" at the offending parent.

Some parents, upon being blasted with invective of this sort, feel themselves pierced through the heart. They interpret the child's rage as either symptomatic of parent-induced psychological trauma or a withering parent/child relationship. If the former, they feel immediate guilt; if the latter, they fear that the child may grow up to not like them. In either case, high anxiety moves them to reconsider the decision that led to the outburst and "correct" it.

Other parents, similarly blasted, become outraged. Interpreting the child's loose tongue as evidence of disrespect, they react punitively. "I won't allow you to talk to me that way!" they bellow, and follow up by swatting the child's rear end or banishing him to his room to "think about it," or both.

In truth, a child's outbursts of frustration are not worthy of guilt, fear, or anger. They merit nothing more, nothing less, than a big "So what?"

Concerning psychological trauma: Children cannot discern the difference between what they need and what they merely want. They also have little tolerance for frustration. Finally, they are given to extremes. Therefore, when they don't get what they want, they are likely to become red in the face, stomp, scream, accuse, slam doors, and so on. So what? All of this, after all, is nothing but the nature of childhood. This is not sign of trauma, but a sign that the child's ability to tolerate frustration is being strengthened. Keep in mind, furthermore, that the better the parental decision (generally speaking), the more upset the child.

Concerning the child coming to dislike his parents: Children do not grow up with a bitter taste in their mouths concerning their childhood simply by virtue of parents who deny them things they don't need in the first place. In fact, I suspect that children are very likely, as adults, to appreciate their parents all the more if their parents make no attempt whatsoever to earn high approval ratings.

The Rosemond children are cases in point. Eric and Amy were denied far more than they were given, were often denied even when their mother and I had the time and the money to provide. Making matters "worse" (from their point of view), Eric and Amy did most of the housekeeping, and were not allowed to watch much television at all (none for four years). They took every opportunity to tell us that compared with the lap of luxury in which many of their friends were growing up, their situation qualified as child abuse. As young adults, however, they have both commented on how well their rather unique upbringing has served them as they confront the realities of life. In other words, whereas they didn't appreciate our rules and requirements as children, they appreciate them now. I'll take the "long run" over the "short run" any day.

Concerning disrespect: Nor are these outbursts of "hate" and slander signs of disrespect. Rather, they are signs of immaturity, impulsiveness, and underdevelopment. They are, again, the normal stuff of childhood. If children did not react in these undercivilized ways, they would not need parents. When they lose control, it is simply necessary that their parents maintain it.

And what, pray tell, is the secret to maintaining one's control as a parent? Why, it is as simple as not taking children and their outbursts all that seriously; it is as simple as understanding that were you the child, you'd be reacting exactly the same way. It is as simple as shrugging your shoulders and saying (to yourself only, of course), "So what?"

Questions, Anyone?

Q: *On a recent talk show, a psychologist said that when a child needs to be punished, parents should use either "natural" or "logical" consequences. This caused me to wonder if I'm doing the right thing when I punish my teenage son for something. When he talks back to me, I generally ground him for a night or two. According to the psychologist, however,*

*that's neither natural nor logical. If not, however, then what
is? I'm confused.*

A: I agree, this business of "natural" and "logical" consequences is nothing short of confusing. Furthermore, the real
world does not operate according to this rule. What, pray tell,
is "logical" about going to jail for five years for embezzling
thousands of dollars from one's employer? Nothing! What's
"logical" about being grounded for talking back to a parent?
Again, nothing! Nonetheless, going to jail will serve as a powerful deterrent against further embezzling, and being
grounded will serve as a powerful deterrent against future disrespect (albeit Rome, if you'll recall, wasn't built in a day).

In short, when it comes to consequences, parents should
simply do what works, whether what works is "natural" or
"logical," or, by contrast, whimsical, arbitrary, capricious,
and/or outrageous. Now, isn't that simple?

Q: *Our thirteen-year-old son is supposedly responsible for
the nourishment and exercise of Betsy, our family's dog. I say
"supposedly" because we must constantly nag him to remember to do either. He'd been asking for a dog for several years,
and he agreed from the outset to accept these responsibilities,
which amount to nothing more than feeding Betsy in the
morning, keeping her water bowl filled, and exercising her in
the afternoon. Everything we've thus far tried has been to no
avail, so we're counting on you for a solution. Please don't
recommend that we give Betsy away, however, because we've
all grown very attached to her.*

A: I assume that by "everything we've thus far tried" you
mean cajoling, berating, complaining, bribing, reasoning, and
threatening. Predictably, these have not moved your son to
begin living up to his promise to take care of Betsy, nor will
they ever. That leaves you no alternative but to stop beating

around the bush and do something about this blatant evasion of responsibility.

Your son isn't going to begin accepting his responsibility concerning Betsy until you dump the lock, stock, and barrel of this problem in his lap. At present, you have a problem, and Betsy has a problem, but other than a couple of nagging parents, your son has no problem at all. Who's upset concerning his irresponsibility? You! And who, pray tell, suffers the inconvenience that accompanies the problem? You! Again!

The proverbial monkey, in other words, is on your back. Ah, but the only person who can solve this problem is your son. He's the only person who can tame this particular monkey, which he cannot, however, begin to do until it's on *his* back. In short, when, and only when, the problem of his not taking proper care of Betsy upsets and inconveniences your son, and *only* your son, will he have reason to solve the problem.

If you haven't done so already, give your son a daily deadline for feeding and exercising Betsy. Vow to give no more reminders, hints, suggestions, or threats. If the deadline passes without his having carried out *both* tasks, say not a word to him. Simply carry them out yourself and ground your son to his room for the remainder of the day and reduce his bedtime by one hour. If, through the week, he neglects his responsibilities toward Betsy more than twice, ground him on the weekend as well. With these rules in place, if your son fails to carry out his chores, who will be upset and inconvenienced? Your son, that's who!!! That's great, because with the monkey finally on his back, he can get about the business of taming it.

People have occasionally asked if this approach might result in the child in question becoming resentful, even cruel, toward the family pet. If the child loves the pet in the first place, as I assume is the case here, then the likelihood of that happening is next to zero. I've ventured the same recommendation many times and have yet to hear of it backfiring. At first, your son may sulk, but keep in mind that pets—and especially dogs—give very positive feedback to their caretakers. It takes a hard-hearted child to reject a pet's expressions of gratitude. In the final analysis, responsibility begets not just self-esteem (the authentic, task-based sort as opposed to the inauthentic praise-based sort), but also feelings of pride in the task itself. In short, this will no doubt improve your son's relationship with Betsy, and immeasurably so.

But first, there's the matter of that monkey.

Q: *Does time-out work with teenagers, and if so, when and how should it be used?*

A: So-called "helping" professionals have given American parents the impression that time-out, properly used, will put an end to any discipline problem with any age child. In fact, I was at one time an avid time-out pusher myself. I used it with my son, Eric, during his younger years and recommended it often to parents I counseled. Eventually, however, I came to the conclusion that *time-out works with children who are already well behaved.* It does not work—not for long, anyway—with children who have developed behavior problems that are outrageous either in kind or frequency. As I said above, the outrageous (referring to a child's behavior) requires the equally outrageous (referring to an effective consequence). As my children grew, I became less and less enamored of time-out and more and more in favor of giving children enough rope with which to hang themselves, lowering the boom, and nipping a problem in the bud. If those ideas sound old-fashioned, it's because they are, indeed. Old-fashioned, however, does not, as I belatedly discovered, mean it doesn't work anymore.

Given that time-out works with children who are already well behaved, I might recommend it when an otherwise good kid loses his balance and falls off the wagon. It happens to the best of 'em, after all, and when it does, a nudge like time-out will suffice to move the child in the proper direction. Giving more than a nudge to a well-behaved child is just a waste of energy, and furthermore, just might backfire. Under no circumstances, however, would I recommend time-out be used in response to teenage misbehavior. Either:

a. the teen in question is reasonably well behaved, in which case, making him sit in a chair will be unnecessarily humiliating (given that time-out has become associated with the discipline of younger children), or

b. the teen in question is not generally well behaved, in which case having him sit in a chair will not suffice to get him back on track. My recommendation will undoubtedly involve something memorable and outrageous, as in *Checkmate!*

Q: *Our fourteen-year-old has become increasingly rebellious of late. In the last year, he started running with a bunch of kids with bad reputations. His grades have dropped, he's violated curfew on several recent occasions, and he's become sassy and disrespectful toward us, all the more so after he's been with his friends. After finding some cigarette rolling papers in his room (he insisted he found them), we tried talking to him but got nowhere. He denied everything and told us we had no right to choose his friends for him. When we brought up the possibility of moving him to a private school next year, he told us he wouldn't go, that he'd run away if we made him. We want to clamp down on this problem before it gets any worse, but we're afraid that doing so might do more harm than good. Do you have any suggestions?*

A: First of all I think you have every reason to be concerned. My experience tells me these sorts of situations—if not nipped in the proverbial bud—will go rapidly from bad to worse. Furthermore, the older the child in question gets, the more difficult it becomes to turn the problem around.

If your son was associating with kids you didn't particularly like, but there was no indication that their influence on him was particularly negative, I would advise you to adopt a "wait and see" attitude. Relationships during early adolescence can be fairly unstable. Sometimes, doing nothing is the best way to get a less-than-desirable one to run its course. It's fairly obvious to me, however—as it should be to you—that your son's friendship with this crowd has gone "over the line." I hope, for example, that you don't believe for one minute he *found* rolling papers and just decided they'd make an interesting knickknack. I'd say there's a 95 percent likelihood he's experimenting with marijuana.

You have enough evidence—bad grades, bad behavior, drug paraphernalia—to put the hammer down, and I encourage you to put it down fast!! Inform him that you have no intention of letting him trash a fourteen-year investment in his future. Since he's obviously misplaced the ability to make good decisions concerning friends, you're going to make them for him; to wit, he's forbidden, absolutely and completely, to have any contact with any of the boys in the group, ever. Otherwise, he can enjoy all of his normal privileges and can continue attending the same school.

Tell him you're going to help him as much as you can by spending a lot of time together as a family and helping him find other activities—including your church or synagogue youth group—that will bring him in contact with a better group of peers. (And by the way, if you don't already belong to a church or synagogue, I'd encourage you to find one that is family-oriented and has a good youth program. You have problems with organized religion? Put them aside for your son's sake.) Now, the kicker: If you even suspect that he's violated the rule, tell him he'll be under house arrest for the entire summer and will go to a new school in the fall.

And yes, this may well make matters worse, but no worse than they would have eventually become anyway. In this regard, there are two things to keep in mind:

- When parents do the right thing in a crisis situation of this sort, they often activate the "things get worse before they get better" principle. In other words, the fact that things get worse doesn't mean parents have made a mistake and should back off.
- It's generally easier for parents to deal with a crisis they bring on themselves than with a crisis that takes them by surprise. You may have to hold on for a wild ride, but any crisis *you* precipitate will be easier for you to control. Not easy, mind you, but *easier.*

Stand ready to stand firm, and may the force be with you.

Q: *Our sixteen-year-old daughter is seeing a seventeen-year-old boy whose reputation leaves much to desired. When we confronted her with what reliable adult sources had told us about him, Angela admitted knowing about his past, but said he'd "changed." We told her she was naive to think she could make a leopard change his spots, but she is adamant about wanting to continue the relationship. She says they've done nothing wrong, and that we have no right to interfere on the basis of rumor alone. We feel like we're in a bind. What would you advise us to do?*

A: If you can't beat 'em—and you certainly can't—then join 'em. You're making the most common of all mistakes made by parents of teens: You're letting your emotions drive your decisions. As a result, you're in danger of not only making decisions that will almost certainly come back to haunt you but also being pulled into a power struggle you can only lose. In short, you risk creating lots of problems and solving none.

Fear and anger are arousing your protective instincts. No one could fault you for wanting to keep your daughter out of harm's way, but the only way you can protect Angela is to restrict her from seeing this young man, and she's made it clear she won't sit still for that. So, if you restrict, she's bound to rebel, and that's when your heartaches begin. Didn't you guys ever read William Shakespeare? He was one of the most brilliant psychologists of all time—if not the most brilliant.

As the father of a young adult woman, I am in complete empathy (that's a psychology word) with your feelings. Nonetheless, you need to rein in your emotions and adopt a more strategic approach to the problem. In so doing, things may get slightly worse (from your point of view) before they get better, but a good tactician is always willing to lose the battle if doing so means winning the war.

In the first place, Angela is right as rain. She and her boyfriend have done nothing wrong. Therefore, you lack just cause to do anything but trust her. Begin your strategic campaign by putting your concerns on the table while, at the same time, admitting to overreaction. Apologize for underestimating her ability to conduct herself properly and make responsible decisions, whatever the pressure this young man puts on her. Don't lapse into lecture or try to extract promises from her. Just move the ball of responsibility gently into her court.

Your next move is to begin including the young man in family activities. Invite him to be a regular guest at dinner. Request his presence on family outings. If he's hiding ulterior motives, an "open arm" policy will make him more than a bit uncomfortable, in which case he's likely to back quickly out of Angela's life. If he's legit, then your family's values can do nothing but have a positive effect on him. Besides, where Angela is concerned, trust breeds trustworthiness.

In the final analysis, Angela can only take responsible control over her life through trial and error. Your job is not to prevent her from making mistakes; it's to control the consequences of those mistakes and see to it she learns from them. Parents who overcontrol by trying to catch their children every time they fall inadvertently set them up for even bigger, more catastrophic tumbles.

CHAPTER FOUR

◆

Drugs, Sex, and Other Cheap Thrills

Okay, here it comes, the chapter you've all been waiting for. The one in which I'm going to reveal how to keep a teenager from ever using drugs, drinking a beer, or having sex. Are you ready? *Lock him in the basement (make sure you soundproof it first) from age thirteen through age nineteen. Tell everyone who inquires as to his whereabouts that he insisted upon spending his/her teen years at a monastery (or, in the case of a girl, a nunnery) in the Urals.* In all seriousness, I wish I had all the answers, but, as you'll see, I only have 98 percent of them.

Cheap Thrills, Part One:
Drugs and Alcohol

With few exceptions, when I talk with the parents of a pre-teen or teen, sooner or later they bring up the subject of drugs. (Please note: I include alcohol in the category *drugs*.)

"What," they ask, "can we do to prevent him/her from using drugs?"

They're hoping that I can share with them a magic parenting formula that will guarantee their child will abstain from any and all drug use forever. I wish I could, but every time I'm asked the above question, I immediately think of God and His first children. If the One and Only Perfect Parent couldn't prevent Adam and Eve from eating the forbidden fruit—the first record of adolescent drug use!—then how foolish is it to think that mere human parents can prevent any one of God's children from consuming forbidden substances?

So, I answer, "You can't."

That's not, of course, what parents want to hear—especially parents who are trying their best to negotiate the most anxiety-arousing phase of the parent-child relationship. They want me to say that if they spend an average of 2.27 hours per day talking and doing things with their teen, attend every one of his/her soccer games and cheer the loudest of all the parents, attend every PTA meeting, and never allow the youngster to watch R-rated movies, he/she will never even entertain thoughts of drugs. They want a pat answer. Instead, I say there's nothing, absolutely nothing, they can do. Invariably and understandably, parents are shocked to hear me say that.

"We can't?!!"

"That's right," I say. "You can't. The only person who can stop your child from using drugs is your child, and the sooner you accept that, the better for all of you."

As I pointed out in Chapter One, every child has a mind of his/her own. In the final analysis, every child is a free agent. Parents have influence, to be sure—a lot of influence, in fact—but parents don't have the power to guarantee anything. Parenting is not the only variable in the equation. As one learns from reading Genesis 2–3, you can be a perfect parent (assuming the possibility exists), and your child will still make bad choices. Not "is likely" to make bad choices, but "will"! There's no doubt about it.

But parents don't let go of idealistic fantasies easily. "Wait a second," they counter. "We understand what you mean, but there must be something we can do to make it more likely he/she will say 'no' when the opportunity to use drugs arises."

"But you asked a different question," I point out. "You asked if there was something you could do to *prevent* drug use. Now you're asking if there are things you can do to make saying 'no' more likely. To that, the answer is yes. You can limit television watching, make your marriage the number-one priority in your family (or, if single, take good care of yourself), say 'no' to your child's requests ten times more than you say 'yes,' help your child, at an early age, learn to occupy and entertain himself, assign him to a regular routine of chores around the home and pay him not a red cent for doing them, teach your child spiritual values, avoid the tendency to micromanage during the teen years, etc., etc."

In effect, I tell these persistent parents to read my other seven books, the themes of which can be summarized with one of Grandma's favorite sayings: *Good citizenship begins at home.* Saying "no" to temptation—i.e., keeping one's narcissistic impulses under wraps—after all, is a hallmark of good citizenship. It is *pro-social* to say "no" to drugs, alcohol, pre-marital sex, drag racing, and every other cheap thrill imaginable. It is *antisocial* to say "yes" to those things. Therefore, the more effectively parents use what I refer to as the *Classroom of the Family* to teach citizenship skills (pro-social behavior), the more *likely* it is their children will say "no" to cheap thrills.

But there are no guarantees!

Besides—*Warning! I'm about to say something unexpected, so brace yourself!!!*—the fact that a youngster uses a drug isn't so bad. You read me right. It's bad, granted, but it's not the end of the world. Children need to make mistakes.

The most valuable lessons in life, in fact, are learned as a consequence of making mistakes. One would hope a child doesn't make life-threatening mistakes—and drug use can certainly be life-threatening—but the very best of parenting opportunities comes about not when children do the *right* things, but when they do the *wrong* things!

Fact: As a parent, you can do nothing to guarantee your child will never make a certain bad choice.

Fact: Therefore, when a child makes a bad choice, it isn't necessarily because of bad parenting. (More on this in a moment.)

Fact: Good parenting is doing the *right* thing when a child does the *wrong* thing.

Fact: To do the right thing when a child does the wrong thing requires clear thinking.

Fact: You cannot think clearly if you believe your child's bad choice is because of bad parenting—that it's your *fault*, in other words.

Fact: When your child makes a bad choice, your *child* needs correcting, not *you*.

Fact: When your child does the wrong thing, you can think clearly and do the right thing by keeping all of the above facts in mind and saying to yourself, "My child's bad decision is *his* fault, not mine."

A slight caveat: There are indeed parents who create circumstances that make it almost inevitable that their children will indulge in drug and alcohol binges, sexual promiscuity, and so on through the list of cheap thrills. If you smoke pot openly around your child, your child is 99 percent more likely to smoke pot (and probably use other drugs as well). If you are sexually promiscuous, and you parade your promiscuity in front of your child, your child is 99 percent more likely to become sexually promiscuous. And so on. But *you*—the parent reading this book—are not that kind of parent. As I've already said, parents who do those sorts of things don't read parenting books.

You, the reader of this book, are trying to be the best parent you can be. You're trying your best to be a good role model, to discipline properly, to instill good values in your child, and so on. Therefore, when your child makes a bad decision, *it's not your fault!* When your child makes a bad decision, it's your job to do the right thing, and guilt prevents clear thinking, which is essential for doing the right thing. So, keep it straight. When your child makes a bad choice, it's your child who needs correcting, not you.

"Okay," a reader asks, "so what's the right thing to do when you find out your child has used a drug?"

I don't know.

"What?! You don't know?! You're supposed to be a parenting expert, for Pete's sake! You're supposed to know these things!"

In the first place, I am *not* a parenting expert for Pete's sake! I don't even know which Pete you're talking about. At this point in my life, I am a parenting expert for my grandchildren's sake. Furthermore, the only correct answer to your question is "I don't know" because there is no one right thing to do when you find out your child has used a drug. There are, in fact, a lot of right things a parent can do in that sort of situation.

One Right Thing to Do: One parent I know, when his fifteen-year-old son came home obviously high on marijuana, simply took him aside and said, "Son, I want you to know that you can't smoke pot or drink alcoholic beverages without my knowing about it, sooner or later. In this case, I know sooner, as in right now. You've been smoking pot."

The youngster was speechless, to say the least. All he could do was stammer, "Ah, um, well, ah, I, uh, what?"

"What nothing," his father continued. "I don't intend to

punish you for this, and I'm certainly not going to start following you around, spying on you. If you want to smoke pot or do any other sort of drug badly enough, you're going to do it, and I can't follow you enough to prevent it. In fact, since you now know that you can't hide it from me, and I'm not going to try and stop you, you might as well just do them right here, at home. What do you say about that?"

The startled son blurted, "Dad! I'm not going to smoke pot here at home!"

"Why not?" his father asked. "Mom and I are going to know about it, either way."

"Because, well, I mean, I'd feel really stupid smoking pot in front of you guys."

"Ah-ha!" his father said. "I'm going to suggest that you'd feel stupid about doing it in front of us because smoking pot *is*, in fact, stupid. And you're smart enough, even when you're stoned, to know that it's stupid. In that regard, I'm going to say just one thing: You are going to hear adults say they wish they'd never done drugs as teenagers, but you are never, ever going to hear an adult express regret that he or she *didn't* do drugs as a teenager. Think about it."

And the father turned and walked away. That was all he said, but it must have been enough, because the son never smoked pot again. Had the father overreacted as a consequence of not thinking clearly, however, there's no telling what might have happened. As my grandmother used to say, "Blow a lot of hot air on a smoldering twig, and it just might become a forest fire."

Another Right Thing to Do: Remember Billy and the yellowed paper cylinder? If it isn't fresh in your mind, then you just might want to reread that uncommon story (page 140). Was there something Billy's parents could have done to prevent him from using drugs? Absolutely not. When he began hanging with the wrong crowd, they could have started micro-managing—trying vainly to prohibit the associations in question (which would only have driven them underground, where they'd have been more difficult to see), trying vainly to follow Billy's every move (which would only have caused Billy to become ever more devious), and so on through the list of counterproductive things micromanaging parents do. Instead, Billy's smart parents gave him enough rope to guarantee he would hang himself, which is exactly what he did!

In both of the above stories, parents did not *cause* their children to do drugs. They didn't make parenting mistakes of the sort that make teen drug use all but inevitable. The parents in question were good parents whose children, once they became teenagers, decided to use drugs. In both cases, the parents, once the drug use was discovered, did not panic. They simply did the right thing. The first youngster's father simply let him know that he couldn't hide it, and that there'd be consequences if it continued. Billy's parents sold his car. Checkmate!

Just as there are a lot of right things to do when you discover your child has used a drug, there are a lot of wrong things to do, as well.

The Wrong Thing to Do: From the time she entered tweenagerhood, Mary Louise had been disrespectful to her parents, disobedient, defiant, and downright rebellious, often flaunting her disdain of their rules and expectations. They had tried counseling, to no avail. (By the way, take it from me, a psychologist: The chance that a child can be counseled [talked] out of bad behavior is slim at best. Enough said, however, because the fact that psychology has failed to live up to its promises concerning children and therapy will be covered in depth in a later book.) They had tried to get her more involved in family activities and church, to no avail. They'd tried "everything," in fact, to no avail. Mary Louise's parents were decent, hardworking people who contributed in numerous ways to the betterment of their community. They could hardly have been rightly accused of doing anything to cause Mary Louise to do what she began doing. Which was: She began hanging with a crowd of kids who are, to put it bluntly, destined to become among the scummiest of the scum of the universe. These were *bad* kids, from *bad* families. At age fourteen, her parents let her begin dating a boy who was fours years older! They thought, naively, if they allowed the relationship, it would run its course. Ha! Mary Louise and her boyfriend's relationship quickly became sexual. Everyone who knew the family and the situation, everyone who'd seen the two of them together, could tell at a glance that Mary Louise had become sexually active. Her parents seemed, however, to be in a deepening state of denial. They asked Mary Louise if she and her boyfriend were having sex. She denied it, and they were satisfied. Mary Louise began drinking and smoking pot. People had seen her around town obviously inebriated. They mentioned it delicately to her parents. Her parents asked her if she was drinking and using drugs. She denied it, and they were satisfied.

Comment: Mary Louise's parents are in the throes of what I call *It Can't Happen to Us Because We Care too Much Syndrome* (*ICHTUBWCTMS*—pronounced "iktubwictimes"). This is a not-so-rare-these-days state of parental denial typical of parents who think only children of bad parents do bad things. Silly, tragic them.

Mary Louise's behavior just got worse and worse. She started lying about everything, even when the truth would have satisfied her parents. She cursed at her parents, even spit at her mother on one occasion. You get the picture, I'm sure.

So, when Mary Louise turned sixteen, guess what her parents did to send her the message bad consequences follow bad decisions? *They bought her a brand-new car!!!* This was their way of showing her how much they cared. As you might well imagine, things went from bad to worse, and who knows where Mary Louise's long decline will end. Sad, because Mary Louise's parents had the wherewithal and the resources to do what Christine's parents did under almost exactly the same circumstances.

By Contrast, Yet Another Right Thing: At age fourteen, Christine began hanging with the wrong crowd. She dropped out of all her activities, her grades plummeted, she started coming home drunk, lying, cursing her parents, and so on down the line. She was doing pretty much what Mary Louise had done, but Christine's parents were by no means suffering from *ICHTUBWCTMS*. They were very much aware of what Christine was doing and tried "everything." They made her go to counseling. That, of course, didn't work. They went to counseling. The counselor tried to persuade them to accept that they were a dysfunctional couple who'd created a dysfunctional family and that Christine was only acting out low self-esteem created by the family dysfunction and that blah, blah, blah. They stopped going to counseling. Smart. They tried spending more time with Christine. She began avoiding them like the plague. And so on.

One day, when in school, the principal's office sent someone to get Christine out of class, saying her parents had come for her. She was dumbfounded. Why had her parents shown up in the middle of a school day? Whatever it was, it had to be earth-shaking for her father to have taken a day from his very important job.

"What's up?" Christine asked her parents.

"Something has happened," her mother said. "You have to come with us."

"What's happened?" Christine asked.

"We can't talk about it here," her father said. "Let's go. We don't have much time."

The three of them got into the car, where Christine's older brother was waiting.

"What's going on?" Christine asked him.

"I don't know," he answered. "Mom and Dad got me out of school, too. We're going somewhere is all I know."

"Where?" Christine asked her parents.

"We can't discuss it right now," said her mother. "We'll let you both know when the time is right."

And off they drove, through the day and into the early evening. Little did Christine know, but her brother knew exactly what was going on. He'd been as concerned about her as anyone, and was there to assist, if assistance was needed.

Around seven o'clock that evening, they pulled onto the grounds of a large facility. The sign said THE WOODHILL SCHOOL (not its real name, of course). They drove up to the administration building and Christine's father shut off the engine.

Christine's parents turned around and looked at her. "Welcome to your new school," her father said.

Christine's eyes got wider than the back end of a Cadillac. "Whaaat?!!!" she screamed. "I'm not going to school here!!!"

"Oh yes, you are, young lady," said her father.

There were words exchanged, but Christine realized she was outgunned. Finally, with feigned resignation, she walked inside to meet the headmaster, the counselor, and several of her new peers, all of whom had been headed downhill, just like Christine, when their parents, just as suddenly, had put them at Woodhill.

"You'll like it here, Christine," they all told her.

"No, I won't!!!" she yelled. "I'll run away!!!"

Her father turned and looked at her. "There's nothing anyone can do to prevent that, Miss Christine," he said. "But if you run away, we'll find you sooner or later, and we'll bring you back. You're going to be here at Woodhill, like it or not, until you graduate from high school."

Everyone nodded. "That's right, Christine," said the headmaster. "Once we accept you, we accept you for the long run. There's nothing you can do to make us kick you out or refuse to accept you back."

"But," said one of the teens in the room, "you're going to like it here, Christine. All of us were kids just like you once. We haven't changed. We're still cool. We've just changed our behavior, that's all. You're going to like us, you'll see."

At the end of her first year at Woodhill, Christine came home for the summer. It was a delightful two months for all concerned. Christine showed no interest in her old "friends," voluntarily spent lots of time with her family, and was the picture of charm. In mid-August, just before it was time for her to go back, her parents said, "We miss you when you're gone."

"I miss you too," Christine said. "But Woodhill is where I belong. It's my life now, and I need to go back."

All's well that ends well.

Comment: The difference between Mary Louise's parents and Christine's parents is the difference between parenting a teen with your eyes closed and parenting a teen with your eyes open. It's the difference between thinking it can't happen to me and understanding "it" can happen to anyone. It's the difference between wringing your hands over what your teen is doing and taking action. It's the difference between trying to buy your child's loyalty and letting your child know there are consequences for making bad decisions. It's the difference between spending lots of money for a new car and spending lots of money for admission to Woodhill School. And, for all of these reasons, it's the difference between a teenager who continues down the same path and one who is rescued from the foolish, self-destructive things she's doing because of the foolishness bound in her heart (Proverbs 20:15).

Concerning drugs and teens, three facts stand out:

1. More teens are experimenting with/using drugs than ever. By conservative estimate, one in four high school students smokes marijuana on a regular basis.

2. The age at which the average "experimenter" first experiments is lower than ever, and getting lower all the time. Drug use has been on the rise among sixth, seventh, and eighth graders since the mid-1980s.

3. The drugs with which teens are experimenting are more dangerous than ever, and getting more dangerous all the time. In the 1960s, most drug-using teens limited themselves to smoking marijuana, which made their throats sore before it got them stoned. Today's teen drug-user is likely to not just use pot, but cocaine, LSD, and amphetamines (uppers) as well.

The inescapable conclusion: No parent can afford to adopt an "It won't happen to my child because I've been too good a parent" attitude. It doesn't seem to matter how well a child has been parented, because all children are "at risk," as the expression goes.

The question becomes, "Why would a teen begin using drugs?"

Not surprisingly, the psycho-socio-familial explanations abound:

- David Elkind, the best-selling author of *The Hurried Child* and *The Hurried Teen*, observes that many children, from early ages, are pressured to achieve academically, athletically, and socially. Under stress, says Elkind, children live in almost constant fear of failure. Hurried children become more self-centered and more likely to take impulsive risks, thus opening the door for involvement with drugs.

- Other experts relate the problem to children who, because they've been given too much too soon by well-meaning parents, have no tolerance for frustration and believe something can be had for nothing. These children want the prize to be located at the *top* of the Cracker Jack box. Drugs satisfy the overindulged youngster's learned need for intense, immediate reward.

- Still other experts link teen drug use to family dysfunction, lack of self-esteem, lack of parental involvement, and something called "addictive personality" (which I'm fairly certain is insidious to being human).

To my knowledge, I'm the only so-called "parenting expert" (I'm still not sure what that means) who explains why more and more teens are using more and more powerful drugs at earlier and earlier ages thusly: *Availability.* Maybe no one else tenders that explanation because it doesn't sound sufficiently intellectual. Experts, after all, want to sound like experts, which is to say they tend to explain things in complex terms, using lots of big words.

I say the teen drug problem boils down to something as simple as availability because it could be said that every generation of teens was more pressured than the one before, parental overindulgence is nothing new, family dysfunction is nothing new, and so on. There is no explanation for teen drug use that reflects anything new under the sun except availability. It's easier to get drugs today than has ever been the case.

Make available something that offers a cheap thrill and humans will consume it. When the cheap thrill is also forbidden, the emotionally immature person is drawn to it like a moth to flame. Most teens are emotionally immature. Therefore, teen drug use is on the rise.

And if that wasn't bad news enough, school-based drug education/prevention programs like D.A.R.E. have been a dismal waste of our tax dollars. These programs don't work because they bark up the wrong tree: To wit, they presume that human children can be proactively "self-esteemed" out of being negatively influenced by peers to experiment with drugs. A "psycho-social" approach such as this might work if low self-esteem were the root cause of the teen drug problem, but it isn't. As I said, it's availability, which means the only way to stop teens from using drugs is to put an end to availability. That would require marshaling the efforts of federal and state government; therefore, drugs are going to continue to be readily available for a long time to come.

Parents need not feel helpless in the face of the teenage drug epidemic. They can take preventive steps. Here are some suggestions for proactive prevention (but remember, there are no guarantees!):

- *Protect your children from stress.* Keep them out of organized sports, pageants, and other adult-supervised competitive activities until early adolescence. Accept their limitations, academic and otherwise. Be understanding of their personalities, too. If they aren't outgoing, don't try to force them into social situations. If they don't like to lead, don't make them assume leadership roles. There's no greater motivation for children than knowing their parents love them for themselves.

- *Prevent your children from becoming self-centered.* Put the marriage, not the children, first in the family. The marriage is the foundation on which the stability of every family member rests. When children occupy the family spotlight, they grow up feeling that their desires come first. When parents' needs are emphasized, youngsters learn social responsibility and become more sensitive to others' wants.

- *Establish your authority early on and discipline well.* Parental authority is the cornerstone of a child's sense of security, and security is the foundation of success. A child's unshakable belief that his parents are powerful people who can protect and provide for him under any and all circumstances liberates and energizes the child's potential for creativity and productivity.

- *Assign your children regular chores around the home.* Begin their "family citizenship" training no later than age four, and do not, under any circumstances, pay them for their contributions to the general welfare. Not only do chores help children learn basic domestic skills, they instill responsibility, feelings of accomplishment, and a sense of obligation and family loyalty, all of which help to prevent self-defeating behaviors like drug use.

- *Prevent the "I've got nothin' to do" syndrome.* Keep television watching to a minimum, and don't ever let it become your child's primary source of entertainment. Some experts are now comparing the blissful state of passivity that television watching induces in children with a drug "high." Marie Winn, author of

The Plug-In Drug (highly recommended by yours truly), contends that youngsters who become dependent on television at an early age are more likely to transfer that dependency to drugs during their teen years.

- *Keep toy purchases to a minimum.* Instead, help your children develop resourcefulness, the antidote to boredom and the key to any success story, by steering them toward creative activities and reading.

- *Give your kids a healthy say in how they use their discretionary time.* Today's parents have a tendency to overstructure their children's free time. That's very well intentioned, to be sure, but youngsters whose lives are constantly being organized by adults are likely to have difficulty learning how to use time wisely or creatively.

- *Help your children develop tolerance for frustration.* Learn to say "no" when necessary and *mean* it. A child who can't take "no" for an answer invariably has parents who have trouble saying it. Children develop tolerance for frustration only if their parents expose them to it. The more immunity your youngster develops to frustration, the more he or she will persist in the face of adversity.

- *Help your children to resist peer pressure and think for themselves.* Listen to them. Let them know that their ideas and opinions count, even though you may not always (seldom?) agree. There is no better insurance against the negative effects of peer pressure than open lines of communication between parent and child.

- *Maintain a good sense of humor about your child's mistakes and your own as well.* Nothing pushes teenagers away from their families quicker than par-

ents who take "parenting" matters—and themselves
—too seriously.

Y'all Have Any Burning Questions?

Q: *We recently discovered that our sixteen-year-old
daughter is smoking with her friends. Neither of us smoke—
nor have we ever—and she knows she's breaking a family
rule, but we can tell she does it anyway. In fact, she doesn't
deny it. She makes good grades, isn't a troublemaker, and we
don't disapprove of her friends (although we disapprove of
them smoking). Apart from this one problem, she's not rebellious. How can we get it through her head that smoking is
damaging her health?*

A: You've told your daughter you don't want her smoking. She smokes anyway. You've told her smoking is bad for
her health. She smokes anyway. You've berated her, lectured
her, become angry at her, pleaded with her, threatened her,
and perhaps even offered her bribes if she'd quit smoking.
She smokes anyway. What more can you do? Nothing!

Obviously, *you* can't get it through your daughter's
head that smoking is dangerous and *you* can't get her to stop.
She will stop when *she* realizes on her own the dangers of
smoking.

There's a prayer that reads: "God grant me the serenity to
accept the things I cannot change, the courage to change the
things I can, and the wisdom to know the difference." I'm
afraid your daughter's smoking falls into the first category. Accepting that this is something you cannot change would bring
you great peace of mind.

In the corporate world, bosses who try to change things
they can't change are known as micromanagers. It's well
documented that micromanagement in the workplace breeds

resentment, distrust, poor work habits, communication problems, and conflict. Likewise, the more effort you put into trying to stop your daughter from smoking, the more deceptive she will become, the worse the problem will get, and the more your relationship with her will suffer.

Inside the parent who tries in vain to change something a child is doing (or not doing) almost invariably churns the fear that the problem is somehow due to bad parenting, as in: "If I'd only [done something differently] my child wouldn't have developed this problem."

The fact is, children have minds of their own and, therefore, free will. Some of the choices a child makes reflect aspects of his or her upbringing, and some do not. In the latter category are choices that have to do with genetic influences (temperament), the peer group, and the often incomprehensible "foolishness" Proverbs tells us is "bound in the heart" of every child. Given that neither of you smoke, I'd venture to attribute your daughter's smoking to 50 percent peer group influence and 50 percent foolishness.

Count your lucky stars. Your daughter makes good grades, chooses reasonably good friends, and tells you the truth, even concerning her smoking. If the only thing she does to disappoint you during her teen years is smoke, you are fortunate indeed.

Q: *What do you say to parents who are afraid their children might begin abusing drugs or alcohol as teens?*
A: I tell them the biggest thing they have to fear is fear itself. Without realizing it, parents who are highly anxious concerning this possibility may actually increase the chances their children will develop drug and alcohol problems. Under the circumstances, substance abuse becomes a way for the child to assert autonomy and secure center stage in the family. The formula is, again, simple: availability (which we've already es-

tablished) plus anxious micromanagement equals increased likelihood of rebellious drug use.

I sense that what a lot of parents truly fear concerning drugs is the feeling they've failed. The fact is, impeccable child rearing is no guarantee a child won't use drugs. I can't say this loudly enough: *Parents are not responsible for everything their children do and/or don't do!!!* (See Put It in Perspective Principle Number Three, page 8.) Again, a parent's job is not to prevent his/her children from making mistakes, but rather to make certain they learn from their mistakes.

Q: *Are you saying parents shouldn't worry about drug and alcohol use?*

A: I'm saying worrying about the possibility isn't going to prevent it, and may well make it more likely. I remind parents that teenagers (a) have minds of their own, (b) are prone to rebellion, risk-taking, and experimentation, and (c) tend to make impulsive decisions. For these reasons, *all* teens are at risk for some degree of drug and/or alcohol use. The fact that a teenager may indulge in experimentation along these lines doesn't mean his upbringing was faulty or that a full-blown problem is going to develop. A realistic understanding of the teen years enables parents to keep their "cool" should they become aware that experimentation has taken place.

Q: *Like yourself, a lot of today's parents experimented with pot and other drugs as teenagers and young adults. If their children ask, should they tell them the truth?*

A: The answer to that question depends on too many factors to list. Personally, I wouldn't volunteer it unless the information was essential to making a point (and I can't imagine what the point might be), and I wouldn't advise admitting it to a child younger than seventeen. Even then, I wouldn't advise telling a youngster who was experimenting or suspected of experimenting with drugs or a youngster who was running with a group of "suspect" kids. Under any of the above circumstances, the child might well conclude that since you used drugs and you're now okay, the dangers of drug use have been exaggerated.

If parents have no reason to worry about drug use, and a fairly mature child asks the question, and the parents enjoy an open and trusting relationship with the child, then answering the question truthfully is probably not going to be a problem. Whatever you do, just don't make it sound adventurous or enjoyable.

Q: *If you had just one piece of advice to parents concerning how to prevent their kids from developing drug or alcohol problems, what would it be?*

A: Actually, I have four pieces of advice:

1. *Don't smoke cigarettes.* Although the relationship has not been proved, many experts now believe that nicotine is what's known as a "gateway" drug—one that increases the possibility of further drug use. Not only is nicotine highly addictive, many drug users report that it was, indeed, their first drug of choice. It's a fact that most teenage drug users also smoke cigarettes, and it's also a fact that when a parent smokes, a child is far more likely to take up the habit.

2. *If you drink alcoholic beverages, do so in moderation.* Why a moderate amount of alcohol, but no cigarettes? First, I'd be a complete hypocrite to advise otherwise. Second, alcohol is not nearly as addictive as nicotine. Think about it. You probably know quite a few people who drink an *occasional* alcoholic beverage, whereas you probably know very few who smoke an *occasional* cigarette. Unlike the case with cigarettes, a child doesn't grow up to become an adult alcoholic because he sees his parents imbibe a glass of wine every

now and then. Children are unlikely to ever develop drinking problems of any sort if they see their parents using alcohol "responsibly," assuming there is such a thing. Obviously, and the studies support this, it's better for parents to not drink at all.

3. *Stay married.* That's right, simply make up your minds and agree between you that you're going to hang in there no matter what. Take it from a guy who's been married for thirty years as of the publication of this tome: Staying married is the toughest thing you will ever do, which is precisely why it is the most rewarding thing you will ever do, which is precisely why you should do it. Not to mention the fact that children whose parents stay together are less likely to engage in any sort of antisocial/self-destructive behavior.

4. *If you're a father, get involved and stay involved with your children prior to their teen years.* Not to diminish the contribution of mothers, but there isn't a study that doesn't show a positive correlation between involvement on the part of fathers and good adjustment during the teen years. Do things with your kids, dads! And I don't mean as a family. I mean you!!! Play golf with them, take them fishing, do projects together, go to concerts together, take walks with them, ride bicycles together, go to sports events together . . . the list is endless. There is no excuse—*none!*—for a father to fail to take his children—of both genders!—under his wing and show them, in concrete ways, that they are more important to him than anything except his marriage.

Q: *I've heard that the more organized activities—church youth groups, athletics, Scouting, school organizations, and so on—teenagers are involved in, the less likely it is they'll get messed up in drugs and alcohol. Do you agree, and if so, how much should parents dictate to a teenager concerning extracurricular activities?*

A: I agree that there is nothing so deadly as boredom during the teenage years and believe that parents should promote involvement in the types of events and activities you mentioned.

The recipe for "Teen in Trouble," whether the trouble be alcohol, drugs, or sex, is equal parts peer pressure, parental (especially paternal) underinvolvement, and boredom. Let a teenager just wander in search of something to do, and he'll eventually wander into a crowd of kids who are themselves wandering. Sooner or later, they'll stumble onto the opportunity to experience something forbidden. (There's that availability thing again.) Lacking anything better to do, they will accept, and keep on accepting the invitation.

Several years ago, I did an informal study of well-adjusted teens. These were young people ages thirteen through seventeen who, according to their parents' reports, made good grades, got along well with their parents, enjoyed an active social life, and seemed happy with themselves. Without exception, these youngsters were active in at least one extracurricular activity through their school, church, or community. In addition, every one of them had a hobby. To their parents' knowledge, none of them was using drugs or alcohol, nor were they sexually active.

I know what some of you are saying: "C'mon, John, don't be so naive! Just because their parents don't know something is going on doesn't mean it isn't."

I disagree. Parents who are interested and involved in what their children are doing with their spare time will usually know when something is wrong. They may not know the specifics, but they will *know*, nonetheless. The test for trouble is simple: Ask yourself, "How often do I have a feeling of general discomfort concerning who my child is with, where he is, and what he's doing?" If your answer is once a month or more, then you'd better take a closer look. Parents often ignore the signs; then when the beast finally rears its ugly head, they claim ignorance.

Remember also that most teens will sooner or later drink a beer or two, take a drag of a joint, and tread dangerously close to "too far" sexually. There's a difference between trying and using. The difference is made by parents who care.

Concerning how far a parent should dictate to a teenager how he uses his spare time: I don't see anything wrong with parents mandating that a teen get involved in a certain activity as long as that mandate is the exception rather than the rule. Part of our job, after all, is to help create and maintain "well roundedness" in our children's lives. If we see a gap, we have every right to fill it—if our children won't take the initiative to do so. Oftentimes, their reluctance to get involved in something is based on inadequate information, misperception, or the unfounded fear that they won't "fit in."

There have been a few occasions when my wife and I told our teenage son what he was going to do with his time. Although he might have initially complained about our decision, he always ended up appreciating it.

Sometimes it pays to remind ourselves that we really *do* know best.

Cheap Thrills, Part Two: *Sex*

Once upon a time, it was a topic parents avoided addressing with their children, but that's no longer the case. These days, most parents agree the earlier discussions about sex take place between parent and child, the better. The more questions about sex children ask, however, the more parents ask as well. But before going any further, let's begin discussion of this hot topic at the beginning:

Under normal circumstances, the first opportunity parents

have to talk about sexual matters with their children presents itself around age four or five, when children first become fascinated by the beginnings of life. The first questions are usually one form or another of "Where do babies come from?" The more we say, the more they ask, and in no time at all, we find ourselves dealing with the sexual aspect of this whole mystery.

This age child also begins to realize that boys grow up to be men and girls grow up to be women. Displays of precocious quasi-sexual behavior at this age are the child's way of exploring and, thereby, understanding the mysterious difference between males and females.

Lacking in vocabulary, the young child "acts out" questions. It's the age of "Let's play doctor" and "Show me," which almost never fail to cause parents considerable dismay. The fact is, a child's curiosity does not readily obey the green and red lights that adults set up to define what is "right" and what is not. It never occurs to a child indulging in immature sex play, whether the play is solo or with a playmate, that these delightful games and discoveries are "wrong."

It is important that parents use these occasions, when discovered, to open lines of communication. If the young child's unashamed openness is punished, then later, as a teen, it's unlikely she will feel comfortable approaching parents with questions, concerns, or problems concerning sexuality.

Handled properly, even the most outrageous of a child's early attempts to understand sex can set a precedent for good communication and, therefore, education concerning the topic. The general rules of thumb include:

- Understand that all early sexual exploration is "normal," no matter what form it takes. Keep your outrage under control.
- When setting limits on certain behaviors, avoid using

the terms "right" and "wrong." Instead, talk in terms of age-appropriateness, as in, "You and Melissa aren't old enough to be doing these kinds of things with one another." It's not that you shouldn't be placing moral judgements on such things, but rather that phrasing such things in terms of age-appropriateness is easier for a young child to understand. You do want your child to understand you, don't you?

- Answer the child's questions matter-of-factly. Be concrete, but remember there's no need to be overly explicit. The child doesn't expect or need a lot of details.

Once the young child's questions have been answered and curiosity has been satisfied, sex moves to the back of the burner and stays there until the preteen or early teen years. Parents should now be trying to not only keep the channels of communication open but also establish themselves as *consultants* to their children where sexual matters are concerned. Whether your teen feels comfortable talking to you about sex is a matter of how nonjudgmental you are when the subject comes up as well as how little you pry, which leads me to . . .

The "Talk": As a young teen, one of the things I dreaded, and hoped to forever avoid, was the "Talk." That's when your father walks casually over to you and says, with this real serious, I mean *terminal* look on his face, "Son, I think you and I need to have a conversation." And you act stupid at first, as though you don't have any idea what he's talking about, all the while calculating how you're going to handle this uncool situation. But before you can say anything, he's already started his spiel, and all you want to do is get out of there, but you can't because it's your father. So you pretend to listen.

Or you do what I did, which was to lie: "Hey, listen, Dad, before you go any further, I think I can save you some time.

This guy came and talked to our health class last year about, you know, and, well, he was pretty good and, well, I don't think it's really necessary for me to hear it all over again, but I appreciate your concern and I'll be sure and come to you if I have any questions, okay?"

Boy, did *he* ever look relieved.

As my son approached adolescence, I looked back on that truncated conversation with a mixture of humor and perplexity. I wasn't uncomfortable with the format my father chose, and neither was he. But what was the alternative? In the process of pondering this dilemma, I realized that my feelings of unease as an adolescent were due in part to the fact that sex was, at the time, a threatening subject for me, and so it is for many adolescent males. One way of keeping the anxiety it arouses at bay is for the young teen to deny that he needs to know anything about it.

But a second reason for my discomfort was that I had no choice in the matter. Dad had decided it was time for my education and that was that. In other words, *his* needs dictated the moment. I'm sure he felt obliged to "do his duty" toward me and approached the subject the only way he knew, but I felt backed into a corner and so took the quickest way out.

I came to the conclusion that what my son needed from me was not a rundown of "the facts," but the freedom to ask questions. If his sexual education was going to be meaningful, he would have to feel in control of it.

So, I took the initiative to issue an open-ended invitation. I think we were going somewhere together in the car when, for whatever reason, the time felt "right" for me to say what I had to say.

"Son, as you get older, you're going to become more and more interested in girls and you're going to have questions and . . ."

He interrupted. "Uh, look, Dad, before you go any further, this guy came and talked to our health class last year and . . ."

"Yeah, I know, he was pretty good and answered your questions, right?"

"Right. How'd you know?"

"Same guy came to my health class when I was your age. But I'm not finished. All I want to say is that when you do have questions or anything at all you want to discuss concerning women and men and sex, I'd like you to ask me. I'd rather you asked me instead of one of your friends, because their answers and opinions might not be correct. And remember: There's no such thing as a dumb question."

Boy, was *he* ever relieved. But he *has* come to me with questions on more than a few occasions, and I've taken those opportunities to not only answer his questions but to add a few editorial comments as well. In addition, he occasionally says or does things that allow me to make further adjustments in his attitude.

With our daughter, the only modification my wife and I made in this basic approach was to prepare her for her first period.

Basically, we tried to get across to both of them that the secret to a successful sexual relationship with someone has less to do with techniques and biology than with attitude and values—specifically, how well you respect yourself and how well you respect the other person. You can't package that attitude in one fact-filled conversation. It's something you model for them every day in what you say and what you do. In that sense, a child's sex education begins the day he or she is born.

Preparing Your Daughter for Dating: At thirteen, Phoebe looked every bit of seventeen. The boys at Hormone High, the local testosterone factory, were overjoyed. Her parents were not. Phoebe's father, who bore a striking resemblance to Al Capone, let it be known that under no circumstances would Phoebe be allowed to date until the day after her sixteenth birthday.

Several months after issuing this edict, Phoebe's dad showed up at my back door, looking decidedly out of joint. Under the pretense of working after school on a drama project, he complained, Phoebe had been sneaking off almost every afternoon with a sixteen year-old boy.

"I can't think straight about this," he said, grinding his teeth together, fists clenched. "What do you think I should do?"

"Well," I ventured, getting ready to duck, "have you considered maybe lightening up a bit? You know, giving Phoebe a small measure of freedom along these lines so she doesn't have to sneak?"

"No way!" he bellowed. "I was sixteen once! I know what the boys are thinking when they look at her! Letting her date would be like sending her into the lion's den!"

Our "conversation" was over before it started. Over the next few years, things at Phoebe's house went from bad to worse. I came to expect regular visits from her Magnificent Micromanager of a father, looking for advice he wouldn't take. Once, he caught her at the shopping center with an older boy when she was supposedly spending the night with a girlfriend. On another occasion, he and his wife came home unexpectedly to discover a boy upstairs. This game of hide-and-seek continued until the day after Phoebe's sixteenth birthday, by which time she had proven her point to all but her father, who remained convinced he had successfully held the line. Meanwhile, the same old, same old had started with the younger daughter, who at age thirteen looked . . . yep, you guessed it. Some folks never learn.

Contrast Phoebe's tale with one told me recently by the parents of one Alice, fourteen going on twenty in more ways than one. During a family vacation, Alice confessed to her mother that she'd met an older boy and, smitten, had smooched with him until their lips were sore. Mom promptly asked, "What do you think usually follows kissing, Alice?"

Alice thought for a moment, then answered, "Probably touching."

"And what do you think usually happens after touching?"

"Um, maybe lying down somewhere?"

Her mother followed each of Alice's answers with "And what do you think usually comes next?" until Alice reached the end of the line and said, "I guess that's when people have sex."

This very shrewd mother then asked, "At what point in this sequence do you want things to stop, Alice?"

"Um, I really don't want to do more than kiss right now, Mom."

"And if the boy doesn't want to stop at kissing, what are you going to do?"

Alice was stunned. It had not occurred to her that, fair or not, it was her responsibility to say "when." She and her mother talked at length about sexual responsibility, birth control, sexually transmitted diseases, date rape, and all the other realities appertaining thereto.

I had to applaud this mother (not to mention Alice's father, who agreed wholeheartedly with his wife's handling of the situation) for seizing the opportunity to educate rather than berate. In so doing, she had opened lines of communication and established a precedent of trust concerning this decidedly sensitive topic. Without dogma or condemnation, she had caused Alice to contemplate the downside of sexual activity. Lastly, she had gently forced Alice to confront a discomforting reality; namely, that boys don't generally stop unless girls are clear in saying "that's far enough."

There are some lessons to be learned in these two stories:

- In determining when to allow a female child to date, look more closely at the child than the calendar. From one point of view (the calendar), neither Phoebe nor Alice was "ready" to date. From another, both were old enough to be prepped for responsible relationships with boys. Alice's parents, seeing the writing on the wall, correctly realized that management was a better strategy than micromanagement. Their response to her initial foray into sexuality was proactive. As such, it is likely to prevent disaster.

- Phoebe's father can't be criticized for his stand; it was certainly morally defensible. Nonetheless, his inflexibility caused him to become his own worst enemy. The more Phoebe rebelled against his "iron-handed" approach to her interest in boys (and their interest in her), the more inflexible he became. There was but one direction this situation could go—down. There are times in the rearing of a child when strategic compromise is the only way to prevent parent and child from being polarized. Alice's parents correctly realized that compromise wasn't capitulation; rather, it was a way of keeping Alice "on their team."

- Parents are absolutely correct in perceiving that girls are considerably more vulnerable than boys when it comes to dating. Rules are definitely needed, but rules alone are likely to backfire. The most positive, productive, and preventive approach is one that educates the young girl on her responsibilities. Realistic rules tend to evolve naturally out of this context.

- There is no approach that's guaranteed problem-free. When problems arise with Alice and boys—and they will!—the precedents set will allow Alice and her parents to engage in creative problem-solving rather than warfare.

- Most professionals agree that a warm relationship between father and daughter is the best deterrent to early sexual activity. A girl who feels approved of and respected by her father is not only less needy of approval from boys but also better able to "just say no" and stick to her guns.

- Last but not least, today's parents need to accept that times have indeed changed since they were teens. The biggest change involves the closing of the gender gap. In the world of the nineties' teen, it's perfectly acceptable for a girl to call a boy, for the girl to drive on a date, for the girl to pay for her own meal and movie ticket. As a result, today's teenage girl feels herself to be more in control of her relationships with boys than did girls in bygone eras. Speaking both as a father and a one-time teenage boy, I have absolutely no problem with that.

Preparing Your Son for Dating: When I was in high school—shortly before "the pill" and long before AIDS—the world was a place of clear-cut dichotomies. Things were either one way, or they were the other. Shades of gray did not exist. The most significant of these either/or propositions, from the perspective of a young, hormone-saturated male (like myself), was that of nerd/cool. There was no mistaking the two. Nerds (like myself) were in the chess club and on the debating team, drove their mothers' station wagons, wore glasses, and stayed home on weekends. The guys with "cool" excelled in physically punishing sports, such as wrestling or football, drove fast cars, consumed great quantities of beer and other alcoholic beverages, and "scored" with girls—lots of girls, to hear them talk about it, which they generally did after consuming great quantities of beer and other alcoholic beverages. And thus the line was drawn separating the "men" from the boys.

We just didn't get it, did we? Not even the nerds understood that beneath this bravado (or the worship of it) lay an insecurity that fed on the depersonalization of women. Compounding the problem was the fact that many of our fathers either ignored our emerging sexuality altogether or, at best, made awkward attempts to fill us in on the physiology of sex. The "Talk," as it was known, generally lasted no more than ten minutes and ended with a call for "Any questions?" Eager to terminate this torture, we assured our dads that they'd performed their duties well and hastened for the nearest exit. Needless to say, not all fathers approached this issue in such cursory fashion, but by the time many males of my generation started dating, they were the hormone-powered equivalent of unguided missiles.

When my son began showing an interest in girls, I reflected back upon the foibles and fiascoes of my adolescence and promised myself he would be better prepared for datinghood. Undertaking this as a project meant defining my goals, selecting my strategies, and formulating contingency plans.

What, I asked myself, did I want to accomplish with Eric? The answer was simple: Everything my father had not, including:

- an open, anxiety-free line of communication concerning anything having to do with not only sexuality but with male/female relationships in general.
- a respectful attitude toward both himself and members of the opposite gender (a lack of respect for oneself *always* manifests itself in a lack of respect for others, and vice versa).
- an understanding of the "politics" of dating, including an appreciation of and a respect for the worries, wishes, and expectations—both explicit and implicit—typical of a teenage girl's parents.

I also had to accept there is no science to this, no approach that will guarantee the desired outcome. Do your best, I told myself, and do not blame yourself for mistakes Eric may make. I knew that the success of my venture was less a matter of intellect than a matter of sensitivity and intuition. In order to be "in tune" with Eric, I had to not just make myself available, but spend time with him on a regular basis. My professional experience had taught me that teenage boys who lack relationships with healthy adult male role models often take to acting out very distorted ideas of what makes for a "real man." During Eric's teen years, we built models, played golf, and went to many a rock concert together. The relationship was not completely free of antagonism, but it never lacked for energy.

As a result of this active interest and involvement, I became aware of things that might otherwise have gone unnoticed. On one occasion, for example, Eric invited me into his room to listen to an album he'd recently acquired. The group had done their rock 'n' roll homework well, to be sure, but their lyrics left much to be desired. One song in particular compared women to dogs. As soon as I "got it," I reached out and shut the stereo off. Eric looked confused.

"Do you have any idea what they're suggesting in that song, Eric?" I asked.

"Not really."

We listened to it again, and again, until he got the point. We discussed its implications, talked about the possible consequences of that sort of attitude toward women, and then— after reimbursing him for his mistake—I confiscated the album, following which it conveniently disappeared. Its lack of morals aside, the band in question had actually given me an invaluable opportunity to do some "sex education" with Eric, and for that I was—and still am—grateful.

The most obvious aspect of this entire process involved my

own behavior toward women, and Willie in particular. An attitude of "do what I say, not what I do" would hardly have worked. I also realized that, in the final analysis, little everyday things would count the most. So, I made sure Eric saw me opening doors for his mother, pulling chairs out for her in restaurants, doing my share of the housework, and respecting her opinion whether I agreed with it or not. Chivalry may be dead, but "gentleman" is definitely not, and a gentle-man is what I wanted Eric to become.

If there's one thing I learned through all of this, it was that a young man's education in opposite-gender relationships cannot be accomplished by hit-and-run, as my father had attempted. Nor is it simply a matter of—in the words of Detective Joe Friday—"the facts, ma'am, just the facts." It's a creative process that requires an ongoing commitment not just to the male child in question but to the very health of our culture. One must, in other words, never lose sight of the forest (one's obligations to the culture) for the tree (one's obligation to a child). I also discovered, much to my vicarious satisfaction, that sex and "cool" have absolutely nothing to do with one another. In this area at least, the sins of the father do *not* have to be borne by the son. Hallelujah!!!

On School-Based Sex Education: In the midst of a get-together several years ago, several women cornered me and began telling me about their efforts to implement a sex-education curriculum in their hometown's public schools. It was to begin in kindergarten and continue through high school. Would I help them?

"Is the program going to be abstinence-based?" I asked.

Not really, they told me. Abstinence was going to be discussed, of course, but other methods of pregnancy prevention were going to be given equal time. This all-methods-are-of-equal-value approach is known as "comprehensive sex education."

"I'm sorry," I said, "but I don't believe schools should be promoting anything but abstinence."

They were so shocked that none of them could even ask the logical question, so I answered it for them: "There is no evidence that traditional sex-ed programs work, and a growing body of evidence that such programs may actually contribute to *increased* teenage sexual activity." And suddenly, having identified myself as an ignorant, narrow-minded rightwing conservative religious fanatic, I was alone.

At this point in time, I am alone no longer. In the October 1994 issue of *Atlantic* magazine, Barbara DaFoe Whitehead, vice president of the Institute for American Values in New York, wrote on "The Failure of Sex Education." I recommend that all readers of this book go to their local library, look up the article, and read it. It's a scathing indictment of the muddle-headedness and downright stupidity that was the genesis of such programs.

For her primary example, Whitehead uses the "Learning About Family Life" curriculum adopted by all 595 of New Jersey's school districts. The program is not unlike others currently in place in school systems across the country. It stresses decision-making skills, helps boys and girls as young as six learn to talk with one another frankly about sexual matters, promotes "non-coital" alternatives to sex such as deep kissing and mutual masturbation, and teaches the facts of reproduction and contraception.

Missing are such presumably tangential topics as commitment, responsibility, and the real-life consequences of teen pregnancy: poverty, welfare dependency, undereducation, increased risk (along a number of dimensions) to the child, and so on. As Whitehead points out, although the curriculum contains stories about such things as showing love through sex, amicable divorce, and a "successful teenage mother," there are no stories about the relationship between commitment and love, marriages that work, or the downside of teen pregnancy.

In short, the program echoes one of former Clinton-administration Surgeon General Jocelyn Elders's more bizarre outbursts: "Everybody in the world is opposed to sex outside of marriage, and yet everybody does it. I'm saying, 'Get real.'" As it so happens, it was (and probably still is) Dr. Elders who desperately needs to get real. After two federal studies, researcher Douglas Kirby has found that comprehensive sex-education programs cannot claim to have accomplished anything.

Kirby also concluded that good parent-child communication concerning sexual matters is less of a deterrent to precocious sexual activity than good discipline and supervision. Teenagers with moderately strict parents report lower levels of sexual activity than those with either permissive or rigidly strict parents.

Sex education can, indeed, be effective, but most existing programs flunk the litmus test. Those that send the strong message: "You are not ready for sex, so don't do it" are clearly the most successful. One such program—called Postponing Sexual Involvement—was developed at Grady Memorial Hospital in Atlanta, Georgia. Instead of stressing knowledge or open communication or getting in touch with feelings and values, Grady's program stresses one word: No. Although it doesn't meet Elders's criteria for realism, it's working, and so are similar programs based on the same model.

One such program is called "Best Friends." Founded by Elayne Bennett, wife of former Education Secretary William Bennett, its target audience is girls ages nine through eighteen. "Best Friends," which is now in more than twenty cities nationwide, stresses abstinence from sex and drugs (including alcohol), positive role models, and self-respect (as opposed to self-esteem, which is a code word for perpetual narcissism). The core message is that every young girl has it within her grasp to achieve a good and even noble life. Whether she does or does not depends solely upon the decisions she makes. Toward the goal of helping girls make good life decisions, enrollees are taught—beginning in grade five— how to distinguish a good friend from a destructive one, how to make realistic plans for the future, how to work toward goals, and how to handle boys, especially where intimacy is concerned.

According to a 1995 survey of the "Best Friends" program in Washington, D.C., by David Rowberry, only 4 percent of "Best Friends" girls had had sex by age fifteen, compared with 63 percent(!) of girls in the District of Columbia generally. Among girls who participated in the program, only 1 percent became pregnant, as compared with twenty-six percent of their peers in the city's school system. A 1996 survey of 1,100 "Best Friends" girls nationwide found that 96 percent were drug-free and sexually abstinent throughout their school years. Isn't that remarkable?

To answer my own question, No, it's not remarkable at all. It simply goes to show that teenagers can indeed make good decisions concerning sex, drugs, and alcohol. They simply need to be given good, authoritative guidance from adults who have faith in them.

Chapter Five

◆

A Veritable Potpourri
of Questions and Answers

Q: *My thirteen-year-old daughter has recently started expressing a lot of anger and bottled-up resentment toward me. Just this morning, for example, I remarked on how pretty a certain painting was and she replied, in a snide tone of voice, "It looks stupid to me!" If I ask for her cooperation around the house, she's likely to tell me my request is "dumb." I've tried to find out what's bothering her, but every time I try to talk, she clams up. All of this is very recent and I'm very concerned. How should I go about addressing this problem?*

A: Your question reflects the tendency among today's parents to view their children's behavior through psychological filters. A generation or so ago, a child who had contradicted a parent in a snide manner would have been regarded as disrespectful. The child would have been sternly reprimanded, perhaps even punished. Today's parent looks at the same situation and concludes that the child is "angry."

The nouveau psychological interpretation says that the child is not misbehaving, but only releasing "bottled-up resentiments." This theoretical construction rules out a disciplinary response. Discipline, the parent fears, will not only intensify the child's "anger" but also shut down any chance of talking things out, thus "resolving the problem."

It's important to note that the psychological viewpoint shifts responsibility for the child's behavior from child to parent. A disrespectful child has clearly done something wrong. She requires, therefore, correction. If, on the other hand, we think of the child as being "angry," the implication is that the child's *parents* may have done something wrong. They become responsible for identifying and correcting their own bad parenting.

Through sleight-of-psychobabble, the child becomes a sympathetic figure whose parents are misbehaving (unwittingly?) and causing the child psychological disturbance (i.e., "poor self-esteem"). Since psychological maladies require understanding, it is necessary that the sensitive parent attempt to engage the child in what I call "therapeutic conversation."

"I'd like to talk about what's bothering you and try to resolve whatever problem we have between us" is the manner in which such conversations are likely to begin. Regardless of what the child expresses, no matter how inappropriate and/or off the wall, the parent is required to be "open," "nonjudgmental," and "accepting." These very psychologically correct conversations generally end with (a) the parent apologizing for something, (b) the parent promising to be more patient, understanding, sensitive, etc., (c) both parent and child engaged in emotive catharsis, (d) all of the above.

Something very interesting has happened here: namely, the child and parent are now on level ground. In effect, they have become equals, de facto peers. They have a "wonderful, open relationship," but one conducted such that the child is unable to develop good old-fashioned respect for the parent. This is unfortunate, given that the Judeo-Christian ethic informs us it is impossible for anyone to develop true self-respect without first having developed respect for others, beginning with one's parents. No wonder veteran teachers consistently tell me that today's child is "self-absorbed."

To answer your question, I recommend you take a psychologically *incorrect* approach to this problem. Make it clear to your daughter that if something's bothering her, you'll be glad to listen, but that demonstrations of disrespect will not be tolerated under any circumstances. When she "slips," I'd suggest that perhaps she needs some time alone in her room to contemplate her future.

Q: *We bought our son a car when he turned sixteen. It's been less than half a year and he already has acquired three moving violations. This has resulted in a significant increase in our car insurance. He seems nonchalant about the whole issue. What can we do to help him understand the seriousness of this situation?*

A: You can sell his car. Today. No doubt the reason he's "nonchalant" is because you have always "toted the note" concerning his mistakes. He has no reason, therefore, to believe you won't do so in this situation. He also has no reason to accept responsibility for his mistakes. He figures—and I'll bet my life savings you've given him every reason to do so—that you'll carp and moan, but when all is said and done, nothing will change. To change the way he thinks and acts, you must change your administrative policies.

Hopefully, the following true story will be inspirational: The child in question—I'll call him "Jimmy"—wanted a car for his sixteenth birthday.

"We'll buy you a used car when you turn sixteen," his parents told him, "but only if you're carrying no less than a solid 'B' average. If not, you'll have to wait until your grades come up."

Jimmy's birthday came and his grades were good, so his parents bought him an '86 Buick (a fairly new car when all this happened) with the understanding that he had to get a job and pay his share of the insurance premium.

His parents also told him that if he was ticketed for even one moving violation (thus increasing their insurance cost), the car would be sold. He would go back to riding the bus to school and have use of one of their cars only to and from work and on weekend nights until ten. They would consider buying him another used car when he graduated from high school, but only if he graduated with a "B" average and was going on to college.

Jimmy said he understood and had no problem with his parents' terms, but they doubted he truly took them seriously. "Although we'd never failed to back up our words with action," they write, "we were sure he thought we were just blowing a lot of hot air to try and keep him in line."

Jimmy got a job and began paying his share of the insurance premium. Six months later, he was ticketed for speeding and running a stop sign. He swore up and down that he'd been given a bum rap. His parents told him that if he was innocent, he should hire a lawyer. If the lawyer successfully defended him, he could keep his car. Jimmy went to several lawyers who all said they could probably get the charge reduced, but not dropped.

At this point, Jimmy decided to throw himself upon his parents' mercy. He pleaded for a second chance; he said he'd find a way to pay his entire insurance bill; he swore he'd learned his lesson.

"Oh, please, please, please," he said, almost dropping to his knees, "don't subject me to the humiliation of riding the bus."

His parents held firm, sold his car, and subjected him to the humiliation of riding the bus. Most days, in fact, Jimmy was able to bum a ride off a friend, but there were times when he had no option other than the bus.

At this point, he played his final card, telling his parents that taking away his car had made him "depressed" and his grades were probably going to suffer as a result.

"Oh, that's all right," they said. "It's your life. If you want a car when you graduate, you'll snap out of your depression soon enough. If not, then maybe the military can un-depress you after high school."

The high school counselor even asked Jimmy's parents to reconsider, saying he felt taking the car away was "a bit extreme." And having to ride the bus, he added, was hurting Jimmy's "self-esteem."

Jimmy's parents told the counselor, "If you think it's extreme, and you're worried about Jimmy's self-esteem, you're free to buy Jimmy a car and put him on your insurance policy."

My gosh! That sounds like parents from another era talking, doesn't it? To think that in these "progressive" times, any parents would actually have the gumption to do such a thing is rather amazing, isn't it? Or is *refreshing* the more appropriate term?

In any case, all this happened in 1990. Today, Jimmy is in law school. He wrote a brief addendum to the letter his parents wrote to me. It reads: "I want you to know that as a result of what my parents did concerning the car, I have more respect for them today than I would have if they had relented."

Q: *I have two children, ages fourteen and eight, from my first marriage and am about to remarry. I recently read an article in which a psychologist who's written a book on stepfamilies said stepparents should not attempt to assume full parental authority, particularly in the area of discipline, lest* *the children become confused and resentful. To tell the truth, I'm a fairly traditional female who believes the man should be the head of the household. I want my future husband to take his rightful role, and right away, but now I'm the one who's confused. What are your thoughts on this?*

A: I seem to be swimming against the current of "psychological correctness" with regards to this issue, because I am adamantly opposed to the idea that stepparents should take a backseat where discipline is concerned. I don't even think there should be a period of transition where a stepparent's authority is concerned.

In a situation such as yours, children need to understand that the moment the marriage vows are taken, the new spouse will be vested with full parental responsibilities and equally full parental authority. This should apply, furthermore, regardless of which parent has primary custody. Arguments to the contrary seem designed to protect the egos of certain biological parents (in this case, your ex-husband's) and avoid upsetting stepchildren. As such, they exemplify the notion— implicit, if not explicit, to the counseling philosophy of many a mental health professional—that where family policy is concerned, people's *feelings* should hold sway. And indeed, if the goal is not to ruffle the feathers of either the children or the "real" parent, then having the stepparent take a backseat when it comes to discipline is prudent. Unfortunately, this all but guarantees that (a) the parent-child relationship, rather than the new marriage, will occupy center-stage in the stepfamily, (b) the children will never develop true respect for the stepparent, and (c) the children will make constant, and often successful, attempts to divide and conquer. This set of circumstance places the new marriage immediately at risk. In this regard, it's significant to note that second marriages, when there are children involved, succeed less often than first marriages.

The fact is, children who are expected to give complete respect to a stepparent who has permission to discipline them will not be confused and will get over being upset. I speak with complete authority on this subject because I spent most of my childhood in two stepfamilies. With my mother's support, my stepfather, Julius, assumed full parental responsibility and authority on day one. If I required discipline, and he was on the front line, he disciplined me. I didn't always appreciate his methods, but I respected him and obeyed him. Interestingly enough, my father had no problem with the role Julius assumed in my life but failed to support his second wife's authority where I was concerned. As a consequence, I had no respect for Betsy (to whom I've since apologized), was openly disobedient toward her, and generally treated her like a peon. When I was living with my mother and Julius, it was clear their marriage came first. When I was living with my father and Betsy, it was clear my relationship with my father came first. The difference was night and day. I have a lot of regrets, but both experiences have helped me understand how a family must operate in order to be worthy of being called a *family.*

By the way, whether or not one is a "traditional female who thinks the man should be the head of the household" isn't the issue. The subtle implication contained in that statement—and one I'm sure was not intended—is that stepmothers have less of a right than stepfathers to assume full authority over and discipline stepchildren. The question, simply put, is, "Are you and your future husband going to form a family, or are you going to become, in effect, a single parent with a live-in parenting assistant?"

Q: *My thirteen-year-old son is giving me fits. Daniel ignores me, sasses me, refuses to do what he is told, and refuses to cooperate in any punishment I levy. I would have to literally* *fight him to get him to his room, and I'd have to hold the door (or lock it from the outside) to keep him there. If I take away a privilege, I have to literally fight him to keep him from taking it back. My husband, whom Daniel obeys without question, travels through the week. I don't like taking a "wait till your father gets home" approach, because even though he doesn't seem to mind, I don't want to make my husband the heavy. What should I do?*

A: I'd strongly recommend that you go right ahead and make your husband the heavy. In the first place, you obviously need your husband's support in order to solve this problem, and he obviously doesn't mind giving it. Furthermore, it will profit Daniel greatly to know that his parents are in complete accord on the matter of his discipline.

My experience as the father of a boy who was 9.5 on the strong-willed scale led me to conclude, somewhat belatedly, that the successful discipline of the average male child requires a strong male hand, especially during adolescence. Willie, while she initially preferred a more "understanding" approach, eventually concurred with me when it became obvious to her that maternal instincts are not well suited to the testosterone-driven inclinations of the typical male teen. As David Blankenhorn points out in *Fatherless America,* the socialization of the adolescent is most successfully accomplished when the male parent is on the front lines where discipline is concerned.

My plan is simple and most effective. Best of all, my experience leads me to assure you that if you are consistent, you will solve this problem in no time at all. Whenever Daniel (a) addresses you disrespectfully (in word or in tone), (b) ignores you when you speak, or (c) openly defies an instruction, tell him he has a choice: He can either go to his room for one hour, or he can refuse. In the latter case, or if he goes to his room but does not remain quietly for one full hour, you will not make any attempt whatsoever to make him serve his punishment. Rather, you will simply shrug your shoulders and tell his father when he returns, in which case his father will enforce much worse punishments on the weekend.

The first time Daniel refuses to serve his punishment in his room, he loses the weekend privilege he values most (i.e., leaving the house to be with friends). The second time such a refusal occurs, he loses his second-most valued weekend privilege (i.e., having a friend over). The third time, he loses all weekend privileges and is confined to his room from the time Dad gets home until school on Monday and goes to bed, lights out, at eight every night.

The success of this plan, which has proven itself on many a Daniel and Danielle, depends on your nonchalant consistency. In short, you must never threaten, warn, or otherwise waffle. If, for example, Daniel ignores you, simply say, "That'll cost you an hour in your room, Daniel." If he protests that he didn't hear you telling him to do something, say, "Then you'd better tune your ears to the frequency of my voice." If he says you're not being fair, and he won't go to his room, say, "Oh, that's okay. I'll just make a note to tell your father about this." If Daniel then apologizes and tells you he'll go to his room, say, "I accept your apology, and you can go to your room if you want to, but you initially refused to go, so I'm going to tell your father anyway."

This is known as being "mean," which children think their parents are when they discover their parents *mean* exactly what they say.

Q: *We're having a problem coming up with appropriate punishments for our twelve-year-old son. He's not a big problem, but like all children his age, he occasionally misbehaves. You generally recommend a restriction of one sort or another for punishment. My husband and I run a busy retail business,* *which means neither of us is home after school to supervise a restriction. I divide my Saturdays between home and the shop, and I never know when business is going to demand my presence. How can we restrict when we're not there to supervise? In lieu of that, are there other, equally effective means of punishing a child of this age?*

A: Your question raises several equally interesting issues, the first of which concerns the commonly held belief that when a child misbehaves, punishment (a corporal, material, or recreational penalty) is in order. This is not necessarily so. When a child misbehaves, some consequence is due. Punishment, however, is but one of the available options. Other options include:

- a stern (albeit calm) reprimand
- an open discussion of why the behavior took place and how this can be prevented in the future
- a simple acknowledgement of the misdeed along with an equally simple statement of disapproval, as in "I know you got in trouble at school today, and all I have to say is I'm not pleased."

The choice is determined by a number of variables, including the child's age, the nature of the misbehavior in question and whether or not it's chronic, and whether it tends to take place in public or only in the home. It is not necessarily true that consequences must escalate as the severity of the "crime" increases. It is sometimes, in fact, more strategic to take a low-key approach with a serious infraction. Likewise, it might be best to impose a heavy penalty for a problem that's relatively minor, but occurs fairly often. As is the case with adults, children are highly motivated to maintain their standards of living. For adults, the standard is a matter of money;

for children, privilege. A child who knows certain misbehavior will result in curtailment of freedom is a child more likely to walk the straight and narrow.

Then there's the matter of your dilemma. While it's certainly not prudent to assign a restriction you can't enforce, a restriction can still be effective even when enforcement can't be completely guaranteed. Let's say you tell your son he cannot leave the house on Saturday. At noon on Saturday, you leave the house for the shop, returning at three o'clock. During your absence, you son goes outside for two hours to visit with his friends. He will probably go no farther than the yard. After all, he's got to stay close enough to the house to get back inside quickly, as soon as your car comes into view. Even considering his "escape," which was hardly satisfactory, he still served the better part of his sentence. Furthermore, he knows there's no guarantee that the next time you put him on restriction, you'll give him the opportunity to escape. Therefore, the restriction has still served its purpose, which is to penalize the misbehavior in question and deter a repeat performance.

Any punishment has its drawbacks. The fact is, however, *a child does not have to completely cooperate in a punishment for it to be effective.* Just as there is no perfect child, there is no perfect means of discipline.

Q: *Is it ever okay to let a grown child live at home?*

A: Valid reasons for letting a grown child come home to "roost" include divorce, job loss, and prolonged illness. These and other relatively traumatic circumstances might temporarily interfere with the young person's ability to be self-supporting.

"Roosting" is also acceptable during major, but not necessarily traumatic transitions in the child's life. These would include the period between college graduation or military service and a job. If a young person wants to live at home for a few months prior to getting married so as to build a nest egg, that's fine too.

Q: *What, if any, understandings should exist between parents and a grown child who lives at home?*

A: Whatever the circumstances, the arrangement should not be "open-ended." Parents and child should set goals, along with a specific plan of action and time frames for reaching those goals. For example, the agreement might stipulate that the young person will be out of the house in six months. The first month will be spent finding a job, the second and third paying off debts, the fourth and fifth building a financial cushion, and the sixth finding an affordable place to live.

During this period of dependency, the young person should be required to make some form of contribution to the household. If unable to pay, he or she should perform services around the home (or in the family business) which function as payment. Once the young person has income, a sliding scale of financial reimbursement can be worked out. He should, in other words, "earn his keep."

Q: *(Concerning the above Q&A) What if grandchildren are involved?*

A: Grandchildren are children first and grandchildren second. In other words, they are the primary responsibility of the parent, not the grandparents. The parent should expect the children to behave as befits a guest in someone else's home. They should respect the grandparents' property and privacy. When needed, the parent should discipline the children. It goes without saying that the grandparents should support, and not interfere with, the parent's philosophy and methods of discipline.

Q: *How much control should parents exercise over a grown child who lives at home?*

A: No more than they would exercise over any other temporary boarder. This arrangement involves three adults, not two adults and one child. The young person should be treated as an adult, and be expected to act as such. Likewise, the parents should act like adults, rather than parents. This means, for example, that the parents set no specific restrictions on the young person's comings and goings. It also means that the young person comes and goes with due respect for the parents' lifestyle and values. The important thing is that *any and all expectations along these lines be spelled out in advance.*

Q: *What if the young person violates the agreement or behaves in ways the parents disapprove of?*

A: The parents should not lecture or punish the young person for behavior they disprove of, but should express their concerns in a straightforward manner. Violations of the agreement should be discussed, the goal being to reach understanding as to why the violation occurred and prevent a repeat performance. Perhaps the violation was the result of a misunderstanding, or perhaps the agreement was unrealistic to begin with and needs to be modified. If conflict continues between parents and child, then family counseling is the next step.

Q: *What if the agreed-upon time for leaving comes and the young person isn't financially able to leave?*

A: Inventory what went wrong and why. Set new goals based on the mistakes and miscalculations that were made and try again. If the young person fails a second time to emancipate on schedule, there may be more going on than meets the eye. At that point, it may be appropriate to explore the issues and problems with a trained family counselor.

Q: *How important are fathers and what is their proper role in the rearing of a child, and especially in the life of a teenage child?*

A: One of the most unfortunate consequences of our nearly 50-percent divorce rate is that a large (and growing) number of America's children are being raised in father-absent families. Equally unfortunate is the fact that until recently this hasn't caused widespread concern.

We have tended to believe that the success or failure of the child-rearing process rests almost exclusively in mothers' laps. This is a convenient fantasy, nothing more and nothing less. The fact is that fathers are as necessary to children as mothers. Studies have consistently confirmed that the more actively involved fathers are in the raising of their children, the more successful those children are likely to become—socially, emotionally, and academically.

There is no time in the life of a child when a father is dispensable, but early adolescence is perhaps the most critical period of all. The early teenage years are fraught with insecurities for both males and females. During this critical developmental period, teens are dealing simultaneously with issues of identity *and* sexuality—not an easy task.

The young adolescent female is beginning to look toward males for attention and verification that "Yes, you are pretty and desirable." At this stage of his daughter's development, a father's role becomes extremely important. By showing interest in her, by being affectionate toward her, by playing up to the idea that she is still "Daddy's girl," he remains the Main Man in her life. And because his attentions satisfy her needs for male approval, she is, therefore, considerably less likely to seek that attention, especially in inappropriate ways, elsewhere. To put it bluntly, the less attention young teenage girls get from their fathers, the more insecure they will feel about themselves and the more likely they will be to act out that insecurity through sexual experimentation.

Ah, but it takes two to tango, doesn't it? And so we come to why the presence of a father in the life of a young teenage boy is also one of the best adolescent sexual preventives going. A young male who enters his adolescent years without a consistently available adult male role model is left to create a fantasy of what being a man is all about. All too often, this involves the idea that being a man is a direct function of how successful one is at sexual conquest. Once having arrived at this misconception of the role machismo plays in the psychology of a secure male, the young teenage boy goes looking for ways to confirm his masculinity by . . . guess what? An actively involved father can help a son develop a more balanced, less sex-oriented view of manhood.

Once upon a time not so long ago, nearly every American child spent Father's Day with both his father *and* his mother. Today, that state of affairs is exceptional. It is estimated that only 6 percent of black children and 30 percent of white children born in the year 2000 will live with both biological parents through age eighteen. The comparable figures for children born in 1950 were 52 and 81 percent, respectively. One in three households is headed by a single parent, and nine in ten single-parent families are fatherless. Thirty-six percent of all children are living apart from their biological fathers.

Today, the once-sacred sacrament of marriage is nothing more than a flimsy contract that any partner can walk away from at the slightest whim, "I'm not happy" or "He [she] isn't meeting *my* needs" being the usual excuses. In the words of UCLA professor James Q. Wilson, author of *The Moral Sense* (1994), "It is now easier to renounce a marriage than a mortgage." Indeed, today's young people are more likely to divorce than to default on a home loan.

The consequence to children of this social experiment has been nothing short of disastrous. In recent years, it has become increasingly and painfully evident that children fare significantly better in every conceivable way—developmentally, economically, socially, and academically—when they are reared by two biological (or adoptive) parents. Since the dominoes of no-fault divorce fell, *every indicator of positive mental health and prosocial behavior in children has been in headlong decline.* Compared with his or her 1960s counterpart, today's child is much more likely:

- to commit a violent crime (children are the fastest-growing segment of America's criminal population)
- assault a parent or teacher
- abuse drugs and/or alcohol
- become sexually promiscuous ("active" is the current euphemism of choice) before age eighteen
- have a child out of wedlock
- commit suicide
- become seriously depressed
- develop a reading problem
- be a discipline problem and/or chronic under-achiever in school

And if that ain't enough, the consensus among us old folks is that today's kids tend to be just plain old, downright rude.

In the fiction of the ubiquitous dysfunctional family, husband/father has been the villain, enforcing submission to his authority by abuse and manipulation of both his wife and children. In reality, women and children are safer when there's a man around the house, and children are safer yet when the man is their father. This belies the feminist sport of having children out of wedlock, legitimized by *Single Parents by Choice* (1992) by Naomi Miller, and glorified by Single

Mothers by Choice, a national organization founded and directed by a female social worker. The point, of course, behind the aforementioned book and organization is that fathers are irrelevant. To that I say, paraphrasing Gloria Steinem, a child needs an unwed mother like a frog needs a bicycle.

It's time we faced up to the fact that keeping a reliable visitation schedule, always being on time with one's child support payments, and maintaining good communication with the mother of one's children just isn't good enough. The only fatherhood that's good enough is the fatherhood of permanent commitment to marriage and children, the fatherhood of constancy through thick and thin, of providing and protecting, of loving strength and tough love.

Here are some suggestions for father-teen involvement:

- Find at least one activity you and your teenager can enjoy doing together—hiking, canoeing, tennis, stamp collecting, or just walking. Then, make the time to do it on a regular basis.
- Support your teenager's hobbies and extracurricular activities. Show interest by attending performance and sports events. If you can find the time, become a sponsor and/or volunteer.
- Work to become less the disciplinarian and more the mentor. It's important that the two of you begin making the transition from parent-child to adult-adult, as it won't be long before your teen isn't a teen any longer. In many ways, these next few years will set long-standing precedents in your relationship. Make sure they're positive ones!
- Communicate! Let your teenager use you as a sounding board to talk about things like sex, troubles with friends, and other personal or social issues. Make the time to talk with your teen about college plans and

future aspirations. In all these ways, you can help your son or daughter clarify and develop a permanent set of sound, positive values. Remember that parents are a child's most important and most influential teacher.

- Keep an open mind concerning your teenager's choice of clothing, music, and, most important, friends. Looks can be deceiving during adolescence, so keep the reins on any tendency to jump to conclusions about your teen's friends based on their outward appearance. When his/her friends come over, take the time to talk with them, get to know them, and make them feel welcome. Once you get to know them, *then* you can draw conclusions.

- Last, but by no means least, remember that a child is never too old to be told "I love you."

Q: *What can you tell us about depression during the teen years?*

A: The teen years can be the best of times, but for many children they are full of confusion and despair, and the light at the end of the tunnel—if it's there at all—seems dim at best.

Dramatic changes in physical appearance and biochemistry, the often-conflicting pressure of rising parental expectations and the pull of the peer group, the need for peer acceptance, and the rapid advance of adulthood make anxiety an inevitable—and for some, inexorable—aspect of adolescence. Some teens experience more anxiety than others, and some teens handle it better than others. These differences, it seems, are to some degree biologically determined. In effect, certain teens are more constitutionally capable of dealing with the stresses of the age than others. Some ride above the stress, while others succumb to it by becoming depressed.

Nearly all teens go in and out of periods of moodiness, especially during early adolescence. They resist participating in family activities, act generally irritable for days on end, react overdramatically to everyday disappointments, and treat even the most minor of requests as if it was an immense bother. In and of themselves, these short-lived periods of being "difficult to live with" are nothing to worry about. Maddening, yes; life-threatening, no. But true clinical depression is a horse of an entirely different color.

Despite many recent findings concerning its nature and origins, depression during the teen years continues to be largely unrecognized and misunderstood by both the public and a significant number of professionals. The symptoms of clinical depression include:

- persistent feelings of sadness and/or despair
- excessive unexplained fatigue
- loss of appetite
- inability to get a good night's sleep
- pervasive anxiety
- poor concentration
- an inability to derive pleasure from normally enjoyable activities
- social apathy
- suicidal thoughts
- reckless behavior (i.e., "What have I got to lose?")

The clinically depressed youngster loses motivation, feels worthless, and suffers declining self-esteem. As a result, grades often drop and the teen withdraws from both the peer group and family. A vicious cycle begins to develop; the more isolated and unmotivated the youngster becomes, the more social and academic failure he or she experiences. The danger is that at some point the teen will begin to feel that "there's nothing to live for." For this reason, it's vitally important that the signs of teenage depression be recognized early, and that appropriate steps be taken to break the cycle and restore emotional health.

The bad news is that the symptoms are often regarded by parents, teachers, and other adults as indications of a behavior problem. Attempts to "discipline" a teen out of depression, however, are doomed to failure. In fact, they will only make matters much worse.

The good news is that recent and ongoing advances in the diagnosis and treatment of depression are making the chances of full and relatively speedy recovery better and better. The key, of course, is proper identification—the earlier, the better—and treatment by a knowledgeable professional or, preferably, a professional team consisting of a clinical psychologist and a child and adolescent psychiatrist.

Generally speaking, the most productive approach to a case of full-blown teenage depression is a combination of therapy and medication. The goals of therapy are to help the youngster learn to control, and ultimately prevent, the negative thoughts that characterize the depression, prompt higher levels of interest in social activities, and uncover any contributing factors that might be part and parcel of the young person's history or family situation. The purpose behind using an antidepressant medication like Prozac is to stabilize and correct the biochemical aspects of the depression. In either case, it's critical that the right hand (the therapist) and the left hand (the medical doctor) know what the other is doing so that treatment can be smoothly coordinated.

Given early diagnosis and treatment, the prognosis is good. In many cases, symptoms can be alleviated in a relatively short period of time. Recent findings suggest, however, that proneness to depression may, to a significant degree, be inherited. Most professionals now recognize that, as a result of this constitutional predisposition, ongoing treatment is often necessary until well into adulthood.

For more information on the causes, diagnosis, and treatment of depression in children and youth, I recommend *Why Isn't My Child Happy?* an excellent video from Dr. Sam Goldstein of the Neurology, Learning & Behavior Center in Salt Lake City. (Write NL&B Center, 230 South 500 East, Suite 100, Salt Lake City, UT 84102; or call (801) 532-1484.)

Q: *When is the right time for telling a child about AIDS, and how should a parent do the telling?*

A: To begin with, let's get something straight: Devastating epidemics, drug and alcohol abuse, death, war, unspeakable cruelties, plagues of locusts, and other so-called hard issues are nothing new to mankind. They've been around forever, and they will undoubtedly be around forever. For some odd reason, late twentieth-century parents often act as if such things are new to human existence, requiring, therefore, that they learn (from experts such as myself) psychologically correct ways of telling their children about them so as not to upset those children's supposedly fragile psyches.

To be sure, things like AIDS are not trivial, and at some point, every child needs to learn about them. Today's parents would do well to keep in mind, however, that parents have forever had to tell children about such things. Furthermore, there is no evidence that premodern parents did a bad job of this, and there is no evidence that psychologists are helping today's parents do a significantly better job (and remember, I *am* a psychologist). Parents of previous generations dispensed this teaching without the aid of expert advice, so they must have relied upon common sense. In that regard:

- Common sense tells us there are certain things children of certain ages do not need to know. A five-year old, for example does not need to know about AIDS.

- Common sense also tells us there are things children of certain ages *should not* know. What a child is not old enough to understand can be frightening, and parents should take care not to confuse or frighten their children.
- Common sense also tells us that the older children are the more they are able to understand, and the more they need to know. A five-year-old doesn't need to know about AIDS, and would probably be frightened by the information, but a fifteen-year-old who doesn't know about AIDS is three or four years behind the curve and may already be playing with fire without knowing it can be fatal. In short, when it comes to informing children about AIDS and other "hard issues," timing is of the essence.

If there is one general rule for telling children about AIDS or any other unpleasant topic, it is *keep it simple*. Don't use big words and don't go on and on. It's a good idea to make an outline beforehand of the points you want to make and the key concepts you want to get across. That's what a good businessperson does before going into a meeting or making a presentation and it's no less important in this sort of parent-child situation. The more well organized you are, the more effectively you will convey your message. Your discussion with your child should unfold according to the following three stages:

1. You give your child the facts, just the facts, ma'am.
2. You take a clear moral stand.
3. You answer your child's questions.

If, for example, you want to tell your twelve-year-old about the potential health risks of premature sexual experimentation, you should begin by identifying the diseases, including AIDS, which can be transmitted through sexual contact. It might be a good idea to go to the library beforehand and collect statistics on how prevalent these diseases are among teens.

After thus setting the stage, you should make a clear statement of your values, as in, "We disapprove of sex before marriage for reasons other than these, but we want you to understand that in this day and age, sex before marriage is a life-and-death issue. You cannot tell by looking at someone whether or not he or she carries the AIDS virus, so it is best to play it completely safe until you have found your mate for life." You might also want to point out that AIDS can be transmitted by means other than sex, and that is, therefore, wrong to judge a person on the basis of this one characteristic.

Finally, you open the floor for questions and discussion. When it comes to such issues, preteens and young teens often either have difficulty formulating questions or feel somewhat embarrassed asking them. In either case, if your youngster doesn't have any questions, don't push. Just say something along the lines of, "You may need some time to think about what we've said, and questions may occur to you later. If they do, please don't hesitate to ask them. More than anything, we want you to feel free to talk to us openly about this topic."

Q: *We've just learned that my father has a terminal illness. Our thirteen-year-old son is very close to his grandpa. How should we tell him?*

A: At this age, he can be told fairly straightforwardly. Again, it's important that you decide when, how, and who's going to tell him. You probably want to ask your father how he'd like this handled, and even if he'd like to tell your son himself. Whatever feels most comfortable for the adults involved is the way to go.

Q: *Before our daughter goes to junior high school next year, we'd like to have a talk with her about drug use. What should we say?*

A: You should tell her that it's only a matter of time before she has the opportunity to use an illegal drug of one sort or another, and where minors are concerned, I include alcohol in that category. You should tell her that young people generally start using drugs because they are encouraged to do so by friends; therefore, you expect her to choose her friends carefully. You should also tell her that most drugs are wolves in sheep's clothing. They feel good initially, but do tremendous damage in the long run. You should tell her what the most commonly abused drugs are, how to identify them, and what the short- and long-term effects are. After giving her these basic facts, you should make a clear statement of your values, as in "We don't want you using drugs, and we don't want you drinking. If that means you won't be accepted by certain people, then we don't want you having anything to do with those people in the first place." You also need to let her know that sometimes the choices are not easy, and that you are always available to help her make the right decisions. Last, you should tell her you're aware teens sometimes make mistakes, and that if she ever makes one concerning drugs or alcohol, you'll be proud of her if she tells you about it. The even bigger mistake, she needs to know, is keeping it a secret.

Q: *Concerning some behavior problems we're having with our fourteen-year-old, a psychologist recently told us that it's never too late. Do you agree?*

A: I don't have the slightest notion whether or not it's "too late" concerning your teen, but, in general, one of my pet peeves concerning my colleagues in the mental health professions is the tendency of many to tell parents "It's never too late." That simply isn't true and by encouraging parents to so believe, psychologists and other mental health professionals unwittingly contribute to parental procrastination on crucial child-rearing matters. I have concluded that this tendency stems from the desire to make people feel good, to not be the bearers of bad tidings, to encourage optimism. In and of themselves, these are admirable motives, but in this case they are misplaced.

More often than not, the parent who asks, "Is it ever too late?" is dealing with an underdisciplined teen whose rebellion is escalating. The honest answer is, "Yes, in many a parent-child relationship, a point is reached beyond which the parent's influence and, therefore, ability to bring about significant change is negligible. It is impossible to predict, for any given parent and child, when that point will be reached, but the mid-teen years (fifteen to seventeen) seem to be the time of highest risk. The further problem is that the longer parents wait to take charge of a problem, the farther upstream they will have to swim and, therefore, the less likely it is they will ever reach their goals.

I spoke recently with a couple who told me they initially thought their first child's behavioral problems were "just a stage" that he would "outgrow." When the child went to school, they began experiencing extreme "ups and downs" with him. At the "down" end, just when the parents could no longer take the child's unruliness and disobedience, he would suddenly and miraculously improve. Then, just when the parents were beginning to think they were out of the woods, he'd begin yet another downward slide. Up and down they went until junior high school, when all hell broke loose. By the time the parents realized they had a social misfit on their hands, the youngster was fifteen and a budding delinquent. At this point, the parents tried "ToughLove" therapy and tightened up on their discipline, but it was too late.

"We kept telling ourselves it wasn't going to happen to us," the mother told me, "that things were bound to get better. But it did happen to us, and things didn't get better. Today, Robert is in jail, which is where he belongs, quite honestly. When our second child, ten years younger, started doing some of the same things, we wasted not a moment's time. We made it perfectly clear from the outset that we weren't going to tolerate those sorts of things from him, and gave him a taste of discipline that, had we used it with Robert before he went into junior high, might have turned him around. His younger brother is by no means perfect, but he's going to be able to lead a productive life, that's for sure."

In short, parents who are experiencing serious difficulties with a child of any age simply cannot afford to wait to take corrective action. The sooner the better, for all concerned. As my stepfather was wont to say, "Tomorrow never comes."

Q: *Our fourteen-year-old daughter's room is a pigsty. Her clothes are heaped on the floor where she takes them off; her closet looks like the aftermath of Armageddon. Papers, books, and records are strewn everywhere. Gaudy rock posters are all over the walls and her bed is never made (except on the day I change the sheets). Millie and I have had a running battle over the state of her room for as long as I can remember. Her position is that she lives there and so should be able to decorate and maintain it according to her standards, rather than mine. I don't see how she can stand to live in such a mess, much less find anything she wants in there. She says it's none of my business whether she knows where things are or not. What do you say?*

A: I say your daughter's argument is far better than yours. She's perfectly right—whether she can stand the mess or know where to locate her possessions is none of your business. (Bear with me here!)

Here's your argument: Millie should keep her room orderly and clean because she'll be happier if she does.

Question: How do you know? Answer: You don't. Millie has told you she's perfectly happy with her room as it is. It's really quite presumptuous of you to tell her she'll be happier if she does things your way.

I say it's time you told Millie the truth. The first part of the truth is that the reason you want her to keep her room clean is because *you'll* be happier if she does. The second part of the truth is that *you* pay the mortgage, so *your* housekeeping standards should prevail.

Now get in there and insist that your daughter keep her room clean and orderly. Sure, her tastes are different than yours, and you can respect that, can't you? Millie can have her rock posters and her Michael Jackson bedspread and her record collection, as long as they're tacked neatly to her walls, spread neatly on her made bed, and put neatly away in their sleeves. The issue is not what constitutes good taste—it's what constitutes "neat and clean," and whether children should obey their parents.

Apply the Godfather principle and make your daughter an offer she can't refuse. On school days, her room must be neat and clean before she leaves for school or she can't socialize with her friends or talk on the phone after school. On other days, freedom and privilege are earned by first accomplishing the same chore. If she wants to trash her room while she's in there, fine. But it must be untrashed before she can do what she wants to do. Define "neat and clean" as (1) clothes picked up and put away properly, (2) floor cleared of obstructions, (3) closet organized, (4) top surfaces of furniture kept likewise, and (5) bed made. (In the future, have her change her own sheets.)

She's bound to want to fight you about this. Just enforce

the rules, without concern for her dislike of them. The more strict you are, the more quickly Millie will get over it.

Q: *Do parents ever have a right to search a teen's room and/or read a diary? My fourteen-year-old daughter and I are having a dispute over this issue. Although I've never searched her room or looked in her diary, I maintain that, as her parent, I have the right to do so at any time, especially if I think she's up to no good. My daughter says her room is her "private domain" and I do not have the right to even step foot in there without permission, much less conduct a search. Who's right?*

A: That's a tough question. Both points of view have merit, but neither can claim to be the final word. For instance, I agree with your daughter that parents should respect a teen's privacy. With that privilege comes certain responsibilities, however. Your daughter's concept of "private domain" implies that she is responsible to no one but herself where her room is concerned. That is simply not so.

She earns and maintains her privacy by, first, keeping her room clean and orderly, in keeping with the standard that prevails in the rest of the home. Second, she is not entitled to do as she pleases in her room. The rules of the household extend beyond her doorway, and she should be expected to abide by them. For instance, she should keep the volume on her stereo low enough that it doesn't interfere with someone else's peace of mind.

Nor does your daughter have any "right" to shut herself in her room for long periods of time, only coming out to eat and perform other vital functions. With the benefits of membership in the family goes the obligation of participation. For some teens, however, the only question is "What can my family do for me?" They have little appreciation for the flip side of the coin, which is "What can I do for my family?"

In other words, you should expect of your daughter exactly what society expects of us. We are entitled to privacy, but we are not allowed to do as we please with the privilege. Our homes are our castles only as long as we abide by certain rules and regulations.

In most communities, for example, there are restrictions that prevent using a private residence as a commercial business. Nor are homeowners allowed to accumulate garbage in their front yards or disturb the peace of the neighborhood with loud noises. In short, if your daughter wants to be treated as an adult where the privacy of her room is concerned, she must be willing to act like one.

For the most part, you are wrong in saying that parents have the right to search a teen's room at any time. A search motivated by mere curiosity will do nothing but undermine trust and communication. If the teen's conduct is above suspicion, then the parents have no right to violate the young person's privacy. On the other hand, if parents have significant reason to believe that the teen is, indeed, "up to no good," they have more than a right to search for evidence. In fact, they have a *responsibility* to their child to do so.

If a teen has been lying about her whereabouts and activities, violating curfew and other rules with regularity, skipping classes in school, etc., then trust has already been broken and parents have sufficient cause to conduct a search of the youngster's room.

If, however, a search reveals that the parents were wrong to suspect wrongdoing, then the child deserves a "confession," along with an explanation and an apology. Trust is, after all, a two-way street.

Q: *Our son is fifteen, and we're coming to the sober realization that we've done it all wrong. We've given him too much and demanded too little, complained about his misbehavior instead of doing something about it, and defended him* *when he got in trouble at school instead of supporting his teachers. As a result, he's a mess. Is it too late for us to correct our mistakes?*

A: First off, you haven't done it all wrong. It's quite obvious you care, or you wouldn't even be giving your son's problems a second thought, much less evaluating your own contributions to them.

I sense your biggest mistake may have been that you doubted yourselves and consistently gave your son the benefit of the doubt. When he screamed because you wouldn't give him something, you questioned *your* judgment and gave in. When someone else complained about him, you wanted to believe it wasn't true, so you became his apologists.

The mere fact that you ask the question means it's not too late. But understand one thing: At this point, you may have more success rehabilitating yourselves than you will rehabilitating your son. Nevertheless, I encourage you to go for it. If nothing else, you'll be able to live with yourselves more easily.

Stop giving in to his demands. Let him scream, rant, rave, and become otherwise apoplectic over your own rehabilitation. Start expecting him to cooperate in household chores (for free) and behave himself in a mannerly fashion within the family, even if it's only an act. Insist that he behave himself in school and work to his potential. And tell him that you are going to chart this course, and stay this course, whether he rehabilitates himself or not. But, tell him, if he does not rehabilitate himself, it will be a freezing day in the underworld before he gets the use of a car when he turns sixteen, much less one of his own. In short, introduce him to the real world, the world where one must be responsible in order to have privilege, work hard in order to keep a job, and be respectful of others as well as willing to go beyond the call of mere duty (the litmus test, by the way, of self-respect).

If your son never corrects his mistakes, at least you'll be able to say with pride that you corrected your own.

Q: *About two months ago, our fourteen-year-old son got mad at us and ran away from home. We finally found him two days later at the home of a friend whose parents didn't know we were looking for him. He left because we put him on a week's restriction for not coming home on time. He was a perfectly delightful kid until about a year ago, when he began acting like a horse's rear end—talking back, giving us grief every time we asked him to do something, becoming belligerent when he didn't get his way, and so on. We're at our wits' end with him. To make matters worse, he's using this running away thing to get what he wants from us. If things don't suit him, he starts talking about leaving. He obviously knows how upset it makes us. To hear his teachers and friends' parents talk about him, you'd think he was a saint. What should we do?*

A: For starters, you need to stop living in fear of his running away. Based on what you told me in your letter, it's not a likely possibility.

I know, you say he already has run away, but I make a distinction between running *away* and running *off.* A good number of teenagers run off. They get mad at their parents and escape to what is usually a fairly safe haven—a friend's house, a neighbor's barn—for a few days. It's an impulsive, dramatic way of handling frustrations. Kids who run off have every intention of coming home and often make it very easy for their parents to find them. Running away, however, is a horse of quite a different color. This is serious stuff, not soap opera, and a real runaway doesn't want to be found.

Runaways are almost always from very unstable families, where conflict is the norm. Frequently, these kids have been the victims of physical and/or sexual abuse. To escape the dead-end street, they hit the road.

The long and short of it is as follows: Your son didn't really run away; he merely ran off. And there's nothing in your letter to suggest he's likely to decide suddenly to leave on a cross-country hike.

Yes, living with a young adolescent can certainly be the pits at times. It's important, however, to distinguish between normal adolescent behavior and real problem behavior. Here's my "Test for Truly Troubled Teens":

- Was he/she a behavior problem before the onset of adolescence?
- Do other adults (teachers, neighbors, other parents) also have difficulty with him/her?
- Is he/she using drugs or alcohol?
- Is he/she sexually active?

If the answer to all four questions is "no," then there's every reason to believe this, too, will pass. If the answer to even one of them is "yes," then I would advise that you get some professional help, and fast.

Your question suggests a "no" to all four. Therefore, I don't think you have anything to fear, save fear itself. In that regard, you mustn't allow your son to intimidate you with threats of running away. The next time he lets one slip, shrug it off by saying, "Help yourself, but when you decide to come home, remember that you're gong to be grounded a week for every day, or part of one, you are gone." That'll give him something to think about.

The more you tiptoe around him in order to prevent another incident, the worse his behavior will become. When he needs discipline, discipline him. In fact, it sounds like a major crackdown may be in order.

I won't wish you good luck, because luck has nothing to do with it. Instead, I'll wish you good "hanging in there."

Q: *Six months age, we moved from the East Coast and settled in a nice community in the Midwest. The adjustment has been somewhat difficult for all of us, but it seems to have particularly affected our fourteen-year-old son. This once outgoing and popular child has formed no close relationships since the move. In fact, he seems to avoid children his own age and has taken to associating with children several years younger. We have spoken to him about making more of an effort to find a friend, but he stays put, spending most of his free time in his room, watching television. He has also become more dependent and attached to his father and me. How can we help him?*

A: I suggest that you begin by talking with your son about how generally upsetting the move has been to everyone in the family, how difficult it was to leave old friends and find new ones, and so on.

The disruption of a move often causes a young adolescent to regress to earlier forms of behavior. He may seek out younger children because they are more accepting, and because his status among them is virtually guaranteed. He is also likely to act more dependent on his parents.

Be understanding and supportive. Encourage and help him expand his "range" away from home. A gentle assist from you in the form of arranging for his involvement in activities sponsored by the church, YMCA, and so on may be helpful.

Finally, I can't urge you strongly enough to remove the television from his room and limit his access to the family set to a maximum of one hour in the evening. His absorption in television is a way of retreating from the challenge of carving out a niche for himself in his new surroundings. Every hour spent staring at the tube further dampens his initiative and increases his inertia.

Q: *Our thirteen-year-old has recently started threatening to run away from home. He is the second of three children and is almost exactly three years younger and three years older than his brothers. He complains about everything. He says we expect too much of him, he never has anything to do, we are "easier" on his younger brother, his older brother gets to do more than he does, and so on. It seems as though he's miserable nearly all the time. He can be loving and cooperative but has not been for at least three months. Should we be concerned about his threats? We hear them two or three times a week. What should we do?*

A: I don't think there's much possibility that he actually will leave for good—not anytime soon, that is. Teens who run with the intention of staying gone don't talk about it much beforehand. They just *go,* and the pressures that push them to that extreme are far more serious than the typical "Tweenage Blues" you're describing. In a similar vein, people who repeatedly threaten suicide are seldom the ones who (except through miscalculation) end up in the morgue. In both instances, the threat is a dramatic way of calling attention to oneself: "Hey! You better look at me, 'cause it might be your last chance!"

There are victims and there are "victims." Included in the former are real-life runaways and real-death suicides. A "victim," on the other hand, is nothing more than a parody of tragedy. Included in the latter are, quite often, middle children and "tweenagers." Congratulations! You've got two for the price of one!

In one sense, the middle child is a "tweenager" throughout his childhood. Born both too late and too early, he rails against the injustice of having an older sibling who enjoys more freedom and a younger one who seems to get more attention.

The middle child wants the best of both worlds, without having to pay the price. He wants to be gloriously independent and securely taken care of at the same time. The lure of becoming a victim is almost impossible to resist in this irreconcilable dilemma. "I'm gonna run away!" is a frustrated, exaggerated expression of this conflict. It is both a battle cry for freedom and a plea for more attention. As the middle child moves into his "tweenage" years, his middle-ness is compounded. Woe is him! Insult upon injury! The straw that broke . . . and all the rest.

I would be less concerned about his threats than the feelings behind them. Understand that this is a particularly stressful transition in his life and an equally important time in the life of your family. For instance, concern over threats of running away can mask the more salient issue of, "What does being a member of this family mean when you are thirteen years old?" In short, the solution to this problem is equal parts understanding and conversation.

Q: *Our three children, ages fifteen, thirteen, and eleven, constantly bicker with one another. We've tried talking to them about how important it is to have good relationships with one's siblings. We've tried mediating. We've tried punishing. Nothing works. They tell us they don't like one another, which absolutely breaks our hearts. Do you have any ideas?*

A: Yes, but first, you need to come to grips with the realities of sibling relationships. You need to understand that unlike spouses and friends, siblings do not *choose* one another. Rather, they are thrown together by "accidents" of birth. Conflict between siblings, therefore, is to be expected. Furthermore, siblings are *more* likely to have conflict than are spouses and considerably more so than are friends, given that friends don't usually live together. The long and short of all this is you can't mandate that siblings have affection for one another. The good news is, most siblings put their childhood differences aside as adults and become as close as their personalities will allow.

Whereas parents can't stop siblings from having conflict, they can take steps to effectively contain the *level* of conflict. Doing so simply requires that you create and enforce a "Do Not Disturb the Peace" rule, which says: Children can have conflict, but they must (a) keep it down, (b) not engage in physical aggression of any kind toward one another, and (c) not tattle on one another.

On any given day, the first time the rule is broken by any two of the kids (or all three simultaneously), you simply identify the infraction and issue a warning, as in, "You aren't keeping it down, so I'm giving you your warning for the day." It's extremely important that you make no attempt to find out what happened or what they're arguing about. Nor should you make any effort to mediate the conflict. Just issue the warning and walk away.

If, on that same day, they subsequently violate the rule a second time, you "lower the boom," which means you confine them to their respective rooms for the remainder of the day. Now, here's the rub: You confine *all three of them* to their rooms, regardless of who was involved in the second incident. (A child who was not home when the second incident occurred begins his or her confinement immediately upon returning home.) The children will, of course, protest that this "all or none" policy isn't fair, in which case you should simply say, "We're glad you think so. Actually, we're not trying to be fair. Perhaps, just perhaps, when you guys begin to show respect for our need to have a peaceful home and family, we will be more fair, whatever that means. In the meantime, you will only waste your time if you complain about it."

This very "unfair" policy will force your children to resolve their conflicts quietly, without force or histrionics. If they don't, they will all pay an equal penalty. There are no villains or victims, just three children in the same boat. And they must learn to paddle this boat cooperatively if they are to stay out of hot water.

Any adults out there in Reader Land who think this is scandalously unjust should consider two things:

1. All three siblings have been equally involved in getting the snowball of sibling conflict rolling downhill; therefore, it is entirely just to hold all three responsible for its effect on the family, regardless of who is involved in any given incident.

2. Over time, each of the three children will experience the inequity of this policy equally.

What I'm recommending is nothing new. Remember how effective it was when a teacher kept the whole class after school because of the misbehavior of one or two students? It wasn't "fair," but it worked, didn't it?

Q: *Our twelve-year old son has always been well behaved, responsible, and honest. This year, he started junior high school and began hanging around with several kids who are troublemakers. As soon as we found out, we forbade the association. He says we're trying to choose his friends and seems determined to hang around with them anyway. It's the first really major conflict we've ever had, and quite frankly, it's a bit scary. What should we do?*

A: Nothing. This is actually a great opportunity for both you and your son to learn some very important lessons. You can learn to let go, to stop being so protective. In turn, he can learn to be more responsible for the social choices he makes. None of you is going to learn anything, however, unless you allow him the freedom to make certain mistakes.

Learning generally takes place by trial-and-error. This means that many attempts and many mistakes must be made before a particular skill is truly mastered. If the learner is prevented from making mistakes, the learning won't ever take place. This applies to learning to hit a baseball or drive a car as well as to making good social decisions.

We can all recall making a decision that brought us face to face with the pavement. Instead of wallowing in self-pity, we picked ourselves up, dusted ourselves off, and carried on, slightly scarred perhaps, but a whole lot wiser. Looking back, we realize that even if someone had warned us we were headed for a fall, we'd probably have fallen anyway. These painfully learned lessons are necessary to growing up and learning to accept the consequences—good or bad—of the choices we make.

You should not only let your son associate with these boys, you should actually hope and pray he *does* get into trouble with them. Let's face it, the worst that could happen at this age isn't likely to ruin his life. Let your son make his mistakes with these boys and, as a result, learn to pick his friends more carefully.

Tell him this: "You were right. We *have* been trying to choose your friends. We'd really rather you didn't hang around with those boys, but we're no longer going to try to prevent it. Whether you influence them in right directions or they influence you in wrong directions is up to you. But hear this! If you get into any trouble with them, not only will you never again be allowed to associate with them but there will also be a significant period of time in your life when you won't be allowed to associate with anyone. You have the freedom you want, but you'd better take care of it, because along with that freedom comes a lot of responsibility."

Make it clear that if he should happen to get into trouble, you're going to hold him completely responsible for his own behavior. You will not give *any* consideration to such excuses as "It wasn't my idea," or "I didn't do anything but stand and watch," or "They told me if I didn't help, they'd beat me up."

If he wants to bring these boys home with him, welcome them into your home. Who knows? Maybe your example will open their eyes to a better set of values.

Q: *Our son began seventh grade this year. He's always had a problem taking responsibility for his homework. As a result, his father and I have had to make sure he kept up with his assignments. When I went to talk with his primary teacher about the problem, she politely told me to stay out of it. She would take care of it, she said. With more than a little trepidation, I agreed. Unfortunately, Andrew is abusing his freedom. Most of the work I've seen has been hurriedly done. When I pointed this out to the teacher, she calmly told me she and Andrew were "working things out" and for me not to worry. Hah! I'm not supposed to worry while I see my son's grades go down the tube?*

A: You've discovered the truth in the adage, "Things get worse before they get better." In fact, I'm convinced that not only *do* things get worse, they virtually *must*.

When parents assume responsibility for a problem that rightfully belongs to a child, they end up compensating for the problem without truly correcting it. These compensations have the unintended effect of allowing the child to stay irresponsible. In your case, you've taken it upon yourselves to do for Andrew what he should have been doing for himself. You've made sure he brought his books home; you've stood over him, figuratively or otherwise, while he did his homework; you've checked to make sure the work was up to par.

You've been doing what many golfers do when they develop a slice. Instead of correcting the defect in their swing that causes the ball to curve maddeningly to the right, they compensate by aiming to the left of the target. In so doing, the problem doesn't get solved, but the consequences of it become less noticeable. In fact, the compensation makes the problem *worse* because it gives the slice time to become habit. The longer the golfer compensates for it, the harder it is to solve.

Like the golfer, you've been "aiming left." As a result, Andrew has learned to rely on you to take up the slack in his academic life. And, like our golfer friend, your compensations have succeeded in making Andrew's problem less noticeable. He's still irresponsible, but his grades don't show it.

If the golfer stops aiming left, his next ten shots will go in the woods. In other words, as soon as he stops compensating for it, the problem will seem to get worse. But by making the problem more noticeable, it finally becomes possible to correct it.

Likewise, Andrew's teacher realizes that in order for him to begin taking responsibility for himself, you are going to have to *stop* taking responsibility for him. Having done what she told you to do, you are in a panic because all of your past accomplishments seem to be going down the tubes. But that's just the point! The accomplishments were yours, not his! It's time Andrew learned to walk on his own two feet. As he does, he's bound to stumble and perhaps even fall flat on his face. That's all right. He seems blessed with a teacher who sees the problem and knows how to solve it. Trust her. She sounds like the answer to a prayer.

Q: *I have really blown it! My fifteen-year-old daughter and I have an absolutely lousy relationship, and I'm to blame. It all started when she was about ten and I realized that she had a mind of her own. The more I tried to influence her, the more she let me know that she had her own tastes and ways of doing things. I became increasingly angry and disapproving, and she became increasingly defensive and belligerent. I began saying "No!" just to prove I still had control over her. She, in turn, began to rebel. Meanwhile, communication got* *worse and worse. Today, our relationship turns around insults, sarcasm, and yelling. I know I've made her feel terrible about herself and made it almost impossible for her to please me. It's beginning to show in her grades and her choice of friends. I discussed this with a counselor, who told me I was being too tough on myself, that Leslie had to accept equal responsibility for the problems before we stood any chance of straightening them out. Do you agree that there's nothing I alone can do to save this situation?*

A: No, I don't agree. Your counselor's advice presumes that Leslie is an adult, and therefore capable of assuming equal responsibility for the problem. Furthermore, she shouldn't *have* to bear half the blame for the deterioration in the relationship. I agree wholeheartedly with you: It's *your* fault. As Leslie approached adolescence, you began wanting her to be an extension of you, to carry on your hopes and dreams and your choice of clothes and furniture and friends and probably, in the long run, husbands as well. When she didn't let you take over her life, you took out your anger on her. It's an old story, one that fathers and sons act out as often as mothers and daughters.

As you already know, you created the problem, and *you* have to fix it. And, yes, it can be fixed. For starters, I recommend an invention of mine called "An Apology a Week." The name says it all. Once a week, you apologize to Leslie for one of the many blunders you've made over the past five years. I'm not talking about a tearful, dramatic scene, complete with organ music, but a short, simple statement of fact: You've messed things up, you know it, and you want to clear the air.

Pick a time when you and Leslie are alone and not likely to be distracted for the next five minutes. Say you're riding along in the car together and out of the blue you start talking: "You know, Leslie, I've been thinking lately about something I did several years ago that was really dumb. I'm talking about when I persuaded you to take piano lessons, which you hated, and which I finally let you quit, after many battles over practicing. Shortly thereafter, you asked for guitar lessons, but I refused because of the piano incident. You argued that the piano was my idea and that you shouldn't be punished for not liking it, but I wouldn't budge. Well, you were right. I was mad and acted like a child because you wouldn't let me run your life. Things like that have made it very difficult for you to be open with me. I don't know if you'd still like to take guitar lessons, but if you do, I'll provide them with no strings attached. I mean, there are no strings attached to my offer. If you discover you don't like the guitar, you can quit with my blessings."

I'm not suggesting that you close each apology by giving her something. Nonetheless, an occasional "peace offering," if it seems to fit the situation, would be helpful. Once you've delivered the apology, say no more and don't expect anything in return from her, even an acknowledgment that she heard you. Initially, she's not going to trust what she hears from you and may think you're trying to trick her into giving you an apology for something she's done. Don't apologize more than once a week, either, lest you begin to sound insincere.

At best, it's going to take a few weeks for her to begin warming up to you. To begin with, she may reject your attempts to establish positive communication. If so, simply acknowledge her anger by saying something like, "I don't blame you for still being mad about it, even after all this time," and let the matter drop. I have found that an apology a week can go a long way toward diffusing a conflict-ridden parent-child relationship, but it's not going to completely turn the trick. In addition, find ways of spending time with Leslie without seeming to force yourself or your likes upon her. Remember, she is her own person.

A few words of caution: An apology is not the same as begging for forgiveness or putting yourself down. Nor does this mean you should start letting her get away with misbehavior. The idea is not to give away power, but to retrieve the power you threw away.

Q: *My boyfriend and I have been seeing one another steadily for two years and plan to marry as soon as our financial situations improve. We've both been married before, but I'm the only one who has children (fifteen and thirteen). My boyfriend wants us to move in together, but I'm reluctant. I've always been sort of old-fashioned about such things. I'm afraid it would be confusing for the kids. He argues that it would be more convenient and cheaper, which is true. But I still don't think it's right. He says we'd only be doing what most people do. He also thinks it would help us determine whether marriage will work for us or not. What do you think?*

A: You can call me old-fashioned, too, because I think it's downright irresponsible of unmarried adults to live together when children are involved. It doesn't take a genius to realize that the arrangement sends the message to children that marriage is nothing special, much less sacred; rather, it's just one of many equally valid options when it comes to male-female relationships. Clearly, those are culturally debasing ideas, and I firmly believe adults have the moral responsibility to see to it that children do not arrive at them. "Convenience" should not be the determining factor in decisions of this sort.

I certainly understand your boyfriend's feelings, by the way, and don't mean to imply that he's immoral. He's simply looking at the practical side of the issue, and from that point of view he's probably correct: Living together *would* be cheaper and more convenient but, under the circumstances, it's *wrong*. I realize it's politically and psychologically "incorrect" these days to make moral pronouncements, but you asked my opinion, so there it is. (Actually, it's only "incorrect" to say someone is doing/has done something *wrong*. To say that what someone is doing/has done is perfectly okay, even though that, too, is a moral judgement, is currently acceptable. Strange, eh?) To my very out-of-step way of thinking, moral standards do not swing in the cultural breeze; they are constants that anchor civilized society. Without them, we have moral anarchy, which is one step away from chaos.

Your children, by the way, would not in all likelihood be the least bit "confused" if the two of you chose to move in together. The term is used entirely too carelessly concerning children. The fact is, children are extremely quick to draw very unconfusing conclusions concerning such things as divorce, living together out of wedlock, custody battles, and so on. The problem is that these conclusions are often *not* ones that will serve them well in later life.

By the way, if you and your boyfriend were both childless, I *still* wouldn't approve of your living together, but I wouldn't feel as strongly about it (and it's very likely that my waffling on this point is a sign of my own moral weaknesses). I should point out, however, that the popular notion that living together is a good way of determining whether a marriage will work is one of those things that sounds right but is dead wrong. Living together and being married are not nearly the same, as any couple who have tried it both ways can tell you. In fact, recent research indicates lovers who live together are *less* likely to eventually marry, and if they do, they are *more* likely to divorce. In short, living together is a bad idea for both the two of you and the children.

I have an idea: Tell your boyfriend that if he's convinced living together will improve your respective financial situations, then he should marry you so you can live together!

Q: *Our thirteen-year-old son Brian has recently started having problems falling asleep. As soon as he closes his eyes he begins having frightening thoughts of dying during the night. He knows that this fear is groundless, but he says he can't stop thinking it. We've also noticed that he's started organizing everyone's place setting before we sit down to a family meal and insists upon wearing a favorite jacket to school, even on warm days. We shared all this with the school counselor, who assured us that Brian's doing fine in school and is popular with his peers. Nonetheless, she thinks he must be "troubled" and referred us to a child therapist. What do you think?*

A: I'm certainly in no position to make any definitive statements concerning Brian's psychological state, but I can tell you that obsessions (i.e., recurrent fears of dying in his sleep) and compulsions (i.e., arranging place settings, wearing the same clothing) are fairly common during early adolescence. In an older individual, similar symptoms would indicate the need for evaluation and treatment. At Brian's age, however, they are not necessarily indicative of a psychological disorder. The relatively high incidence of such problems during the "tween" years (eleven to fourteen) suggests they are related to the dramatic physical and psycho-social metamorphoses that define this transitional stage.

As puberty yanks the rug of childhood out from under him, the tweenager no longer knows who he is, how he's supposed to act, or where his loyalties lie—all of which are rather anxiety-arousing, to say the least. Obsessions express this anxiety while compulsions become a means of controlling it. Obsessions are most likely to occur when the youngster is unoccupied—in Brian's case, while he's trying to fall asleep. "Silly" rituals like rearranging place settings serve the need to stay occupied and in so doing keep anxieties at bay. Favorite pieces of clothing and the like are "transitional objects" that function the same way a "blankee" does with a toddler who's trying to adjust to a new preschool setting.

Given that Brian's symptoms are confined to a few specific times and places (as opposed to being pervasive), his schoolwork isn't suffering, and he isn't withdrawing from social relationships or showing other signs of being depressed, I'd recommend a "wait and see" attitude toward the issue of therapy. Rushing Brian to a therapist— especially if he's not crazy about the idea—has the potential of making him feel *more* uncomfortable with himself. At present, I'd simply tell him that if his symptoms become intolerably uncomfortable, you're willing to make an appointment for him with someone who can teach him how to control them. Should you begin to feel that Brian's symptoms are worsening, I'd advise that you make an appointment for yourselves with a qualified child mental health professional for the purpose of obtaining a recommended course of action.

In the meantime, his fears and rituals should not be discussed unless he brings them up. More one-on-one time spent doing "guy things" with Dad will almost certainly move things in the right direction. In addition, if Brian's not already so involved, encourage his participation in a sport or after-school activity. Above all else, take every possible opportunity to reassure him that what he's going through is not at all unusual and that "this too will pass." More than anything, Brian needs to know that albeit these aren't the sorts of things young teens confide to one another, he's definitely not alone.

Q: *In your newspaper column and your books, you emphasize the importance of children having respect for adults. I'm a teenager who's read two of your books (believe it or not), and it seems to me that some adults have very little respect for* *children. Isn't respect a two-way street? If so, I think it's time you said something about how important it is for adults to show respect for kids.*

A: You're absolutely right! Respect is a two-way street and it is important that adults demonstrate proper respect for children, just as they expect it in return.

Unfortunately, many adults want the respect of children, but don't really understand why respect for adults is so important to a child's development or how to properly achieve it. These adults seem to think this is a matter of children acknowledging the superiority of adults and demonstrating proper gratitude for being fed and clothed and protected from the elements. Because they think in superficial terms about this issue, these adults (and I truly hope I'm stepping on a lot of toes out there in Reader Land) get all bent out of shape when children act the least bit rebellious or ungrateful.

But the object is not to uplift adults by having children feed their egos, but to assist children toward their own uplifting. Jesus, Buddha, Mohammed, and Confucius all said—each in different ways—that one must develop respect for others in order to develop self-respect. In other words, what goes around eventually comes around. The young child takes the first step toward self-respect by learning respect for his or her parents. After respect attaches successfully to one's parents, it begins to generalize to other adult authority figures, then one's immediate social group, and then to all mankind. In the process of bestowing respect upon others, respect for self matures.

And yes, it is indeed necessary for adults to demonstrate respect for children, but the adult-child relationship is not, and cannot be, democratic. Therefore, showing respect for children is not a matter of treating them like equals. Rather, it's a matter of (1) accepting children for what they are, (2) patiently nurturing them toward what they are capable of be-coming, and (3) expecting a lot of them. I'd like to say a few words about each of the above:

1. Accepting children for what they are means accepting their misbehavior—not approving of it, mind you, but accept-ing it. Adults who don't accept that all children misbehave get all bent out of shape when they do. It takes most of eighteen years to fully civilize a child, and the process is one of con-stant trial and error, with an emphasis on *error*. As the errors occur, adults must be ready to correct them. But to effectively correct, one must communicate well, and to communicate well, one must be reasonably composed in the face of a child's errors. Above all else, this requires that one respects the fact that the child is a child.

2. To be patiently nurturing means not only giving ade-quate love and affection but also involves delivering proper discipline. Those are the two sides of the coin of good par-enting. Love without discipline in equal measure is indulgent, and discipline without an equal measure of love is simply punitive. Walking this balance beam, and walking it with grace, is the task set before all parents.

3. Expecting a lot of children means setting high standards for them. It is, of course, possible to set unreasonably high standards but the more common mistake is to set standards that are too low. In the real world, mediocrity is not rewarded. Therefore, to accept mediocrity of any sort from a child is dis-respectful. Parents should expect children to do well in school, display excellent manners, treat other children fairly, and perform chores (for no pay) around the home. Within reason, the higher parents set their standards, the more they "elevate" their children. And that, in the final analysis, is what respecting children is all about.

Q: *My ex-husband and I have been divorced now for nearly two years, but he doesn't seem to be able to let go of his bitterness. Almost every time our two children, ages thirteen and twelve, visit with him they come home with tales of negative, critical things he's said about me. Making matters worse, most of what he says is completely untrue. I don't want to put the kids in the middle, but it's becoming increasingly difficult for me to bite my tongue. What would you suggest I say to them?*

A: As little as possible. Or, put another way, a lot less than you'd like to say. This is definitely more a matter of *don't* than do, as in:

- Don't try to explain yourself to the children.
- Don't try to explain to them why their father is saying these things about you.
- Don't even deny what he's telling them.
- And don't, under any circumstances, try to "one up" him in the scandalous tales department.

In the first place, responding to your ex-husband's vitriol lends it credence. The more you talk, explain, and deny, the more you invoke the Methinks Thou Doth Protest too Much Principle. Put another way, the more you defend yourself against his "assaults by proxy," the guiltier you begin to appear.

Your ex-husband is undoubtedly well aware that the children are relating his gossip. This is a fairly common way for one ex to get the other's goat, and you are evidence of the fact that it usually works. Do yourself a big favor by not making the mistake of thinking that the children are your allies and will keep your rebuttals in confidence. They are no one's allies; rather, they are in the middle, where their father has put them. Therefore, just as they blab to you, they will blab to him. In a situation of this sort, the children are always double agents, albeit unwittingly. The more you say in defense of yourself, the more he will hear, and the more his criticisms of you will escalate. In short, don't be your own worst enemy.

Your number-one objective is to come to the aid of the children. Their father is manipulating them, pure and simple. He probably feels justified in what he's telling them, but it's manipulation nonetheless. You can't stop him from doing what he's doing, but you can limit the damage by acting completely unfazed by anything he says (or more accurately, the children *say* he says). In keeping with the fact that the more adults talk, the less children understand and the more anxious they become, you need to respond calmly and evenly to your ex-husband's childishness. The next time the kids come to you with a "Guess what Dad said?" listen politely and say (pick one that feels comfortable):

- "Oh, I understand why your father would say such a thing. Look, kids, we are divorced. Therefore, he can talk about me all he likes."
- "I'm sorry that your father tells you such things. It must hurt and confuse you a great deal. I'm not going to confuse you any more than you already are; therefore, we're not going to talk about it."
- "You know, kids, if you don't want to hear this kind of thing from your father, you should tell him so. I can't do anything about it, but you can."
- All of the above.

In any or all of these ways, you project self-confidence, which is what the children need from you. Their father is undermining their sense of security. You need to shore it up. If you do so successfully, then regardless of what he says about you, you are the champion.

Q: *My husband was killed two years ago. I have some concerns about how our two children, ages fifteen and eleven, are dealing with his death. The older child, a girl, has never seemed to need, or want (I'm not quite sure which) to talk about it. She's very well adjusted, does well in school, and has lots of friends, but I worry that she may be holding anger or unhappiness inside. Our son, on the other hand, wants to talk about his father a lot. Usually, these conversations involve memories he has of doing things with his father. He, too, is well adjusted and shows no outward sign of problems. Do you think I have reason to worry about either of them?*

A: If your children were continuing to have significant problems dealing with their father's death, their behavior would reflect evidence of depression and/or anxiety. They would be underachieving in school, having difficulties in social relationships, and/or engaging in inappropriate and/or erratic behavior.

In the absence of these indicators, the fact that a child doesn't *need* to talk about a parent's death is not a problem. In that case, forcing the issue is not only unproductive but is also likely to create problems where none existed before. You've done the right thing by letting your daughter know that if and when she wants to talk about her father, you're always available. If she doesn't accept the invitation, I wouldn't push it. Nor would I attribute any deep meaning to her silence.

As for your son, his questions and remembrances are a means of "staying in touch" with his primary role model. In a sense, your son is still trying to please his father. He tries to figure out what his father would approve of, what advice his father would give him under various circumstances, things his father would be encouraging him to become involved in, and so on. These mental exercises serve to keep him aligned with an appropriate masculine standard. All of this is very healthy, natural, understandable, and good.

Regardless, you mustn't let him beat any given issue or question into the ground. If you find yourself repeating the same things over and over again, do yourself and your son a favor by telling him, firmly but gently, "I'm not doing anything but saying things I've already said. I think we need to agree that this is something we're not going to talk about anymore." Just as it's important for parents to set limits on a child's behavior, it's sometimes necessary for parents to set limits on how much discussion will take place concerning a certain topic.

As a general rule, children tend to be hardest hit by the death of a parent if the death occurs either during early childhood (four to six) or early adolescence. The young child is just beginning to understand that life is finite and death is forever. The death of a parent at this time confirms the child's worst fears and can precipitate significant anxieties and phobias around the issues of separation and loss. The young adolescent is beginning to shift his or her primary base of security away from parents and into the peer group. The death of a parent at this critical developmental stage can result in significant feelings of guilt and depression. During middle childhood (six to ten), children tend to bounce back fairly quickly from the death of a parent. Nonetheless, signs of childhood depression should never be ignored.

Q: *Our eleven-year-old daughter recently told me she has been having "scary thoughts" lately, including thoughts of dying, us being killed, and other vague feelings that something terrible is about to happen. The thoughts not only frighten her but also—concerning the ones about us getting killed—cause* *her to feel guilty. We have a good relationship and she's been open with us about this. We recently read an article about a psychological disorder that involves obsessive thoughts of this sort. Could something serious be going on here? How should we handle it?*

A: The psychological disorder you read about is called obsessive-compulsive disorder (OCD). It often begins during adolescence and is characterized by obsessive thoughts and/or compulsive ritual behaviors that the individual feels compelled to perform. Recent research suggests that OCD results from a chemical imbalance within the brain and is best treated using a combination of medication and psychotherapy.

I am in no position, of course, to make a diagnosis. Chances are, however, your daughter's problem isn't serious. Persistent disturbing thoughts of one sort or another are fairly common with preteens and teens. Often, they are a by-product of the transition from childhood to adolescence.

Along with physical changes that are taking place during this time, profound changes are taking place in how a child organizes and processes information. Specifically, the child becomes capable of thinking in far more complex and abstract terms—in other words, like an adult. Comparing the child's brain to a computer, it's as if the child's "thinking program" is suddenly and significantly upgraded. This new capacity is exciting, but some aspects also may be initially confusing, even frightening.

When my daughter, Amy, was about twelve, she began having fears of dying. They usually began after bedtime, preventing her from falling asleep. When she shared her anxieties with me, I explained them in terms of "mental growing pains."

"At this point in your life, Amy," I told her, "you're beginning to change from a child into an adult. You can see the changes happening in your body. What you can't see are the changes happening in your brain that affect the way you think about things. As you go through this transition from thinking like a child to thinking like an adult, it may sometimes feel that you're not in control of what's going on in your mind. Sometimes, a frightening thought may just pop into your head, or the same thought may occur over and over again. No matter how powerful these thoughts may feel, however, they don't have the power to cause things to happen that wouldn't have happened anyway.

"The important thing," I went on to say, "is that you talk about these things with either Mom or me. The worst thing you can do is bottle them up inside because then they have nowhere to go and they just start bouncing around in there and make you feel more and more confused. The best way to get them out of your head is to talk about them, and that's one reason why we're here."

Amy and I continued to have occasional talks about this over a period of about six months. Each time, I provided the same reassurance and basically the same explanation. To my knowledge, the thoughts didn't go away that quickly, but Amy became less and less fearful of them and, therefore, better able to control them without talking.

The fact that your daughter shared the problem with you indicates you have a healthy relationship in which there is good communication and lots of trust on her part. With you there to provide the foundation of support and security, there is little chance that this will develop into something major. If, however, the problem persists longer than a few months without any improvement, it would be prudent of you to seek professional help.

Q: *Several times in the past six months, we have found panty hose, usually several pairs at a ime, in our twelve-year-old son's room. (He will be thirteen soon.) He says he took most* *of them from his aunt's house. He denies ever wearing them, but can't (or won't) explain why he is so interested in them. We don't understand what the problem is, since he seems like a well-rounded boy in every other way. He is active in sports, makes good grades, and has lots of friends. What do you think is going on, and how should we handle it?*

A: What you probably have is an otherwise well-rounded twelve-year-old boy expressing his emerging sexuality in a rather unusual, but no means abnormal, way. Furthermore, as he's told you, he probably doesn't know why he's attracted to panty hose; he just knows he is. Let's face it, part of the mystery and magic of sex is that words are inadequate to express why it feels so darn good. It just does. For instance, if I try to explain why I'm sexually attracted to my wife, I end up describing her. Fine, but why am I attracted to that particular combination of characteristics? I dunno. I just am.

Where sexuality is concerned, adults tend to have conveniently forgotten some of the strange sexually curious things some of us did as young teens. Furthermore, where sex is concerned, we tend to define "normal" in adult terms. So when a twelve-year-old elopes with a pair of panty hose, we freak out because we forget (some of us) that we did strange things at that age, too, and eloping with panty hose doesn't fit our preconceived notions of what is normal.

Another facet of the problem is that we think of the differences between children and adults in purely quantitative terms. A twelve-year-old possesses less "adultness" than a thirty-year-old—he is smaller, less practical, and so on. But childhood is not just the lower eighteen rungs of life's ladder; it is a different ladder altogether. Children play at a different game, particularly when it comes to things like sex. In fact, the basic difference between children and adults is that children learn about such things *by playing,* while adults think of learning as a very serious undertaking.

Around the age of twelve, your son became increasingly, irresistibly, attracted to the female body. He could hardly contain his curiosity! But he had to. The average twelve-year-old has enough presence of mind to know that the female body is off limits for another few years. But it just so happens that there are these things called panty hose that women wear over a very intriguing area of their anatomy. So . . .

He's only playing. Just learning, in a safe and harmless way. In this case, panty hose are "transitional objects"—items the youngster uses to help him come to grips with the changes taking place in his body, in his mind, and in his emotions. He is interested in them because the "real thing," besides being off limits, is too threatening for the moment.

If your son's behavior were extremely unusual in other respects, if he isolated himself from other children his age or seemed depressed—then more concern would be appropriate. But even in that context, panty hose would be the *least* relevant detail. (And make no mistake about it, if he were sixteen or older and had an obsession with women's underwear, I'd second your concerns and recommend professional help.)

Take this ideal opportunity to let your son know that you understand how panty hose could be so intriguing (but *don't* analyze his interest for him). Tell him that as his body matures and his feelings about women change, you are there to help answer his questions and discuss his concerns. If the door is open, he will walk through it, and when he discovers that you're willing to listen without judging or criticizing him, he will seek your counsel more often.

Q: *What are your thoughts on junior high school versus a school (in this case, parochial) that houses grades kindergarten through eighth grade in the same building?*

A: I don't like junior high school. Never have, never will. The virtual extinction of the traditional neighborhood elementary school is one of the prices we've had to pay as school districts everywhere undergo consolidation.

The problem, to begin with, is that junior high school requires more independence, initiative, and responsibility than many tweenagers have. Many a child of junior high age, although smart enough to do the work, lacks the maturity to do it in that setting.

The junior high child is dangerously "on his own," a problem compounded by the fact that junior high teachers are generally more subject- than student-oriented. Not only is a junior high teacher less likely than his/her elementary school counterpart to initiate help for a student who may be having academic problems, but communication from teacher to parent is also less likely to take place.

I risk sounding like I'm down on junior high teachers, but I'm not. It's not their fault; it's the system. These are caring people who do the best job they can within the limitations of a situation that imposes distance between themselves and their students.

That's the academic side of the issue, but the problems spawned by the lessening of structure and supervision don't stop there. There are negative behavioral and social consequences to junior high as well. As the physical and psychological distance between home and school increases, so do the odds students will begin acting as though they are ready, even entitled to, complete independence from parental authority.

The move from elementary to junior high school creates the dangerous and completely false illusion in many children that they no longer need supervision and structure, that they are capable of managing their lives without interference from adults. It's a rite of passage that occurs two years earlier than it did for children of my generation, and rebellion is the logical outcome.

More than several times have I heard the parents of a junior high student lament: "Everything was fine until she got to seventh grade. Then everything went haywire. She began concealing things from us, demanding more freedom, and disobeying us at every turn."

One day, as I sat waiting for my daughter to come out of the junior high she then attended, I marveled at the parade of children trying not to look or act like children. I saw young girls wearing heavy makeup and sexually provocative clothing, boys strutting their comically macho stuff, girls getting into cars with older boys, and members of both sexes smoking and cursing.

May God forever bless the "immature" children of the world, those who are without pretension to be more than just children. The ones who molt their innocence prematurely don't know what they are missing—but they will miss it for the rest of their lives.

Granted, junior high school isn't the only reason today's young people stray in such great numbers these days. The media's glorification of youth and sexuality hasn't helped either. Nor has the fact that, in many families, children don't have a parent at home after school. Nor has the divorce rate. The difference is that our school systems are a public trust, supposedly responsive to the needs of children. It's unfortunate that none of the many experiments in education that have taken place since the early fifties—open school, junior high, the "new" math, and whole language reading—have proven worthy. Even the lunches are worse.

Encouraging is the fact that a number of school systems around the country have realized the folly of junior high and are converting to middle schools housing grades six, seven, and eight. Whereas junior high, as the name implies, is a step toward high school, middle school is an extension of the elementary grades. It's a step in the right direction, and if parents put enough pressure on school boards, it doesn't have to be the last.

Q: *As the parent of a fourteen-year-old, what signals should I look for to tell me something is wrong?*

A: Parents who are interested in what their teenage children are doing and maintain proper supervision concerning their comings and goings will usually be able to sense when something is amiss. They may not know the details but they will *know* nonetheless. The test for trouble: Ask yourself, "How often do I have a nagging feeling of discomfort concerning what my child is doing or says he's doing with his time?" If your answer is once a month or more, then you'd better take a closer look. Some of the more definite danger signals include (1) dramatic changes in behavior, friends, or attitude toward school, (2) secretiveness concerning whereabouts, (3) outright lying, often concerning unimportant things, (4) refusing to participate in family activities, and (5) prolonged periods of self-imposed isolation when at home.

If you suspect a problem, you should first share—not accuse, mind you, *share*—your observations and feelings with your child and try to engage him in a discussion of the problem. As a general rule, the more defensive a teen becomes when parents share concerns, the more on target the parents probably are.

Q: *What's the dumbest thing you've ever heard concerning teenagers?*

A: Actually, there were two dumbest things:

The first was a story that appeared in my hometown newspaper about two years ago concerning a nouveau parental strategy for keeping close tabs on teens: The supervised co-ed slumber party! No, really, I'm not kidding. According to this article, which came from a wire service, the co-ed sex—oops! sorry, I meant *slumber*—party is sweeping the country.

Typically, parents will host a party on the night of a high school dance. After the dance, the invited kids will meet at the hosts' home, bringing sleeping bags and "appropriate" sleep wear. As the festivities begin, the girls change into night-gowns, the boys into shorts and T-shirts. A floor or area of the house is designated "for teens only," and the parents promise not to intrude unless they hear something going on that's obviously inappropriate. All the kids do, parents swear, is watch television and eat popcorn or dance to their favorite records or just have a rap session. Then they fall asleep, sometimes in boy-girl pairs, under blankets or inside sleeping bags that have been zipped together. But nothing goes on. Honest.

One parent was quoted in the story as saying, "They're not going to have sex in front of each other, much less right under our noses!"

Are today's parents really so stupid?! Apparently, some of them are.

The second dumbest thing was the first report from the federally funded (to the tune of $25 million that once belonged to you and me) National Longitudinal Study of Adolescent Health, which surveyed some ninety thousand students in grades seven through twelve. The findings: *Teens who have strong emotional attachments to their parents are much less likely to use drugs and alcohol, attempt suicide, engage in violent behavior, or become sexually active at an early age.*

My reaction to this revelation was, of course, *they've got to be kidding!* In other words, these researchers spent $25 million of our hard-earned money to tell us what we already knew: to wit, if you demonstrate to a child that you love him, even if he is a jerk sometimes, he's less likely to develop problems than a child whose parents are unaffectionate, critical, and rejecting.

Here's another absolutely astonishing finding: *The presence of a parent in the home when a child comes home from school reduces the likelihood the child will use drugs or alcohol.*

And yet another: *Teens who have repeated a grade in school or are attracted to members of the same gender are more likely to have problems than heterosexual teens who have done reasonably well in school.*

As today's teenager might say, "Well, duh!!!"

There you have it: Dumb and dumber.

AFTERWORD

◆

Just yesterday, June 4, 1998, I was having a casual conversation with someone I'd bumped into while strolling through my favorite mall. The someone in question had recognized me from the picture that accompanies my newspaper column and he walked over and introduced himself. People who don't know me but know who I am almost always begin a conversation by making some remark about parents and/or children. So, this fellow said something about parents and/or children and I said something to which he said, "Today's teenagers are smarter than we were, you know." I restrained the impulse to disagree and just said something erudite, along the lines of "Yeah."

Here's what I really think: Today's teenagers are not, by and large, smarter than "we" were, the "we" in question being middle-aged baby boomers. They are not even as smart, on average. I have to think the aforementioned fellow was referring to the fact that today's teens appear to be more self-assured and sophisticated than we remember ourselves being. Indeed, they're far more adept at negotiating what we didn't even try to negotiate—adult society. They're not intimidated by adults, that's for sure. And they possess knowledge of things most of us only knew *about*. But that's not smarter. If they were smarter, they'd be doing better in school and committing fewer antisocial acts. But they're not. So, while I'm sure that some of today's teens are pretty smart, on average today's teenagers are dumb. Oh, sure, we did dumb things, but they do dumber things. By far.

But it's not their fault. The problem is their parents. Us. We who were smarter as teens grew up to become parents who dumbed-down our kids. We dumbed them down by giving them too much and expecting too little, defending them when we should have been holding their feet to the fires of blame, helping them when we should have been letting them fall flat on their faces, sleeping in beds *they* made, stewing in *their* juices, and in general violating every child-rearing principle our parents held dear and tried to pass on to us.

How'd this happen? After all, don't psychologists say that a person tends to parent the way he himself was parented? Yes, they sure do, which only goes to prove that psychologists don't know half of what they think they know. Once upon a time, child-rearing traditions were passed from generation to generation. But we baby boomers grew up in times that were driven not by tradition, but rather by the media. My grandparents showed my parents how to conduct themselves. The media has told us baby boomers how to conduct ourselves, and beginning some forty years ago, the media gave platforms to people in the mental health professions who were promoting a new child-rearing philosophy. With the aiding and abetting of the media, these pseudointellectual "experts" were able to sell America on the notion that traditional child rearing was not just out of date, but downright dangerous to the mental health of children. Traditional child rearing was psychologically, if not physically, brutal and caused something called "low self-esteem." To make a long story short, baby boomers bought this drivel and child rearing in America went into a long decline. And as child rearing became dumber, children began doing dumber and dumber things.

As I write these final words, the 1997–98 school year is drawing to a close. For reasons obvious to all except someone who was in a coma from September through May, it may well become known as the "Year of the Gun." By last count, more than twenty students and teachers across the country were killed this past year by children who brought guns to school and opened fire indiscriminately.

If one is to believe what a good number of pundits are maintaining, the problem in Paducah, Pearl, Bethel, Jonesboro, and Springfield was guns. Gun control, therefore, is the solution. In mulling that over, it occurred to me that in eighteenth- and nineteenth-century America, nearly every male child who grew up in a rural area had access to a gun from an early age and knew how to use it—and well—by early adolescence. Nevertheless, no child in those times ever took a gun to school and opened fire on classmates and teachers. So, guns are not the problem. Furthermore, Paducah, etc., is not the issue. It is the tip of the iceberg. The issue is that America's kids have been escalating out of control since the late sixties. In the halcyon days of my adolescence, teens—especially those of the male persuasion—were mischievous. Today—to repeat something I said back in the Introduction—teens have become downright dangerous to themselves and others. That's what we need to come to grips with, and fast.

I think it's this simple: Americans, by and large, no longer understand children. Once upon a time, it was implicitly understood that every child comes into the world carrying a "Pandora's Box" of his or her very own. Contained in this "box" is pure, unbridled narcissism—the "I want, I deserve" impulse that drives every antisocial evil. With this went the understanding that adults must keep the lid of the box closed until the child is capable of keeping the lid closed on his own.

That very realistic appraisal has been replaced by a very romantic one that says, in effect, every child is embodied holiness sent from heaven to grace us with his/her presence. According to this New Age outlook, only the benighted believe every child is capable of evil acts. The New Age view has it that children commit antisocial acts not because of congenital spiritual imperfection but because of either biological imperfections (i.e., bad genes, allergies, bio-chemical imbalances) or socio-familial forces (prime among which is the ubiquitous dysfunctional family). In either case, the causative mechanism is beyond a child's control.

The old-fashioned view has it that a child's potential for evil (not all, mind you, but *part* of every child's nature) can be contained only with liberal amounts of unconditional love and firm discipline. The New Age view posits that love is enough; further, that the misbehaving child needs not discipline but understanding and "help."

And so, because the New Age view has prevailed (albeit, in many individual instances, unwittingly), American children, by and large, have not been properly disciplined for more than a generation. They've been worshiped; at the least, treated with kid gloves. Instead of subduing the narcissistic impulse, adults have unleashed it. What today's child wants, he thinks he deserves. Whatever he feels, he thinks he is justified to act upon.

In a May 27, 1998, letter to the editor, a Charlotte, North Carolina, teacher relates asking his high school civics class what could justify going to school and killing a classmate. To his horror, his students reeled off an "enthusiastic" litany of reasons, including "someone 'dissing' you," "a guy taking your girl," and "someone embarrassing you." The teacher, a Vietnam vet, astutely comments, "The problem we have is not with guns, it's with what has happened to kids."

Yep. And what's happened to kids is narcissism, unbound.

We have a job ahead of us. It's the job of undoing forty years of mental health professional mischief, mischief that ripped the lid right off the Pandora's Box of childhood. As we enter a New Millennium, the biggest challenge America faces is the task of getting the lid back on the box and closing it. What we need in America is a Parenting Crusade. No, come to think of it, we need a Child-Rearing Crusade. *Parenting* is part of the problem. We need to "rear" children again, as in bring them "up." Adults bring children *up* by leading them, not by trying to be their friends. Adults bring children *up* by causing them to look *up*. Adults bring children *up* by being role models worthy of respect, by causing children to say, "I want to be just like him [her] when I grow up." Adults bring children *up* by describing high expectations and pushing them, if need be, to go the distance and then some. Adults bring children *up* by giving them the freedom to make mistakes. Adults bring children *up* by not making excuses for them, by holding them accountable for their behavior, by punishing them when they act badly. Finally, adults bring children *up* by forgiving them their mistakes and always loving them, regardless.

It is my sincere hope that this book will inspire each and every reader to get out there and begin doing some big-time *up*-bringing. Enjoy! To Life! *Mazel tov!* Have a wonderful!

ABOUT THE AUTHOR

◆

John Rosemond is a family psychologist, but don't let that fool you. He doesn't really believe in psychology. In fact, he is a certified psychological heretic, an antipsychologist, if you will, who maintains that psychology is the most successful secular religion ever devised, complete with high priests and priestesses, saints, heretics, and Inquisitions.

To date, John's written eight books on what is commonly called "parenting." He has also—what's the word? produced?—a number of videotapes and audiotapes, all on parenting.

John is one of America's busiest and most popular public speakers. In a typical year, he gives two hundred and fifty presentations to more than one hundred thousand people. He is a man on a mission. Does he get tired? Sure he does, but he says he never gets tired of what he's doing. He's having fun and intends to keep having all that he can until his wife, Willie, makes him stop. She's very tolerant ("More tolerant than I deserve, really," admits John), however, so it's anyone's best guess when that will be.

John and Willie have been married for thirty years and it will last forever, no doubt about it. That must be why Willie persuaded John to put everything in her name last year. Just kidding. Seriously though, Willie and John have two grown children, Eric and Amy. They're both married to stable, intelligent people who have